planning • environment • cities

Series Editors: Yvonne Rydin and Andrew Thornley

The context in which planning operates has changed dramatically in recent years. Economic processes have become increasingly globalised and economic fortunes have fluctuated. Administrations in various countries have not only changed, but old ideologies have been swept away and new ones have tentatively emerged. A new environmental agenda has prioritised the goal of sustainable development, requiring continued action at international, national and local levels.

Cities are today faced with new pressures for economic competitiveness, greater accountability and participation, improved quality of life for citizens, and global environmental responsibilities. These pressures are often contradictory and create difficult dilemmas for policy makers, especially in the context of fiscal austerity.

In these changing circumstances, planners, from many backgrounds, in many different organisations, have come to re-evaluate their work. They have to engage with actors in government, the private sector and non-governmental organisations in discussions over the role of planning in relation to the environment and cities. The intention of the *Planning, Environment, Cities* series is to explore the changing nature of planning and contribute to the debate about its future.

This series is primarily aimed at students and practitioners of planning and such related professions as estate management, housing and architecture as well as those in politics, public and social administration, geography and urban studies. It comprises both general texts and books designed to make a more particular contribution, in both cases characterised by: an international approach; extensive use of case studies; and emphasis on contemporary relevance and the application of theory to advance planning practice.

planning • environment • cities

Series Editors: Yvonne Rydin and Andrew Thornley

Planning, Environment, Cities
Series Standing Order ISBN 978–0–333–71703–5 hardback
Series Standing Order ISBN 978–0–333–69346–9 paperback
(*outside North America only*)

You can receive future titles in this series as they are published. To place a standing order please contact your
bookseller or, in the case of difficulty, write to us at the address below with your name and address, the title
of the series and the ISBN quoted above. Customer Services Department, Macmillan Distribution Ltd,
Houndmills, Basingstoke, Hampshire, RG21 6XS, UK

Urban Resilience
Planning for Risk, Crisis and Uncertainty

Jon Coaffee

and

Peter Lee

 palgrave

First published 2016 by
PALGRAVE

Palgrave in the UK is an imprint of Macmillan Publishers Limited, registered in England, company number 785998, of 4 Crinan Street, London, N1 9XW.

Palgrave Macmillan in the US is a division of St Martin's Press LLC, 175 Fifth Avenue, New York, NY 10010.

Palgrave is a global imprint of the above companies and is represented throughout the world.

Palgrave® and Macmillan® are registered trademarks in the United States, the United Kingdom, Europe and other countries.

ISBN 978–1–137–28883–7 hardback
ISBN 978–1–137–28882–0 paperback

This book is printed on paper suitable for recycling and made from fully managed and sustained forest sources. Logging, pulping and manufacturing processes are expected to conform to the environmental regulations of the country of origin.

A catalogue record for this book is available from the British Library.

A catalog record for this book is available from the Library of Congress.

Printed in China

*For Maggie (JC) and the remarkably
resilient Margaret Shaw (PL)*

Contents

List of Figures, Tables and Boxes

Figures

Tables

Boxes

Acknowledgements

The idea of this book began in 2011, in the wake of the devastating earthquake and associated tsunami that hit Japan's eastern seaboard on 11 March. At this time, in our roles as Director and Deputy Director of the Centre for Urban and Regional Studies (CURS) at the University of Birmingham, we were preparing to host the 2011 UK/Ireland (International) Planning Research Conference entitled *Planning Resilient Communities in Challenging Times*, reflecting the growing importance of urban resilience as it began to be adopted by the academic and practising planning community.

Ideas of urban resilience had become increasingly important in our own work. These were facilitated through dialogue within planning communities about the appropriateness of resilience thinking as a way of framing the responses to the challenging times we continue to face which expose communities to a range of risks, hazards and perceived threats. These include climate change such as: climate change and associated environmental issues; financial constraints, access to credit and economic uncertainty; political and security disorders; and the effects of social polarisation and migration upon community cohesion, all of which have direct implications for urban and regional planning, not least in ensuring spatial and social justice within the implementation of urban resilience strategies.

In undertaking such work we have engaged with communities of planning and planning-related professionals from across Europe, North America and South East Asia as they have attempted to wrestle with the intractable nature of urban risk, the increased complexity of urban and regional systems, and most notably 'change' in the role and function of planning and how the planning profession is expected to play a greater and more pivotal role in ensuring urban resilience.

The empirical research which supplied the data and evidence presented in this book emerges from a range of innovative transdisciplinary work that has sought to investigate how resilience principles have affected the design, construction, maintenance, management and utilisation of the built environment and how such manifestations have interfaced with planning practice. Our research has been undertaken in liaison with an array of built environment professionals; planners, urban designers, architects, surveyors, civil engineers; those engaged in post-disaster reconstruction work; a range of emergency responders, community and voluntary groups; and a number of local, regional and national policy-making communities, who were increasingly embracing the resilience agenda in their everyday work. Our empirical results have fed into emerging UK planning and planning-related policy, as well as professional training and education courses for planners, and have sought to encourage new ways of thinking and acting. Funding for such work has come from a variety of sources – the UK Research Councils and European Commission, and a number of local government and planning authorities in the UK. We would like to especially acknowledge funding from the following sources: the Arts and Humanities Research Council – AHRC: Resilient, mutual self-help in cities of growing diversity (AH/J50028X); the Engineering and Physical Sciences Research Council – EPSRC: Resilience through innovation (EP/I016163/1); the Economic and Social Research Council – ESRC: The everyday resilience of the city (RES-228-25-0034); EPSRC/ESRC/AHRC: Resilient design (RE-DESIGN) for counter terrorism (EP/F008635/); ESRC/JSPS (Japanese Society for the Promotion of Science): Planning responses to 'shock' and 'slow-burn' events: the role of redundancy in regional resilience (ES/J013838/1); European Commission-funded projects as part of the Seventh Framework Programme focused upon urban resilience: HARMONISE (Holistic Approaches to Resilience – grant agreement number 312013) and DESURBS (Designing Safer Urban Spaces – grant agreement number 261652); and funding from the Department of Communities and Local Government, Liverpool City Council and the North East Assembly which funded and assisted research and consultancy on housing markets that forms the basis of Chapter 9.

The research that has gone into this book, although largely carried out by ourselves, has been helped along the way by a host of academic colleagues and a great number of planning policy makers and practitioners, as well as support from family and friends. In particular, we would like to acknowledge the assistance and support of a host of research colleagues across the globe – Rob Rowlands and Jonathan Clarke (Resilient Cities Laboratory, University of Warwick), Lee Bosher and Ksenia Chmutina (Loughborough University), Paul O'Hare (Manchester Metropolitan University), William Hynes (Future Analytics Consultancy, Dublin), Pete Fussey (University of Essex), Richard Browne and Ifor Jones (Birmingham

City Council), Mike Turner and Elad Persov (Bezalel Academy of Art and Design, Jerusalem), Michio Ubaura (Tohoku University), Hiroshi Suzuki (Fukushima Action Research, Institute for Global Environmental Strategies, Kanagawa), Osamu Sohda and colleagues (Waseda University, Tokyo).

Finally, we would like to thank the anonymous reviewers for their useful suggestions, *Planning, Environment, Cities* series editors Yvonne Rydin (University College London, UK) and Andy Thornley (London School of Economics and Political Science, UK) and Stephen Wenham, senior commissioning editor at Palgrave, for their advice and support.

Jon Coaffee
Peter Lee
January 2016

Part I

Towards a Framework for Resilient Planning and Urban Living

Chapter 1

Why Does Urban Resilience Matter?

This century, more than any other, is the century of the city, where rapid urbanisation and greater global connectedness present unprecedented urban challenges. Such increased urbanisation also concentrates risk in cities making them increasingly vulnerable to an array of shocks and stresses. Under such circumstances, city managers are increasingly having to plan for *risk, crisis and uncertainty*: they have to enhance urban resilience. In this endeavour, urban and regional planning has a central role to play in defining urban resilience, addressing underlying risk factors and building resilience to reduce the exposure and vulnerability of people and assets to a range of current and future hazards and threats. Urban resilience provides an operational framework for reducing the multiple risks faced by cities and communities, ensuring there are appropriate levels of resources and capacities to mitigate, prepare for, respond to and recover from a range of shocks and stresses. As Harriet Tregoning, the head of the US Office of Housing and Urban Development's Office of Economic Resilience, and President Obama's 'Chief Resilience Officer', highlighted:

> While not geared toward any single shock or stress, resilience is part of a recognition that the future is going to be considerably different than the past. Resilience favors diversity. It favors more choices. It favors innovation. It favors social connectedness and cohesion. It must focus on the most vulnerable geography and the most vulnerable people, because how people fare in the event of a shock of some kind is extremely different based on whether they have the resources to bounce back. (cited in Mazur, 2015)

Increasingly, the ideas and principles of resilience carry tremendous influence in modifying and, in some cases, significantly changing international urban and regional planning agendas, whether this is

3

dealing with the unique needs and characteristics of places, looking at the short-, medium- and long-term issues, advancing knowledge, objectives and actions or recognising the wide range of stakeholders (who should be) involved in resilient planning. As Porter and Davoudi (2012, p.329) have noted, the emergence of resilience discourse has unsettled traditional planning methods and approaches:

> The concepts and metaphors that resilience thinking brings to planning exert significant power. In this sense there is the potential for it to reframe planning in ways that break down sterile analysis and rigidly conservative interventions, so that we can see them afresh.

In recent years urban crisis and disaster of many forms have focused attention on how urban resilience might be enhanced. In *Designing to Avoid Disaster*, Thomas Fisher (2013) notably highlighted how recent catastrophic events, such as New Orleans' flooding, the Fukushima nuclear plant's devastation by tsunami, the Wall Street investment bank failures and the collapse of housing markets, all stem from what he termed *fracture-critical design*. He noted in the book's preface, that:

> [I]f we, as architects, planners, engineers, and citizens are to predict and prepare for the next disaster, we need to recognize this error in our thinking and to understand how design thinking provides us with a way to anticipate unintended failures *and increase the resiliency of the world in which we live.* (p.ix, emphasis added)

Fisher evoked the idea of a more resilient future as a counterpoint to the path dependencies and cultural assumptions that have contributed to the high impact of a series of disruptive events worldwide. In doing so he described why there is the need for alternative development pathways and new planning cultures – based on the properties of resilience – by which global society can plan its way out of its fracture-critical present through a series of interlinked interventions and innovations focused upon urban design and governance. It is these types of innovative and transformative 'resilient' interventions, and their implications for planning policy and practice at the urban and regional scale, that are the key concern of this book.

This book thus serves as a guide to, as well as a critique of, early attempts to improve urban resilience approaches. As the majority of the infrastructure that will serve cities for the next 100 years is yet to be built, and with rapidly rising rates of urbanisation especially in the developing world (it is predicted for example, that by 2050, 75% of an expanded global population will be urban (UN Habitat, 2011)), planning to deliver urban resilience in the context of increasing complexity will become ever more pertinent to the way in which we view cities and think about their creation and adaptation (see for example Rodin, 2015).

The emerging requirement for urban resilience

In the last 20 years, resilience has not only become a highly popular policy metaphor but also an increasingly politicised concept, incorporating a vast range of contemporary risks, underpinned by an orthodoxy that has pre-eminently focused upon managerial and technical aspects of 'crisis' response and environmental management. After the devastating events of 11 September 2001 in New York and Washington DC (henceforth 9/11) and with the release of the fourth Intergovernmental Panel on Climate Change (IPCC) report in 2007 highlighting unequivocal evidence of a warming climate, resilience has increasingly become a central organising metaphor within the urban and regional policy-making process and, more broadly, in the expanding institutional framework of national security and emergency preparedness (Coaffee, 2006). As policies which incorporate principles of resilience have evolved and been adopted internationally, the ideas underpinning resilience have additionally begun to infiltrate a host of further, more loosely connected, social and economic policies, which impact at the urban and regional scale. This growth in both the scope and importance of resilience has been strengthened by the political prioritisation of the safety and security of organisations, communities and individuals, and the need to enhance preparedness against an array of perceived hazards and threats, including terrorism, earthquakes, disease pandemic, global warming-related flooding, economic crisis and social breakdown. These priorities have been focused predominantly on cities as a result of continued and rapid urbanisation and because of the particular vulnerability of cities as densely populated political, economic and cultural centres.

Urban resilience and change

Urban resilience is ultimately about change. From the perspective of urban and regional planning practice, and in relation to the roles and responsibilities of planning-related professionals, attaining urban resilience requires an enhancement of planning and design techniques and the development of new repertoires of 'doing' planning in order to make cities and their associated critical infrastructure and communities more resistant and adaptable to a complex combination of endogenous and exogenous shocks and stresses. This can be exemplified by the pre- and post-event planning in relation to Hurricane Sandy that hit New York City in 2012.

While the discourse of urban resilience had been readily applied to cities in the name of ensuring safety and security, and enhancing emergency preparedness in the years that followed 9/11, it took another disaster, once again centred on New York, in 2012, to illuminate on the global stage the power of and requirement for urban resilience. As Scott (2013, p.103) narrated in a special issue of *Planning Theory and Practice* which focused on flood risk and enhancing urban resilience:

> The flooding of parts of New York in the aftermath of Hurricane Sandy in October 2012 provided dramatic images of a global city and world financial centre struggling to cope with a natural disaster. At times, many neighbourhoods, particularly in Manhattan, seemed to struggle to function. This moved beyond those directly affected by flooding in their homes and businesses, to the wider city as critical infrastructure was damaged, including electricity sub-stations leading to hospital evacuations following power-cuts, and the closure of public transport networks along with petrol/gasoline shortages disrupting the mobility of New York citizens. While the initial debate in the aftermath of such flooding events often centres on the immediate recovery efforts, increasingly flood risk (and the potential for increased risk from climate change impacts) *raises more fundamental questions concerning how cities and communities should prepare or transform in order to cope with increased exposure to flooding events.* (emphasis added)

Hurricane Sandy was a wake-up call for New Yorkers, forcing them to confront the realities of extreme weather brought about by climate change: 'it provided violent and tangible evidence, if ever it were needed, that extreme weather is here, sea levels are on the rise and that cities must adapt more urgently than ever before' (Wainwright, 2015). In the wake of Hurricane Sandy new logics of risk management emerged, centred on the discourse of resilience, which saw $50 billion of funding invested in resilience initiatives. As a result, New York is emerging as an exemplar for urban resilience through a host of innovative and good practice initiatives. In 2013, in the post-Sandy recovery period, a 'Building Resiliency Task Force' was set up by New York's Mayor's Office to identify measures to protect the city against similar events. Subsequently, the Task Force proposed improvements to the state's building codes and encourage 'Better Planning' to ensure that developments are located in suitable locations (Urban Green Council, 2013). As some scenarios suggest that storm surges of a similar magnitude to Hurricane Sandy (broadly concomitant with a 1-in-100-year event) could occur every three to 20 years and the period between very large catastrophic events could halve over the next 100 years (Aerts *et al.*, 2013), urban and regional planning is becoming increasingly precautionary. This pressing need for future-looking risk mitigation and adaptive strategies inspired the creation of the New York State 2100 Commission and the enactment of long-term planning proposals for the state based upon preparedness, adaption and, most critically, building resilience (NYS, 2013). Moreover, the Commission report outlined a number of 'challenges' for the state emphasising: the need to: 'rebuild smarter' and consider the appropriateness of land uses in relation to risks and vulnerabilities; increase the use of green infrastructure including permeable surfacing and the re-establishment of soft shorelines; ensure there is 'integrated planning'; increase 'institutional coordination' including the establishment of a state-level 'risk officer' to put in place a framework for risk management; and, finally, ensure that there are sufficient 'incentives' for building resilience and education programmes (ibid.).

New York has also seen other important planning initiatives, stimulated by the desire to avoid further significant impacts from extreme weather events, such as *Rebuild by Design*, which aimed to promote urban resilience through innovative planning. Here, after an international design competition that attracted a vast range of novel entries, a number of ideas have been taken forward towards potential implementation, notably BIG Architecture's *Dryline* (Rebuild by Design, 2014). Inspired by the Highline (a public park built on a historic freight rail line elevated above the streets on Manhattan's West Side), the *Dryline* aims to convert the ten miles of Manhattan's hard shoreline, with its bridges and infrastructure, into a continuous network of landscape buffers and 'protective park'. The design incorporates a system of levees, dams and flood walls which improves mitigation to flood events, integrated within a linear public park that finds imaginative uses for the resultant spaces, giving social and environmental benefits.

At a very different scale of operation, the Transition Towns movement (or simply Transitions movement), which originated in the UK, has spread its principles – of decarbonising and relocalising the economy through community-led change – internationally (Bailey *et al.*, 2010). This provides another example of how ideas underpinning resilience have been applied in practice at an urban scale. The movement's manifesto, set out in *The Transition Handbook: From Oil Dependency to Local Resilience* (Hopkins, 2008), articulates a journey that can be taken to prepare for the collective impacts of peak oil and climate change using resilience ideas. Resilience within the Transitions movement is seen as 'the capacity of a system to absorb disturbance and reorganize while undergoing change, so as to still retain essentially the same function, structure, identity, and feedbacks' (ibid., p.54), which translates as being 'more prepared for a leaner future, more self-reliant, and prioritizing the local over the imported' (p.55). The movement envisions a resilient system as one that is diverse (making its constituent elements and connections interchangeable) and with built-in redundancy, modularisation (so parts of the system can reorganise in the event of a shock, thus making the system less vulnerable to disruptions in wider networks), and with tight feedback loops (so that one part of the system can respond to changes in another part). In this vision, increasingly localised systems are seen as the most resilient and better able to respond in a self-organised way to disruption, allowing the community to be increasingly responsible for its own environment. In later work, notably *The Transition Companion: Making Your Community More Resilient in Uncertain Times* (Hopkins, 2011), the Transitions movement provided a more nuanced view of the importance of community resilience, highlighting a number of key factors that help determine its strength: self-determination and local democratic structures; skill diversity within a community; and the ability to agree and implement a collective vision for change. As argued in *The Transitions Companion*, resilience is about more than 'sustaining' current models and practices. Rather, it is transformational, focused upon change and rethinking prior assumptions about infrastructure and systems that should lead to a more sustainable and resilient, low-carbon economy.

Planning for urban resilience

Within the context of change and adaptation, illustrated by the examples above, this book examines the emergence and changing role and remits of urban resilience policies and explores how planning and planning-related professions are increasingly being asked to contribute to this agenda. From a geographical and political perspective we also chart how urban resilience has emerged in the academic and policy literatures and how urban and regional planners, together with other built environment professionals, have sought to embed principles of resilience into city planning and management regimes. This will illustrate new proactive ways of thinking about the role of local planning and the state, and highlight the emergence of a range of risks that must be anticipated and mitigated (or eliminated) with forward-looking adaptive strategies necessitating changes in the role and function of urban and regional planning.

Planning for urban resilience is an international agenda. Emerging urban trends amplify the pressure upon cities to keep citizens safe, healthy, prosperous, well informed and supplied with essential services, and have recently led to an array of global governance collaborations and private sector attempts to develop strategic evaluation frameworks to assess the urban resilience of cities and regions. Notably, the United Nations Office for Disaster Risk Reduction's (UNISDR's) *How To Make Cities More Resilient* campaign launched in 2012 (UNISDR, 2012a) and the World Bank's guidance *Building Urban Resilience in East Asia* (Jha and Brecht, 2012) both aim to increase the resilience of cities to disasters and climate change impacts by utilising a risk-based approach to steer planning decision making. Furthermore, in 2013 the philanthropic Rockefeller Foundation launched, to much fanfare, its *100 Resilient Cities* (100RC) campaign 'dedicated to helping cities around the world become more resilient to the physical, social and economic challenges that are a growing part of the 21st century' (Rockefeller Foundation, 2013). This initiative builds on the experience of the Rockefeller Foundation's Asian Cities Climate Change Resilience Network (ACCCRN), a pioneering effort launched in 2008 to enable Asian cities to build their resilience to climate change, and which defines urban resilience as 'the capacity of individuals, communities, institutions, businesses, and systems within a city to survive, adapt, and grow no matter what kinds of chronic stresses and acute shocks they experience' (ibid.). Key within the 100RC campaign is the two to three year funded appointment of a so-called Chief Resilience Officer (CRO) in each city who works directly with the city's Chief Executive to pursue collaborations across government, private, and nonprofit sectors. As Michael Berkowitz, CEO of the Rockefeller Foundation's 100RC initiative has noted, an effective CRO is a person able to 'work across the sectors and siloes to coordinate, to connect the dots, to advocate, *to keep the resilience issues and resilience perspective in all the decisions that the city is making'* (emphasis added) (cited in Clancy, 2014).

The Rockefeller Foundation has also worked closely with private sector organisations such as Arup in developing a city resilience toolkit that 'gives cities a tool to understand their resilience; to shape urban planning, practice and investment' (Arup, 2014; see also Siemens, 2013). These new collaborations point to the way in which the development of new resilience frameworks for understanding and responding to urban risk, crisis and uncertainty are arguably being shaped and moulded by global institutions for commercial gain and in the interests of business opportunity. Collectively, these emerging approaches also highlight how an overarching and strategic view of urban resilience needs to consider not only the material built environment but also governance and decision-making processes which underpin possible interventions: where they materialise, how they are enacted, whose resilience is being enhanced and, importantly, whose isn't.

Situating urban resilience for planners

This book is specifically situated at the interface of emergent policy and practice literatures as well as the popular and academic literature on the general nature of resilience. Academic interest in urban resilience has grown significantly in recent years and has provided a range of, often critical, perspectives on the emergence and impact of resilience as a socio-political buzzword and operational concept (Walsh, 2013). While there is a general lack of empirically grounded research on urban resilience – which some have argued has resulted in 'a poor understanding of how to operationalize the metaphor of resilience in the particular context of cities [and] weakened the potential of the concept of urban resilience' (Chelleri *et al.*, 2015, p.1) – evidence from academic referencing databases has shown a steep upward trajectory of the academic use of the term since 2005 in urban and regional planning and the associated discipline of urban geography (Serre and Barroca, 2013). This growing literature has illuminated the possibilities of resilience as well as its potential shortcomings. The myriad uses of 'resilience thinking' (Walker and Salt, 2006) in global policy networks increasingly highlight resilience as the pre-eminent approach to govern an increasingly complex world where the new 'doctrine of resilience' is inherently bound up with living with threat, insecurity and vulnerability

(Chandler, 2014; Evans and Reid, 2014). This is underlined by Zolli and Healy (2014) who highlighted how, in an increasingly turbulent world, resilience has emerged to focus on 'the ability of people, communities and systems to maintain core purpose and integrity amid unforeseen shocks and surprises' (frontispiece).

Within the urban and regional planning literature, this book draws from, complements and extends a number of key texts published in the mid–late 2000s that have been influential in driving forward initial interest in city-based resilience. In *The Resilient City: How Modern Cities Recover from Disaster*, Vale and Campanella (2005) took a largely historical perspective on urban disaster recovery, evoking the metaphor of resilience as an inherent 'spirit' of cities to renew themselves in the post-disaster phase. Through a series of urban case study chapters their contribution sought to learn from the past in drawing out how, and why, narratives of resilience emerge and how they are enacted by planners and other built environment professionals. Similarly, *Hazards and the Built Environment: Attaining Built-in Resilience* (Bosher, 2008) highlighted the wide-ranging and transdisciplinary nature of the emerging resilience debate with regard to how disaster risks are reduced in the built environment and through the network of professionals and communities that are required to play a part in the resilience endeavour. It also drew attention to the gap between the actions of planning professionals and those tasked with disaster risk reduction, arguing that a more integrated approach is essential in the new age of resilience. Another contribution around this time was *The Everyday Resilience of the City* (Coaffee *et al.*, 2008b) that tracked the rise of the discourse of resilience, highlighting how it was being infused into a range of policy practices affecting urban areas and subsequently provoking a range of critical academic debates surrounding urban resilience. This was the first such volume to explicitly connect the policy, practices and politics of resilience to cities, providing a systematic interrogation of the consequences of the resilience discourse on urban professionals (including planners) and local communities, and illuminating the role and power of agency in 'resilient' urban systems through the interactions of the state, citizens and the market. *The Everyday Resilience of the City* raised important questions about whether resilience-related policies are a legitimate attempt to empower citizens and other local actors, or simply a further retrenchment of the state and an attempt to alter the social contract between government and citizens, and it prefaced recent approaches to measuring and assessing resilience noted above.

Approaching the study of urban resilience

Drawing on theories of urban resilience that have emerged from these contributions, this book will chart the emergence and progression of different 'styles' of resilient planning practice over the last decade which may be viewed as increasingly anticipatory, localising and responsibilising. Such practices are not without critique and as such the early chapters of this book will engage with the ongoing academic and policy debates regarding the pros and cons of using the discourses of urban resilience in public policy.

Empirically, this book draws from research undertaken by the authors investigating the changing dimensions of a range of urban resilience policies that seek to unpack the role of planning and planners in the growing assemblages of resilience policy and practice at urban and regional scales. Our research in this area has engaged with how the planning profession is expected to play an ever more crucial role in ensuring urban resilience now and in the future, and has highlighted the intractable nature of urban risk, the increased complexity of urban and regional systems and most notably the changing role and function of spatial planning. The data and evidence presented in this book illustrate how resilience principles have affected the design, construction, maintenance, management and utilisation of the built environment and how new governance formations have emerged to advance urban resilience and interface with planning practice. As the book progresses we further highlight a set of important questions that have emerged for urban and regional planners tasked with implementing resilience thinking such as: Why do we need urban resilience? How is resilience operationalised? Who undertakes resilience and for whose benefit? Resilience is increasingly being focused not upon state institutions but upon citizen and community responses. Specifically, in relation to urban and regional planning and when places and communities are increasingly vulnerable, we are therefore interested in the role and remit of resilience planning in challenging times. But do communities have the skills to make effective decisions affecting their resilience and will all voices be heard equally? Moreover, in the context of austerity, how is planning reconciling the challenge of finding solutions and spatial strategies that will deliver 'more for less' while balancing future needs and resources? How does planning ensure spatial and social justice within the implementation of resilience strategies? How is the wider epistemic urban and regional planning community – 'a network of professionals with recognised expertise and competence in a particular domain and an authoritative claim to policy relevant knowledge within that domain or issue-area' (Haas, 1992, p.3) – adopting urban resilience as a concept and approach? And, how does this affect the changing roles and responsibilities of urban and regional planning?

The ways in which ideas of resilience are creating new planning imaginaries, repertoires of action and collaborative relationships is a central theme of this book. In our view, what resilience *is* becomes less important than what it *does* (Coaffee and Fussey, 2015) and in particular the manifold and localised ways in which resilience becomes interpreted and translated into planning practice. Specifically, we argue that changing practices of urban resilience have emerged as both a function of time and in relation to a range of changing socio-political and economic pressures that have rearticulated the meaning and operational function of urban resilience as it has evolved. Emerging in the 2000s, predominantly as a policy connected to countering the threat of international terrorism through securitisation and as a reaction to fears of intractable climate change, urban resilience has now further expanded as a policy metaphor for embedding 'foresight', robustness, inclusivity, cost effectiveness and adaptability into a variety of place-making and planning activities. Until recently, urban and regional planning, both conceptually and in practice, has tended to conceive of such challenges as short-term issues, based on predefined technologies and siloed governance structures and approaches. The strategies adopted have tended, on the whole, to be reactive to particular 'locked in' approaches, technologies and predicted scenarios based on the simple extrapolation of current trends. Emerging ideas in urban resilience have served to increasingly question these pre-existing assumptions about the extent and nature of urban and regional planning, suggesting how a range of adaptive pathways can emerge to give multiple possible trajectories/scenarios for urban futures (Pike *et al.*, 2010; White and O'Hare, 2014). While the word resilience originates from the Latin *resilire* – 'to leap back' – and with 'bouncing back' to a steady state having been seen as a core resilience function, more nuanced understandings are increasingly forward looking and focused upon a new, and increasingly unpredictable, normality. For example, Edwards in his acclaimed *Resilient Nation* report (2009) contended that an understanding of resilience based upon 'bouncing back' is restrictive, while Shaw (2012a) has also suggested that we need to consider a more proactive approach, viewing (urban) resilience as 'leaping forward'.

Further relevant debate explored throughout the book concerns the extent to which urban resilience practice represents transformative or radical change, comprises a superficial rebranding of existing practices (such as risk management, disaster risk reduction or sustainability) or operates in the service of enduring processes such as neo-liberalisation and post-politics. We also reflect upon: the usefulness of urban resilience as the central organising concept used for depicting urban systems' response to contemporary and future disruptive events, and the form future urban resiliency practices will take and how these will interface with and impact upon the planning profession in years to come. Our analysis relates to both material and participatory aspects of planning and ways in which planning has the power to engage with local communities and enhance *community resilience*. Throughout the book we engage with the human side of urban resilience and 'the ability of communities to withstand external shocks to their social infrastructure' (Adger, 2000, p.347). Interwoven throughout the broader narratives of planning and resilience we will articulate how local communities can learn to better prepare for a range of disruptive challenges affecting their locality through the 'adaptive potential' of individuals and communities. This will assist the balancing of resiliency policy, reorienting it away from analysis of deterministic legislative and technological processes, and increasingly grounding it in the more meaningful experience of the world by citizens which is often absent from debates in the urban resilience literature (Coaffee *et al.*, 2008b).

Structure of the book

The book is structured into three main parts which contextualises the broader field of urban resilience and highlights the key urban and regional planning processes at play and the domains in which it can play a useful role, now and in the future.

Part I – *Towards a Framework for Resilient Planning and Urban Living* – locates the field of study and highlights the multiple and varied ways in which resilience is defined and interpreted and why it matters to planners. It will illuminate the emergence of resilience as an important consideration in planning for and managing a range of urban risks, and situates urban resilience in relation to its cognate disciplines, ranging from ecology and engineering to disaster management, economics and planning, that have been used to develop and theorise the concept (see, for example, Holling, 1973; Rutter,

1985; Thoits, 1995; Adger, 2000; Simmie and Martin, 2010). We further connect these ideas to a range of related ideas such as robustness, adaptability and redundancy, recognised as a key properties and means of improving the resilience of urban systems, while unpacking competing policy discourses such as sustainability and sustainable development which are often used interchangeably with urban resilience. More conceptually, we will also note the traditional dominance of the socio-ecological systems (SES) model of resilience which remained relatively uncontested until the 2000s when new approaches to urban resilience emerged and which have become increasingly important to our understanding of the socio-political complexity of contemporary planning policy and practice (Bosher, 2008; Coaffee *et al.*, 2008b). The adoption of the discourse of urban resilience is not, however, without critique and as such this part of the book will highlight the multiple viewpoints regarding the usefulness of resilience concepts and those perspectives that can be used to understand the politics of resilience across different spatial and temporal scales.

Part II of the book – *Processes of Urban Resilience* – will survey the 'state of play' in urban resilience scholarship and highlight the emerging nature of resilient planning across different national contexts. Here we focus upon the reasons that urban resilience is required by critically engaging with the existing literature around two main and interlocking areas of interest: the way in which physical or material alterations brought about by changes to urban design and land-use planning can enhance resilience, and how new governance and management solutions are seeking to better prepare for, and cope with, a range of disruptive challenges. We further highlight the inherent weaknesses within the governance and management of many urban areas that make resilience necessary, while arguing that urban resilience is most effective when it involves a mutual and accountable network of civic institutions, agencies and individual citizens working in partnership towards common goals within a common strategy. Relatedly, we will also unpack the range of national and international approaches to measuring and monitoring city resilience and highlight how an overarching and strategic view of city-based resilience can assist in changing the nature and function of urban and regional planning. Here we also reflect on the extent to which existing urban resilience assessment tools demonstrate a scalable methodology and practical (and increasingly professionalised) tool for risk assessment which can be used to focus city-level investment decisions.

To date, the majority of work in the burgeoning field of urban resilience has not been grounded within the everyday practices of planners, despite the term's increased acceptance and importance; there remains 'an apparent gap between the advocacy of ... resilience in the scientific literature and its take-up as a policy discourse on the one hand, and the demonstrated capacity to govern for resilience in practice on the other' (Wilkinson 2012, p. 319). The ways in which planning policy and practice might close this so-called 'implementation gap' in urban resilience (Coaffee and Clarke, 2015) will be highlighted in Part III – *Urban Resilience in Practice*. Here, Chapters 6 to 9 present a series of thematic vignettes associated with the different ways in which resilience has been deployed in urban and regional planning practice. These empirical chapters, drawing on a range of international experiences, first unpack the two main ways, to date, in which the practices of urban resilience have been deployed by urban and regional planners (climate change adaptation and security) before, secondly, drawing on ongoing debates in the literature about the usefulness of urban resilience with regard to reducing the effects of large-scale disasters (sudden shock events), notably the triple disaster that hit Japan in 2011, and less dramatic events which unfold over longer time periods (so-called slow-burn events), exemplified by the ongoing housing crisis and associated credit crunch.

To conclude the book, we draw together the ideas developed in the previous chapters and highlight how urban resilience can be advanced and enhanced, and provide suggestions for the future research, policy and practice trajectories in urban resilience. This includes the adoption of international agreements signed in 2015 on sustainable development, disaster risk reduction and climate change adaptation. We also address the question of how we can combine multiple resilience perspectives in an effective whole-systems resiliency strategy and highlight how urban resilience can be embedded as a set of principles for envisioning future local place-making activities. This involves, for example, increased emphasis on responding to, or anticipating, major challenges with a long-term view (Connell, 2009), rethinking risk assessment and mitigation strategies, giving increased focus to facilitating adaptive human behaviours and developing individual and institutional coping strategies, and providing the appropriate training to professionals working in the built environment. We represent this myriad of urban resilience issues in a thematic framework through which existing and future urban resilience interventions can be viewed.

Chapter 2

The Origins, Evolution and Critiques of Resilience

Resilience is everywhere today, rapidly becoming a principal framing device for political discourse: 'It falls easily from the mouths of politicians, a variety of state departments are funding research into it, *urban planners are now obliged to take it into consideration*, and academics are falling over themselves to conduct research on it' (Neocleous, 2013, p.3, emphasis added). The term has entered into the lexicon of policy communities, the media and academia to not only assess and understand the resistance to shock events of people, households and communities, but also to describe the properties and ability of interconnected and complex ecological, technical (e.g. engineering), social and economic systems to adapt and change in the midst of failure. As the UK's Leverhulme Trust noted in 2010 in its call for research:

> This is the century in which the human race will have to respond to major challenges resulting from environmental change, from the need to attain sustainable and equitable social structures, from contrasting demographies, from conflicting cultural models and from enhanced global economic uncertainty. Linking these challenges are notions of risk assessment and of the required changes which must lead to adaptive human behaviour. Options are needed for mitigation and for the development of individual and institutional coping strategies. *Central to these strategies is the concept of resilience.* (emphasis added)

With such a diverse range of applications and flexibility in its terminology and use, it is necessary to reflect on the etymology of resilience and whether overuse of the term in so many different contexts is in danger of undermining its meaning and value, and to consider how it might be best applied in practice. For example, while resilience has undoubtedly become a relevant concept for politicians

17

and policy makers alike, the way in which it is used is often subject specific. Nevertheless, it offers a new vocabulary to make sense of a range of disruptive challenges (Buckle *et al.*, 2000). As Vernon (2013) highlighted:

> Resilience is a wonderful metaphor. It somehow conveys in a single word the qualities of bending without breaking, of healing after an injury, of tensile rather than brittle strength. [...] Resilient people pick themselves up after being knocked down, draw on their reserves of ideas and strength to deal with difficult challenges, or hunker down until the gale has blown itself away. Resilient economies bounce back, and resilient ecosystems restore themselves after the fire or the flood has passed.

Resilience has become an all-encompassing metaphor which can be applied in a variety of national and international contexts – a translation term that allows 'connections to be made between different stands of research with common terminology and consistent threads of analysis, without needing to make assumptions that the phenomena under investigation are the product of similar processes that apply regardless of cultural context' (Gold and Revill, 2000, p.6; Coaffee, 2006). However, for others, resilience has in the last few years become a 'catch all' phrase used to vaguely express a wide range of responses (social, economic, security-related, psychological, ecological, governmental, etc.) to threats of many kinds and pinning down the actual operational meaning of resilience has proved difficult and led to confusion, especially over terminology. For some this might indicate it is meaningless or unhelpful jargon (see, for example, Hussain, 2013).

Other commentators have argued that there increasingly is a broad-brush, yet normalised, notion of resilience that pervades everyday life (Coaffee *et al.*, 2008b). This state of affairs poses critical questions regarding the relationship between broader 'resilience policy' for dealing with disruptive challenges (such as flooding), emergent social policies directed at the civic realm (such as community empowerment – now often badged as community resilience) and the qualities of individuals, households and communities to withstand shock and slow-burn events (such as the global economic recession). Some also view ambiguity over resilience terminology and its use as a positive feature. For politicians it allows ideological flexibility, offering new ways to make sense of a range of complex disruptive challenges across multiple scales of action (Coaffee, 2013a).

For research purposes resilience can be seen as a 'boundary object' (Brand and Jax, 2007) or a 'bridging concept' between the natural and social sciences (Davoudi, 2012) that can now be applied in a variety of specific national and international contexts. As Beilin and Wilkinson (2015, p.1213) note, 'the difficulties and the challenges for resilience are absolutely in the "particular", the "local" and the implementation of resilience as a process' (see also Anderson, 2015).

Some of the confusion over the vagueness of resilience concepts and discourse comes from its association with sustainable development or sustainability, with many proclaiming that resilience is replacing sustainability as the central organising concept of the age as a result of increased volatility that requires a different framing and response (Vale, 2014; Zolli and Healy, 2013). In essence, where sustainability often assumes a present and future of equilibrium, resilience is based upon a change paradigm, which makes it particularly helpful for managing a complex and uncertain future: 'where sustainability aims to put the world back into balance, resilience looks for ways to manage in an imbalanced world' (Zolli, 2012). We can also compare the two concepts in terms of their transference into an ever-increasing array of policy discourse. As with resilience, when sustainable development (and sustainability) emerged with the publishing of *Our Common Future* by the UN, authored by Gro Harlem Brundtland (1987), it was clearly understood as a central policy metaphor for dealing with environmental change, yet then became overused in an array of policy discourses, losing its initial meaning as it did so. As the late, great Sir Peter Hall (2002, p.412) noted in *Cities of Tomorrow*, regarding the surge in popularity surrounding the 'holy grail' of sustainable urban development in the early 1990s:

> The problem was that although everyone was in favour of it, nobody knew exactly what it meant [...] though they could all quote by heart the definition of sustainability from the Brundtland Report of 1987 [...] it was not at all clear how this mapped onto actual everyday decisions in everyday urban contexts. The general objectives were easily enough understood [...] but the difficult part was the next step: to translate these objectives into actual contexts. Consequently and quite predictably, everyone defined them to suit themselves.

Will 'resilience' become the new 'sustainability' due to its overexposure in the policy realm? In order to unpack the operationalisation and usefulness of resilience in the contemporary world, in this chapter we acknowledge the ways in which different disciplines have approached the concept of resilience and its theorisation. We do this in three main sections. We first draw attention to, and critique, so-called *equilibrium* models of socio-ecological systems (SES) resilience that have dominated resilience discourse since the early 1970s and have focused upon bouncing back to a pre-defined state in response to stress or perturbation. Second, we highlight more *evolutionary* approaches that have emerged within the resilience literature and which, by contrast, focus upon a bounce forward and 'new normal' model of resilience, seeking to construct an approach more applicable to increasingly complex and non-linear systems. As the chapter progresses we connect these two approaches to resilience to a range of related concepts, such as robustness, resourcefulness, adaptability and redundancy which are recognised as key properties and means of improving systemic resilience. The third section provides a critique of contemporary resilience policy through three key, and inter-related, lenses – anticipation, localisation and responsibilisation – all framed through an overarching assessment of resilience as having been captured by neoliberalism and associated governmentalising agendas by which governments seek, through a range of organised governing practices, to shape an uncritical citizenry best suited to deliver its policy priorities.

The dominance of the socio-ecological equilibrium model

Resilience (from the Latin *resilire*) literally means 'to leap back'. It is a metaphor that has been discussed at length in the academic literature with various disciplines and sub-disciplines laying claim to its etymological evolution and applying it within different experimental, and largely theoretical, contexts (Coaffee, 2013a). While ecologists, psychologists, disaster managers, geographers, economists and social scientists have all contributed to the academic discussion of resilience with the idea subsequently creeping into a range of policy debates over the last decade (for a review see Coaffee *et al.*, 2008b; Walker and Cooper 2011) and more recently urban and regional planning practice (see Chapter 3), the resilience literature has, until recently, been overwhelmingly dominated and influenced by *ecological* and *engineering* approaches.

The use and application of the term resilience is broadly acknowledged to have emerged from C. S. 'Buzz' Holling's 1970s studies of systems ecology and his subsequent work with the Resilience Alliance (a research network comprised of scientists and practitioners from many disciplines who collaborate to explore the dynamics of socio-ecological systems). Holling's ideas, best portrayed in the classic 1973 paper *Resilience and Stability of Ecological Systems*, represented a paradigm shift in thinking, demonstrating a more dynamic process which he termed the *adaptive cycle*, differentiated from earlier understandings of ecological systems which assumed a stable basis. The adaptive cycle focused attention upon processes of destruction and reorganisation, which were often marginalised in classical ecosystem studies in favour of growth and conservation. Including these processes sought to give a more complete view of system dynamics.

The adaptive cycle was essentially an equilibrium model in which system resources go through periods of production, consumption and conservation and in which resilience is the ability of a system to either bounce back to a steady state or to absorb shock events and persist under stress. Here resilience was defined as a system's ability to 'absorb change and disturbance and still maintain the same relationships between populations or state variables' (Holling, 1973, p.14). In essence, Holling's model proposed that external shocks, such as forest fires, created new opportunities for resource exploitation and that the ability of species and systems to persist was based on an ability to adapt while still maintaining core functions in the face of this inevitable cycle of change.

The adaptive cycle of a resilient system was represented by four phases of system development, involving exploitation, conservation, release and reorganisation of resources. The exploitation–conservation phase represents a slow accumulation of system resources ready for a period of release–reorganisation. The phases of the adaptive cycle are depicted against two axes which represented the system potential and connectedness (see Figure 2.1). The connectedness and potential of the system increase during the exploitation–conservation phase as connections embed and augment system potential for resource production and release. Walker and Cooper (2011, p.147) provide a summary of this process, linking it to classical ecological study:

> Where classical systems ecology focused only on the phases of rapid successional growth (r) followed by the conservation phase of stable equilibrium (K), the Resilience Alliance argues that these phases are inevitably followed by collapse (Ω), and then a spontaneous reorganization that leads to a new growth phase (α).

Figure 2.1

The adaptive cycle of a resilient system

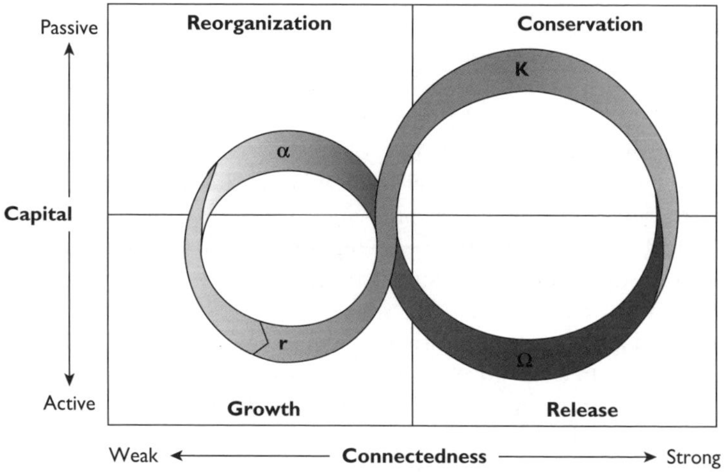

In Holling's (1996, p.33) words, such a dynamic adaptive cycle measures ecological resilience – the magnitude of change a system can absorb before it 'flips' and changes structure to another 'stability domain'. Ecological resilience in this definition focuses upon change and unpredictability *but* with a view to return to equilibrium.

A related definition – that of engineering resilience which Holling (1996) coined in comparison to ecological resilience – concentrates on stability and an equilibrium steady state where, specifically, resistance to disturbance and speed of return to normality is measured. Here, while ecological resilience was seen as the magnitude of disturbance that could be absorbed before a system changed its structure, engineering resilience is seen as the capacity of a system to move back as quickly as possible following a disturbance to its original equilibrium state. Such engineering resilience, although used extensively to measure the performance and resilience in technical systems, is seen by some as only a partial measure of overall system resilience (Walker *et al.*, 2004).

More contemporary approaches to resilience have borrowed heavily from Holling (1973) and Gunderson and Holling's (2002) adaptive–equilibrium models of resilience. For example, Zolli and Healy (2013) suggest that understanding of the adaptive cycle can be helpful in many other settings, such as how businesses can exploit new markets, while Fisher (2012) has suggested that designers can utilise an understanding of this model to improve resilience in the built environment. Walker and Cooper (2011) have also suggested that an understanding of the adaptive cycle was used by neoliberal economists to promote how an unregulated financial system would be self-governing. For example, Rose (2007) defined economic resilience in equilibrist terms as 'the ability of an entity or system to maintain function (e.g. continue producing) when shocked' (p.384; see also Chapter 9 of this book). More generally, Beilin and Wilkinson (2015, p.1206) have also emphasised how engineering resilience is often measured though techno-rational approaches to risk assessment and management that seeks to control the future and create the stability required to retain normal functioning. Others have also highlighted how engineered resilience, largely focusing on returning to a (imagined) stable state, has been prominent in disaster management literature and still dominates desired programme outcomes (Folke, 2006).

Increasingly, such equilibrist approaches associated with the so-called social–ecological systems (SES) have been critiqued as their influence has spread, particularly into the area of climate change adaptation. In general, such SES approaches are viewed as inherently conservative, and as noted above, have a core aim of system stability. They also tend to focus upon endogenous (internal) stresses with little attention given to exogenous (external) factors that might disturb or shock the system. More broadly, the development of SES based on equilibrium ideas is perhaps not best suited to modelling systems involving complex social dynamics which are less easy to conceptualise with theoretical models (Davoudi, 2012; Alexander, 2013). For many, SES resilience approaches fail to account for political and power relations within a complex social system which affects those whose needs are being met (resilience for whom?) and how distributional resource issues are mediated by political action. In essence, as Brown (2013, p.109) highlighted, an SES approach to resilience 'promotes a scientific and technical approach akin to "imposed rationality" that is alien to the practice of ordinary people [...] is depoliticized and does not take account of the institutions within which practices and management are embedded' (see also Cannon and Müller-Mahn, 2010). Early contributions in relation to urban and regional planning also problematised the use of the term and critically asked 'resilience of what to what?' (Beilin and Wilkinson, 2015, p.1206; see also Carpenter *et al.*, 2001) and, more broadly, questioned whether it is relevant to use resilience thinking at all within the social sciences (see also Chapter 3).

In an attempt to introduce greater social resonance and complexity into understandings of ecological resilience, the SES approach was 'updated', in particular through Gunderson and Holling's (2002) *Panarchy* which was premised upon a hierarchy of adaptive cycles and named after the Greek god Pan – 'the epitome of unpredictable change' (Holling, 2001, p.396). This approach attempted to reconcile some of the limitations and contradictions of the earlier theories by providing a conceptual framework to account for the dual, and seemingly contradictory, characteristics of all complex systems: stability and change. The panarchy model outlines phases that are neither fixed nor sequential, rather operating as multiple, nested adaptive cycles that function and interact independently (Davoudi, 2012; see also Chapter 9). Panarchy also recognises that internal functions can introduce change, as in social systems, in effect working from the bottom up as well as the top down (Figure 2.2).

The panarchy framework places great emphasis on the interconnectedness of system levels, between the smallest and the largest, and the fastest and slowest. In this framework, the large, slow cycles set the conditions in which the smaller, faster cycles operate, although the smaller, faster cycles can impact upon the larger, slower cycles. Here there are many possible points of interconnectedness between these adjacent levels, with two of particular note. First, *revolt*, which occurs when fast, small events overwhelm large, slow ones, for example when a small local power cut causes cascading impacts through a range of interdependent infrastructure systems causing wider scales of disruption. Second, *remember*, which facilitates a return to stability by drawing on the potential that has

Figure 2.2

A panarchy of nested systems

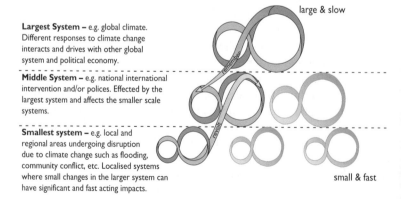

Largest System – e.g. global climate. Different responses to climate change interacts and drives with other global system and political economy.

Middle System – e.g. national international intervention and/or polices. Effected by the largest system and affects the smaller scale systems.

Smallest system – e.g. local and regional areas undergoing disruption due to climate change such as flooding, community conflict, etc. Localised systems where small changes in the larger system can have significant and fast acting impacts.

large & slow

small & fast

been accumulated and stored in a larger, slower cycle. For example, after a widespread power cut, it could refer to the processes and resources such as knowledge, experience and memories of coping with prior events that help to guide the system back to its normal operating state. Sometimes, though, this return is to a different path than the former state and is referred to as a hysteresis effect – referring to how a system responds to a loss of resilience, or more specifically, the return path taken following some disturbance or change due to cumulative effects which serve to increase resilience again (Ludwig, Walker and Holling, 1997).

However, such a model, despite its acknowledgement of complexity and social systems, is still, for many, too divorced from reality of non-linear complex adaptive systems to be applied appropriately in a range of socio-economic and political policy spheres, failing to take into account the unevenness of space, inequality, power, or the agency of actors within social systems. Therefore, while the term resilience has its roots in physical science (physics and engineering) and natural science (ecology, biology and biosciences) it is increasingly seen as a 'political, cultural, and social construction' (White and O'Hare, 2014, p.943) that is not amenable to wholesale transfer from the natural to the social sciences. As Cote and Nightingale (2012, p.475) have contended, resilience in SES has 'evolved through the application of ecological concepts to society assuming that social and ecological system dynamics are essentially similar', further arguing that resilience ideas have grown in 'remarkable isolation from critical social science literature' (cited in Brown, 2013). It is to this critical social science literature that we now turn in exploring emerging 'evolutionary' approaches to resilience.

Towards an evolutionary approach

The thinking and practices of resilience are increasingly contested, leading a number of researchers to argue for a more evolutionary approach to be adopted to consider the nature of constantly changing non-equilibrium systems (see Carpenter *et al.*, 2005). As Majoor (2015, p. 257) noted, 'here the existence of an equilibrium or state of normality has been replaced by the insight that the world is inherently complex, uncertain and unpredictable'. Thus more nuanced ideas of resilience have moved away from unquestioned equilibrium approaches and have sought to embrace adaptation and change as a means to ensure that a systems functioning continues (Prior and Hagmann, 2013). Edwards, in *Resilient Nation* (2009, p.17), contends that an understanding of resilience based upon 'bouncing back' is 'too narrow, too short term and too reactive', while Shaw (2012a) suggests that we need to consider a more proactive conception of 'leaping forward'. Here, in contrast to equilibrist models that seek a recovery to a (pre-existing or new) stable state, resilience is considered as an ongoing process that seeks to understand and adapt to the complexities of constant change (Coaffee, 2013a). Work, particularly in evolutionary economics (Simmie and Martin, 2010) and urban planning, has adopted and modified important aspects of the adaptive cycle and panarchy models to broaden the description of resilience beyond bounce-back approaches (Folke *et al.*, 2010) and to incorporate 'the dynamic interplay between persistence, adaptability and transformability across multiple scales and timeframes' (Davoudi, 2012, p.310).

The widening of the resilience metaphor and application within a broader policy arena is logical as it is in correspondence with the complexity and interrelated nature of truly 'global' or 'globally significant' events that combined exogenous and endogenous forces, such as climate change/environmental disasters, and how these influence anthropogenic systems at a variety of spatial scales. Events during the early part of the twenty-first century such as Hurricane Katrina in 2005, the global economic recession and credit crunch between 2008 and 2013, and the 2011 Great East Japan earthquake demonstrate a need for responses which are multi-agency (vertical and horizontal integration) and multi-scalar (global–national–regional–local) where the initial shock poses a threat to integrated 'systems' and often illuminates more persistent stresses at a local and regional scale.

On the one hand so-called evolutionary resilience approaches have advanced as a reaction to the acknowledged limitations of equilibrium models, often creating a binary opposition to highlight difference. On the other hand we do not want to fall into the trap of dismissing the attributes associated with equilibrium models as, in many ways, these have been appropriated and expanded upon by more recent theories, ideas and practices. Therefore we would argue that at present we are witnessing a transitionary period between equilibrist and evolutionary approaches based on the advancement of a number of key attributes: preparedness and persistence; adaptability, responsiveness and resourcefulness; redundancy and diversity; and cycles and feedback. Below we expand on these attributes in more detail.

Preparedness and persistence

Preparedness is increasingly utilised in resilience approaches to anticipate potential shocks and stresses and to allow ample preparation for such events. Such 'anticipatory planning' is also frequently used to reduce future uncertainties and often takes the form of enhancing core capabilities amongst key 'responders'. For example, the London Resilience Partnership's 2013 strategy document highlighted a number of 'core' functional capabilities that underpin their preparatory resilience work and which help them identify vulnerabilities and accumulate knowledge:

- *Risk assessment* – assessing the hazards and threats to London, and understanding what impacts these could have – this then drives what capabilities need to be developed;
- *Training and exercising* – all plans and procedures need to be exercised, to make sure they work in practice, and those who have a role in responding to an incident trained to be able to fulfil that role;
- *Coordination and information sharing* – identifying and agreeing the principles by which coordination of multi-agency response and recovery to an incident occurs;
- *Communicating with the public* – making sure people who live, work and visit London are aware of the risks and how they can prepare, and that in the event of an emergency they are given accurate, timely information. (London Resilience Partnership, 2013, p.8)

Linked to a better understanding of risk and vulnerability is the related concept of *persistence* – the ability to withstand a given level of stress (Davoudi, 2012) – that is often connected to infrastructural and human systems. Persistence in this context can be related to classical engineering models of resilience and viewed in terms of the 'robustness' of a system. This type of definition is particularly common in the sub-field of critical infrastructure resilience. As a recent US study noted:

The *robustness* component of resilience is the ability to *maintain critical operations and functions in the face of crisis*. It is directly related to the ability of the system to absorb the impacts of a hazard and to avoid or decrease the importance of the event that could be generated by this hazard. Robustness can be seen as the protection and preparation of a system facing a specific danger. (Argonne National Laboratory, 2010, p.6, emphasis added)

While robustness in most instances can be seen as a short-term protective measure, the physical and technical ability of a system to persist in light of a stress or challenge in the longer term, or within a dynamic social context, can be influenced by what Davoudi (2012) referred to as 'institutional rigidities' which can stifle adaptability and innovation both in the short and long term. (In their panarchy model, Gunderson and Holling (2002) outlined the idea of a 'rigidity trap' where particular adaptive cycles decline due to maladaptation as a result of a high degree of connectedness within institutions that are often seen as lacking diversity and are inflexible to change.) Thus in evolutionary resilience great emphasis is placed upon the institutionalism and governance of resilience and in particular ways in which organisational flexibility and learning can be fostered alongside public 'awareness raising' campaigns that encourage individuals to be resilient by taking appropriate risk mitigation measures and preparing for an emergency (Coaffee and Clarke, 2015).

Adaptability, responsiveness and resourcefulness

Adaptability is a key concept in evolutionary resilience which 'captures the capacity of a system to learn, combine experience and knowledge, [and] adjust its responses to changing external drivers and internal processes' (Folke *et al.*, 2010, p.18). Adaptability (often seen through the lens of adaptive capacity, see Chapter 4) is frequently perceived as a function of the type and quality of networked linkages and multi-scale cooperation. Pike *et al.* (2010), for example, argue that more flexible linkages can enhance system responsiveness and allow multiple evolutionary trajectories to emerge, thus fostering greater system resilience. In contrast, tight linkages can be seen to enforce path dependency. Where such adaptability is arguably most required is at the local level where adaptive capacity and resources are demanded most in relation to local government's resilience needs:

> In disasters, local governments are the first line of response, sometimes with wide-ranging responsibilities but insufficient capacities to deal with them. They are equally on the front line when it comes to anticipating, managing and reducing disaster risk, setting up or acting on early warning systems and establishing

specific disaster/crisis management structures. In many cases, a review of mandates, responsibilities and resource allocations is needed to increase the capacity of local governments to respond to these challenges. (UNISDR, 2012b, p.7)

In order to mobilise adaptability an additional key component of evolutionary resilience is required – *resourcefulness* – which is seen as the network of actors across multiple scales that are expected to play a role in better coordinating and mobilising assets and creating an enhanced capacity to act in the face of risk, crisis and uncertainty. In the emerging resilience literature this has perhaps two distinct meanings. First, and from a more technical perspective, it refers to efficiency and the ability to get back to normal functioning (rapidity) and operationally the ability to skilfully prepare for, respond to, and manage a crisis or disruption as it unfolds. Here, resourcefulness comprises the steps taken prior to an event to prepare for possible threats and the application of the training and planning once an event unfolds. Second, resourcefulness can be seen as an alternative to resilience, which, for an increasing array of critical resilience scholars, is seen as lacking social justice. MacKinnon and Derickson (2013, p.263), for example, see resourcefulness as 'one in which communities have the capacity to engage in genuinely deliberative democratic dialogue to develop contestable alternative agendas and work in ways that meaningfully challenge existing power relations'.

Redundancy and diversity

A critical difference between equilibrist and evolutionary resilience approaches is the assumptions concerning the role that redundancy plays in the ability of communities to absorb shocks and how this underpins resilient systems. Redundancy is recognised as a key property and means of improving the resilience of systems and relates to alternative sources, sub-systems, roles or strategies that provide a back-up function for each other and increase the resilience of the whole system. Redundancy has also been defined as 'the extent to which elements, systems, or other units of analysis exist that are substitutable, i.e., capable of satisfying functional requirements in the event of disruption, degradation, or loss of functionality' (Bruneau *et al.*, 2003, p.737). In natural and engineering systems redundancy provides the capacity and ability to absorb and still persist. By contrast, redundancy in social systems is characterised as inefficiency and arises from the pursuit of efficiency within urban economic systems.

Redundancy can, however, be an essential resource in the resilience process, necessary for adaptive capacity. In resilience language this is about reducing path dependencies and optimising paths through utilisation of resources to enhance alternative path development. In technical systems, with the drive for optimisation, having a Plan B was seen as wasteful. In more evolutionary resilience approaches, having a diversity of options as 'back up' is seen as a vital asset that fosters adaptability, innovation and self-organisation.

Cycles and feedback

Resilience is increasingly being understood as a never-ending journey – a cyclical process involving a number of overlapping stages, with distinct emphasise and policy priorities (Coaffee, 2013a). This resonates with SES emphasis on adaptive cycles and feedback loops but grounds it within more contemporary approaches to complex adaptive systems. As such, resilience has become an increasingly central organising metaphor within the policy-making process across all aspects of a 'resilience cycle' of mitigation, preparedness, response and recovery (see Figure 2.3) – a cycle that encourages the continual

Figure 2.3

The integrated resilience cycle

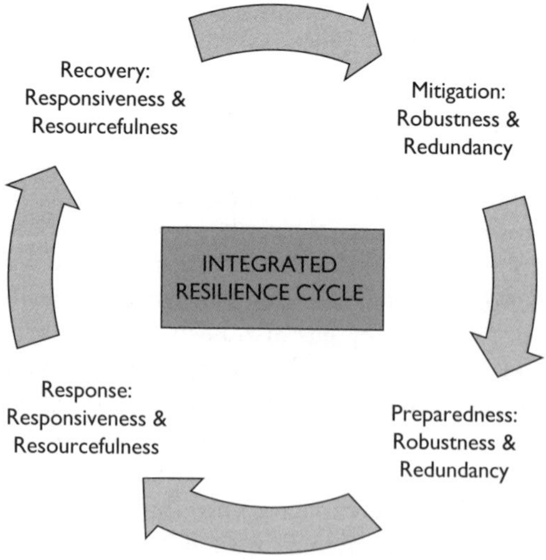

reappraisal of plans and strategies. The different aspects of the cycle pay attention to different attributes of evolutionary resilience (noted in the sections above). In many ways the resilience cycle draws heavily on the traditional emergency or risk management cycle of prevention, preparedness, response and recovery, but places much greater stress upon the preparedness phase of the cycle.

The mitigation part of the resilience cycle is focused upon strengthening the capabilities in order to better cope with future disruptive challenges, often with a focus upon robustness and redundancy. Mitigation involves taking sustained actions to reduce or eliminate long-term risk to people and infrastructure from a range of stresses and their effects. Mitigation is the initial phase of the resilience cycle and should be considered before an incident or emergency occurs. Mitigation should also be integrated with each of the other phases of the resilience cycle to facilitate a long-range approach. Typical mitigation techniques will be used to protect people and structures; reduce the costs of response and recovery; and undertake risk assessment.

Preparedness is mainly focused around anticipating events and creating a response capability often connecting to principles of robustness and redundancy. This phase involves enhancing the ability to anticipate disruptive changes and to put in place a management regime to respond effectively to, and recover from, local disruptive changes. While it is not possible to mitigate for every hazardous incident or threat, good preparatory activity can help to reduce the impact of incidents by taking certain actions before an event occurs. Preparedness activities are integrated into response and recovery operations and tend to include a range of stakeholders and multiple interlocking scales – local, regional, and national agencies, organisations and citizens. Preparedness activities are typically operationalised at the local level and might include tools to: analyse probable threats and risk assessment; develop resilience plans that address identified hazards, risks and response measures; design response management structures and train staff in key areas of response operations; conduct scenario planning and exercising; designate facilities for emergency use; and set up appropriate warning systems.

The response phase of the resilience cycle involves action taken during, and immediately after, an incident or event occurs, focusing on minimising damage and disruption and allowing a system to re-establish functionality as rapidly as possible. Response often focuses upon responsiveness and resourcefulness and typically involves conducting operations to reduce the impact from a hazard or threat to acceptable levels (or eliminate it entirely). In the case of a disaster situation this might involve evacuating potential victims, providing care to those in need and restoring critical public services and infrastructure. At this stage of the cycle many measures focus upon the collation of critical information required, including information about: lifesaving needs, such as evacuation and search and rescue; the status of critical infrastructure, such as transportation, utilities, communication systems, the status of critical facilities, and the potential for cascading events (events that occur as a direct or indirect result of an initial event). In other words, response involves putting preparedness plans into action and typically involves conducting a situation assessment to determine the most appropriate response activities.

The recovery phase of the resilience cycle seeks to utilise the attributes of responsiveness and resourcefulness and involves short-term or long-term phases of rebuilding and restoration so that individuals, businesses and governments can function and protect against future disruptive challenges. The ultimate goal of the recovery phase is to return the systems and activities to normal, or a 'new normality', based on a better appreciation of risk. Recovery begins right after an event with, for example, damage assessment. Some recovery activities may be concurrent with response efforts. Long-term recovery includes restoring economic activity and rebuilding community facilities and housing, and putting in place mitigation measures to ensure against future challenges.

Resilience for whom, and by whom? A critique of contemporary resilience

The shift in resilience approaches focused upon moving equilibrium ideas towards an alternative evolutionary and transformative doctrine required in an age of increased volatility and uncertainty is not without critique. Much of this critique concerns the alleged tarnishing of resilience ideas through continued processes of control enacted through neoliberalism and a post-political, or depoliticising, landscape characterised by: the disciplining role of consensus towards an uncontestable moral (rather than political) ordering (Mouffe, 2005; Hay, 2007; Swyngedouw, 2009); the rise in experts as a substitute for proper political debate (Zizek, 2008; Fischer,

2009); the rise of governance beyond the state (participatory governance, delegation to experts or transnational networks); and a fatefulness in formal politics regarding, in particular, economic globalisation. Here, post-politics can be understood as the foreclosing of political choice, the delegation of decision making to technocratic experts, growing public disengagement from politics and ultimately the closing down of political debate and agency (Flinders and Wood, 2014).

Resilience has been recognised by a range of transnational organisations and governance coalitions as a means of further pursuing an explicitly neoliberal agenda (Swyngedouw, 2005). Many argue that the prevailing imagination of resilience has dominated debates on how we live with incalculable and volatile risk – debates that focus on the cultivation of a certain kind of citizenship that sits neatly within neoliberal rationalities, are politically exploitable and often fail to address alternative imaginaries and the possibilities of more radical social and political transformation. In the contemporary era resilience has thus become central to the discussion of shifting social and political histories and to the framework of agents and agencies operating under the guise of national security and disaster mitigation and as an active rationale for the *modus operandi* of governance underpinning crisis (Buckle *et al.*, 2000). In more practical terms, through the lens of resilience policy we can chart new forms of precautionary governance, attempts to create resilient citizens, the drawing in of a range of stakeholders to the resilience agenda and the corresponding adoption of new roles and responsibilities in enacting policy priorities.

This emerging canon of work in 'critical resilience studies' thus seeks to critique the way resilience policy and practice has become a vehicle for 'neoliberal decentralisation' (Amin, 2013), indicating a shift in the state's policies which reflects a desire to step back from its responsibilities to ensure the protection of the population during crisis and to delegate to certain professions, private companies, communities and individuals. Such a Foucauldian interpretation argues that resilience encourages individuals to autonomously act in the face of a crisis or a disaster (as part of a wider emerging governmentality – or 'conduct of conducts'), which precipitates citizens behaving and adapting according to prescribed moral standards, often driven by neoliberal requirements (see, for example, Joseph, 2013; Zebrowski, 2013). As Welsh (2014, p.16) highlighted in relation to what he considers a problematic deployment of resilience discourses through different modes of governance, resilience is seen as: 'a post-political ideology of constant adaptation attuned to the uncertainties of neoliberal economy where the resilient subject is conceived as resilient to the extent it adapts to, rather than resists, the conditions of its suffering'. It is to these key concerns, organised around the interconnected themes of *anticipation, localisation* and *responsibilisation* that this chapter now turns.

Anticipation, pre-emption and the colonisation of the future

Today, the mitigation of risk in all its guises has proved to be the catalyst, if not the defining priority, behind an array of policy discourses linked to resilience. This has led to a change in thinking by policy makers and professional practice with new working definitions and new ways of thinking, seeing and responding to risk being developed in response to a wide range of dangers hazards and disasters.

Such policies – often explicitly badged as resilience – are increasingly anticipatory and pre-emptive in nature and, for many, come wrapped up in a cloak of fear. Anderson (2007, p.159), for example, has noted how 'fear, dread and anxiety accompany the emergence of anticipatory logics of governance' and how 'heightened concerns about a range of risks, now in almost every conceivable sphere of thought and life are argued to have generated a culture of fear'. Specifically in relation to the so-called post-9/11 'War on Terror', Elmer and Opel (2006, p.477) highlighted how 'what if' scenarios, relating to the likelihood of the US being attacked, have been replaced by 'when, then' scenarios. In other words, the inevitability of further risk is assumed, and pre-planned for. Such anticipatory logic, often then, provides the justification for state-level affirmative and pre-emptive action with a number of commentators arguing that this emergent politics of fear is being manipulated by governments through 'planning for emergencies' guidance to citizens or public 'threat assessment levels' (see, for example, Mythern and Walklate 2006). Notably, Massumi (2005) argued that the public US threat-alert system for terrorism is intended to 'calibrate the public's anxiety' and 'make visible the government's much advertised commitment to fighting the "war" on terror' (p.33). This is not a new concern. Massumi's earlier work (1993, p.viii) on the politics of fear highlighted that for some time, and particularly after World War Two, the 'social landscape of fear' has intensified, with a low-level 'ambient' fear now insinuating itself within everyday life (see also Deleuze, 1992; Hardt and Negri, 2002).

For many authors this perpetual fear amounts to a permanent state of emergency where exceptional conditions become normalised as the status quo, and where new discourses – in this case, resilience – emerge to reassure the public that they are safe (Coaffee and Wood 2006). As Agamben (2005), writing in the wake of 9/11, noted, such exceptionalism within particular locales becomes normalised with little social scrutiny under attempts to anticipate future risk and threats. Arias (2011, p.370) also argued, this 'biopolitical paradigm organises life in such a way that it is understood as constant contingency, which, thus, constantly requires exceptional measures'. Exceptionalism is, as Minca (2006) further commented, firmly rooted in the notion of crisis and has become the new biopolitical *nomos*; the 'dominant paradigm of government' (Agamben, 2005, p.3). The spreading domestication of exceptional risk and security, considered at one time to be unacceptable or temporary, has become mundane, everyday and unchallenged (normalised) in particular spatial contexts and under the rubric of resilience.

Here normalising exceptionalism within resilience policy is often operationalised largely through a variety of foresight documents, forward-looking security strategies, future threat assessments and risk registers, and associated simulated practice exercises, which in effect have attempted to embed the need to be constantly prepared for an array of risks and threats:

> Symbolically, the deployment of resilience discourses reformulates crises and uncertainty as not uncontrollable, but as an opportunity to proactively confront threats and even to provide general betterment. Particularly in circumstances where individuals, communities, and businesses can do little to be immunised from risk, resilience – embedded within a language of assurance and comfort – offers hope and confidence. *Resilience is therefore opportunistically tailored to fill 'policy windows' yielded in the wake of crises or in response to emerging perils.* (White and O'Hare, 2014, p.939, emphasis added)

This form of anticipatory and precautionary governance, often focused upon worst-case scenarios, also raises serious questions about the power of political rhetoric in shaping policy and the role of citizens and other stakeholders in decision making and the enacting of policy. Resilience policies engage and encourage:

> a culture of preparedness. The state now assumes that one of its key tasks is to imagine the worst-case scenario, the coming

catastrophe, the crisis-to-come, the looming attack, the emergency that could happen, might happen and probably will happen, all in order to be better prepared. (Neocleous, 2013, p.4)

Through such a requirement to attempt to anticipate the future through preparedness activities, resilience thinking has become embedded in a range of interlinked policy objectives – from health to housing, and from the environment to urban and regional planning – in ways the state had previously found impossible to do. As Neocleous further asserts 'resilience' is 'the concept that facilitates that connection: nothing less than the attempted colonization of the political imagination by the state'. (ibid.)

Localisation and the rescaling of the governance of resilience

Recent years have witnessed considerable evolution and deployment of concepts and practices of resilience at multiple scales of governmental action: on one hand developing an array of national policy guidance and strategies while on the other hand ostensibly decentralising responsibility to the local scale (Coaffee and Fussey, 2015). In most countries that have operationalised resilience-like policies, this is premised on a command and control approach from central government, and actualised through meta-strategies linked to national security or emergency management. Here central government can influence the approaches of associated stakeholders and communities through resource allocation and compliance mechanisms and through the development of specific and general plans. For example, in the UK centralised resilience policy has a number of guiding principles (see Box 2.1) that influence the way in which resilience is subject to a multi-scale governance fix (Coaffee and Wood, 2006).

For the UK, like many other countries that are rolling out resilience policy at a range of scales, subsidiarity is a key guiding principle (Box 2.1). Such ongoing devolutionary processes generate questions over the capacity and connectivity of resilience practice, the degree to which existing hierarchies become translated at the local level and the generation of new hierarchies within newly configured networks of local practice. Here there has been a shift, from traditional Euclidian, Cartesian and Westphalian notions of scale and territory as a fixed, stable, bounded container, to a more diverse set of arrangements where networked relations are

Box 2.1   *The guiding governance principles of UK resilience*

Preparedness – All those individuals and organisations that might have to respond to emergencies should be properly prepared, including having clarity of roles and responsibilities.

Continuity – Response to emergencies should be grounded in the existing functions of organisations and familiar ways of working, albeit delivered at a greater tempo, on a larger scale and in more testing circumstances.

Subsidiarity – Decisions should be taken at the lowest appropriate level, with coordination at the highest necessary level. Local responders should be the building block of response on any scale.

Direction – Clarity of purpose should be delivered through a strategic aim and supporting objectives that are agreed and understood by all involved to prioritise and focus the response.

Integration – Effective coordination should be exercised between and within organisations and tiers of response as well as timely access to appropriate guidance and appropriate support for the local or regional level.

Communication – Good two-way communication is critical to an effective response. Reliable information must be passed correctly and without delay between those who need to know, including the public.

Cooperation – Positive engagement based on mutual trust and understanding will facilitate information sharing and deliver effective solutions to issues arising.

Anticipation – Risk identification and analysis is needed of potential direct and indirect developments to anticipate and thus manage the consequences.

(UK Resilience Guidance, 2005, p.4)

continually rescaled and renegotiated. New agencies and networks populate a growing landscape of resilience practice that, in turn, brings an assortment of organisational priorities and approaches. Although driven by developments such as globalisation and devolution, resilience-related 'politics of scale' hold strong resonance with the emerging and fluid geopolitical landscape of more traditional security concerns (Coaffee and Fussey, 2015). For example, over the last decade responses to a range of security threats have increasingly highlighted the importance of sub-national and localised responses to new security challenges, which require analysis through a different frame of reference than the realist state-centric security studies orthodoxy, 'placing the needs of the individual, not states, at the centre of security discourses' (Chandler, 2012, p.214). As has been argued in academic discourse, 'security is becoming more civic, urban, domestic and personal: security is coming home' (Coaffee and Wood, 2006, p.504). In a similar way, the focus of resilience policy is increasingly being directed towards smaller spatial scales and everyday activities.

In many respects, such localised resilience practices mirror broader trends in public governance of the past 20 years where the regulatory state 'steers' via strategy and the 'rowing' of implementation is carried out locally (Osborne and Gaebler, 1993). Here, resilience practices become nested in the local area, providing a fit with wider government ambitions to create a new, more community-driven, social contract between citizens and the state (Coaffee, 2013a). As a result resilience approaches become realised not through state institutions, but upon localised networked responses, with governance dispersed more widely across key stakeholders and sectors. Enhanced citizen resilience is, however, more often than not, still articulated through the lens of emergency planning with the belief that greater resilience will be produced by 'communities and individuals harnessing local resources and expertise to help themselves in an emergency in a way that complements the response of the emergency services' (Cabinet Office, 2011, p.4). In the UK, this push for resilience is also connected with the ideals of place-based resilience as promoted under the government's 'Big Society' commitment to 'reduce the barriers which prevent people from being able to help themselves and to become more resilient to shocks' (ibid, p.3). Such initiatives encourage the development of community or institutional resilience, and of the 'responsible citizen', in accordance with new techniques of governmentality: the replacement of state-centric 'protective' security approaches with those emphasising 'self-organising' human security.

Yet for all the focus on local and subjective individual performance of resilience functions, the persistence of state governance from a distance (Joseph, 2013) enables multiple extant hierarchies and separations of tasks to remain and exert themselves. At the same time, the proliferation of resilience discourse has led to increasingly broad coalitions of practice and a cluttered organisational landscape (Coaffee and Fussey, 2015). The localisation and diversification of the governance of and responsibility for resilience-focused practices therefore generates a series of questions around where influence lies during a time of crisis.

Responsibilisation: The changing roles and responsibilities in resilience practice

Related to the critique of resilience as rescaled and localised, another common argument made in the critical resilience literature concerns the movement of responsibility for resilience against a range of perturbations towards individual actors and local scales of operation. In a particularly staunch criticism, this process of redistributing responsibility and governance to the local level has been labelled a form of 'neoliberal citizenship' (Neocleous, 2013, p.5). Others have likened this relocation of resilience practice to a means of protecting economic and political elites from fulfilling responsibilities for the vulnerable, human and nonhuman (Walker and Cooper, 2011, p.156).

As the push for evolutionary resilience policy that can respond in a flexible fashion to multiple risks across a range of scales has been encouraged alongside specific planning for high-likelihood or high-impact 'events', the changing institutionalisation of resilience has come under scrutiny. In particular, new governance approaches to enhancing resilience emphasise joined-up approaches to decision making involving a greater array of individuals and organisations within strategic resilience efforts. In other words, the emergence of resilience has disrupted the traditional relationship between the state and the individual with 'governing from a distance' and as Rose (2000, p.324) noted, this places the onus upon individuals and communities to 'regenerate and reactivate their ethical values' in order to 'regulate individual conduct'. This shift in emphasis has broader implications for the participation and responsibility of the citizen as an actor in embedding resilience into everyday life and demonstrates the ways in which *everyone* is now intended to be involved in the performance of resilience with modes of behaviour encouraged through the discussion of resilience: 'we are all risk managers and resilient subjects now' (Coaffee, 2013a, p.8).

The governance of resilience, and particularly the interactions between citizen and state, is, therefore, progressively 'responsibilising' (Garland 1996); putting the onus for preventing and preparing for disruptive challenge onto institutions, professions, communities and individuals rather than the state, the traditional provider of citizens' security needs (Coaffee *et al.*, 2008b; 2013a; Welsh, 2014). Ever-increasing numbers of local, public-facing individuals and agencies thus become drawn into resilience roles. As recent work on resilient subjectivity in late modernity has also argued, resilience policy appears to be part of 'a complex of scientifically grounded techniques of the self, necessary to optimize autonomous subject in an age of high uncertainty' (O'Malley, 2010, p.488). Such 'optimisation' projects targeted at so-called 'neurotic citizens' (Isin, 2004) are now widespread, and seek to shift responsibility for resilience and risk management to general local-level governing practices and non-government subjects. In essence, resilience policies and practices transfer responsibilities for exogenous shocks and locate their response endogenously.

The underpinning rhetoric of the need to be resilient is becoming increasingly influential in public policy making as resilience moves from the periphery to the centre of government action. This has seen resilience policy evolve from a rhetoric of absorbing shock towards being more pre-emptive and then on to embedding resilience thinking as an everyday and localised activity. This has led concomitantly to the dispersion of security and risk management-related responsibilities to all levels of government and to an increasing collaborative network of locally based, resilience-focused, professionals and communities (such as urban and regional planning). Increasingly, non-state actors are being 'captured' within new modes of governmentality and held accountable or responsible for managing resilience through the implementation of incentives, targets and legal obligations. From an ideological perspective 'resilience has also become a valuable political strategy facilitating neoliberal shifts in the responsibilities for risk governance from the state toward the private sector and communities, not least given how the costs to manage risks are perceived to be increasing' (White and O'Hare, 2014, p.940).

This decentralisation of responsibility to meet resilience objectives does, however, run alongside a parallel centralisation of power to shape the agenda back towards the state through a constant stream of nationally derived guidance (MacKinnon and Derickson, 2013). This is a far more pervasive and widespread responsibilisation of citizens and local actors than that highlighted previously (see, for example, Dean, 1999), cloaked in the softer and more palatable language of resilience which has facilitated 'a shift' in dominant security discourse in terms of scale of intervention (Chandler, 2012). Additionally, many have argued that this is assisted by the political neutrality of resilience which, as Welsh (2014, p.21) asserts, can become defined by 'a set of consensual socio-scientific knowledge that reduce the political to the policing of change [...] diverting attention from questions of power, justice or the types of (socio-natural) future that can be envisaged'.

Viewed through this lens, everybody now has a moral responsibility, whether vague or defined, in developing resilience within government frameworks with an implicit agenda of civil responsibilisation, and the passing on of the risk management baton from state to citizen. Governments and institutions, having lost their ability to fully manage contemporary risk, have diffused their responsibility to a plethora of 'authorities' and 'institutions' and 'communities' who are subtly steered by the hand of supposedly apolitical 'experts'. This, for many, is seen as an expression of 'neoliberal governmentality' and represents a new relationship between the state, associated transnational networks, and civil society actors.

The transition towards evolutionary resilience

While there are a number of attempts to measure and assess resilience (see Chapter 5) it is not easily amenable to *precise* calibration and is highly dependent on context. The malleability and flexibility in the use of the resilience concept has, however, made equilibrium approaches to resilience politically acceptable and durable. Such approaches seek to preserve system stability – to bounce back – after a perturbation and focus upon short-term and reactive measures predominantly concerning endogenous risk. By common consensus such resilience approaches do not transfer well from natural to social systems analysis, but importantly have paved the way for a more complex and transformative approach to resilience to emerge, albeit with a high degree of critique. As Welsh (2014, p.17) has highlighted, 'the dangers and difficulties of translating theories and concepts between epistemic communities have not been lost on researchers instrumental in developing and popularising the discourse outside its ecological heartlands'. However, confusion over resilience terminology need not detract from its utility (Strunz, 2012) and as Prior and Hagmann (2013, p.2) note, 'given that many threats or disruptions to society must increasingly be addressed in a systemic manner across disciplines, confusion and contradiction pose methodological limits for the operationalisation of resilience approaches'. The challenge for policy making is in accurately capturing the nature of the problem across scales and the appropriate mechanism to underpin resilience policy.

Evolutionary approaches – often portrayed as the binary opposite for equilibrium approaches – focus upon adaptability and flexibility with the function of restoration to a new normality and an increasingly complex and volatile world: 'evolutionary resilience promotes the understanding of places not as units of analysis or neutral containers, but as complex, interconnected socio-spatial systems with extensive and unpredictable feedback processes which operate at multiple scales and timeframes' (Davoudi, 2012, p.304). Such approaches tend to be proactive and focus predominantly on the medium- to long-term exogenous risk. We would contend, though, that as a move towards resilience is always in a state of becoming, such constantly transformative approaches are vital in aiding our understanding of how society responds to volatility and unpredictability. We would also contend that in practice – and in its current guise – evolutionary resilience is rare. Rather, we would see an ongoing paradigm shift occurring *from* equilibrium *to* evolutionary approaches. In this transition we see resilience is as much about a set of transformative learning processes as it is about outputs and outcomes. As we have also highlighted in this chapter, the implementation of resilience is not without its challenges, in particular related to the way in which its increased usage as a policy metaphor appears to be altering the traditional social contract between the state and citizen which is leading to the dispersion of responsibilities to all levels of government and to an increasing array of locally based professionals and communities.

Such resilience rhetoric is, however, often vague and imprecise. The malleability of resilience has parallels in human geography and social policy. The concept of social exclusion, for example, is incontestable – no politician would argue for more social exclusion! But in shifting the focus from *distributional* disadvantage (poverty) to *relational* disadvantage (social exclusion) the creation of the illusion that politicians care about disadvantage without tying policy makers down to identifying a threshold for relative deprivation or a poverty line is achieved. Social exclusion's malleability hides its political *raison d'être* – that of reducing the state and emphasising the role of the market and community (and family) as a means of social inclusion (Lee, 2010). Likewise resilience's malleability allows the state to walk clear of responsibility, to cloak its mantra of resilience and caring for communities affected by crisis events by putting them at the centre of their solution. White and O'Hare (2014) also liken the rise of resilience to that of sustainable development in the 1990s with each term becoming a 'perfect symbol of its time [and with] the very same fuzzy qualities which aided its rise remain unaddressed, they may serve to undermine the effect of a promising notion to manage change in an uncertain world' (p.947). However, there is no doubting the potential of resilience, like sustainability before it, to stimulate change in the way we think about urban development, both now and in the future:

> Resilience, like sustainability before it, is an idea with potentially transformative power. Resilience is all about our capacity to survive and thrive in the face of disruptions of all kinds. If we were to take resilience seriously (highly recommended in our increasingly disruption-prone world), we would make some far-reaching changes in how we live. (Mazur and Fairchild, 2015)

Despite much of the criticism of resilience and resilience policy – that it draws in an anticipatory and precautionary logic, that it is a depoliticising and reactive tool of government, and that it responsibilises professions and individual communities – we, like others, prefer to focus upon how its usage and the implementation of its 'principles' might be repoliticised so as to illuminate and change its uneven and problematic deployment and 'to ultimately recast resilience as a potential antidote, rather than complement, to perpetual neo-liberal vulnerability and insecurity' (Paganini, 2015). The potentially positive force of resilience to transform the status quo and shine a light on how future vulnerabilities might be tackled, as we will see in the next chapter on the urban resilience turn, is having a significant influence upon urban and regional planning and can provide a proactive and optimistic set of frameworks and imaginaries for assessing and adapting to a range of contemporary and future risks.

Part II

Processes of Urban Resilience

Chapter 3

The Resilience Turn in Planning Policy and Practice

In their 2011 work on the politics of resilience Walker and Cooper note that 'resilience as an operational strategy of risk management has more recently been taken up in financial, urban and environmental security discourses' (Walker and Cooper, 2011, p.143). In the last decade ideas of resilience, and its underpinning principles, have also slowly infused into urban policy-making circles. Resilience perspectives have become increasingly rooted in urban and regional planning with policy makers and the public increasingly turning to planners in times of risk, crisis and uncertainty to provide protection from a volatile future:

> As urban areas expand [...] how to plan for resilience will continue to raise important questions for city governments and planners. *Urban planning approaches that recognise these challenges* and aim to maximise synergies between municipal government, the planning profession, hazard scientists, civil society, private sector, residents and other critical stakeholders *can prove highly effective in managing risk and emerge as a key component of resilience.* (Valdes and Purcell, 2013, emphasis added)

Resilience can be viewed as the latest in a long line of natural and ecological metaphors to be applied to the theory and practice of planning (Evans, 2011). The impact of a resilience discourse as a framing device for planning practice has been significant: 'from relatively discrete beginnings, resilience now has potentially profound implications for the theory and practice of spatial planning', note White and O'Hare (2014, p.3). MacKinnon and Derickson (2013, p.258) go further to suggest that 'organic conceptions of cities as systems displaying natural traits such as growth, competition and self-organization have proven particularly influential' albeit with serious implications for urban governance. As demonstrated by the socio-ecological systems (SES) approach (see Chapter 2) such an ecological modelling approach was often inward focused, serving to artificially separate urban systems with wider exogenous forces such as flows of capital, and with an assumption that social systems would imitate natural resilient processes.

Urban resilience, viewed in this way, is 'in danger of a realignment towards interventions that subsume politics and economics into a neutral realm of ecosystem management, and which depoliticize the causal processes inherent in putting people at risk' (Cannon and Müller-Mahn, 2010, p.633). Appreciating the shortcomings of transplanting a SES resilience framework to planning is resulting in a range of evolutionary resilience approaches and a focus of attention on the emerging complex urban condition underpinned by the political prioritisation of the safety and security of communities against an array of perceived hazards and threats, as well as concerns with social cohesion and economic austerity.

In this chapter we will illuminate this recent resilience 'turn' in urban policy and practice (Coaffee, 2013a) that has attempted to address a wide variety of contemporary urban concerns through a range of possible adaptations (Edwards, 2009; Coaffee and Fussey, 2015). In an urban context, resilience, in its broadest sense, refers both to the practical design of places and the management of persistent stresses and orchestration of responses to catastrophic events (Coaffee and Rogers, 2008). Urban resilience takes place at numerous overlapping spatial and temporal scales and can be achieved through a number of means:

> Some emphasize long-range strategies, while others react to current development proposals. Some try to reduce development in hazardous areas, while others accept such development but focus on site and building design to reduce vulnerability. Some redirect public investment, but most seek to regulate or influence private development. Some are regulatory, and others are voluntary. (Burby *et al.*, 2000, p.100)

Until recently, academic and practical approaches to enacting urban resilience have tended to treat different areas of resilience enquiry as distinct, with research methodologies and disciplinary structures impeding integrated approaches (Bosher and Coaffee, 2008; see Chapters 1 and 2). More recent work, however, suggests that it is not only possible but also positively productive to integrate divergent research methodologies to address questions of urban resilience in a range of settings and in relation to a range of risks. In this chapter we will unpack *why* resilience approaches traditionally associated with crisis management have become an increasingly popular way to frame the practices of urban and regional planners and embedded within formal planning policies (Coaffee *et al.*, 2008b; Shaw, 2012a). Drawing on a range of international examples of urban and regional planning practice we illustrate how ideas of resilience have evolved over the last decade and how urban resilience has metamorphosed from a largely reactive, managerial and technical approach towards a proactive system-of-systems socio-technical and localised approach. In so doing urban resilience has not only become an increasingly central organising metaphor within the policy-making process and in the expanding institutional framework of emergency preparedness in a general sense, but a key imaginary in urban and regional planning. Specifically, we argue that resilience is slowly but surely extending, and in some cases supplanting, sustainability discourse as the key planning policy driver in the current urban age.

The urban resilience zeitgeist

The modernist architect Mies van der Rohe famously asserted that architecture was the 'will of the epoch translated into space', high-lighting how built environment styles and the processes which create them are different in each era, often reflecting the spirit of the age. In the twenty-first century – the century of the city – resilience priorities have converged upon contemporary cities by virtue of their accumulation of population and critical infrastructure as well as a lack of foresight in previous developmental regimes (Coaffee *et al.*, 2008b; Fisher, 2012). The heightened growth in importance of resilience and its embedding within urban affairs has been intimately related to advancing ideas of risk and practices of risk management. Beck's (1992a) environmentally focused *Risk Society*, published in the wake of the Chernobyl nuclear catastrophe in Ukraine, starkly illuminated the magnitude and boundless nature of the risks global society now faces and how this is transforming the way in which risk is imagined, assessed, managed and governed, but not eradicated. In the years that have followed the publication of *Risk Society* many commentators have subsequently mapped the significant increase in occurrence and cost of a range of urban disasters and catastrophes that impact both locally and globally. For example,

Godschalk (2003) identified the worldwide impact of natural disasters in 2001 as resulting in 25,000 deaths, $36 billion in economic losses and $11.5 billion in insured losses, while more recently Fisher (2012, p.3) has highlighted the dramatic increase in weather-related catastrophes, such as floods, storms and drought, the occurrence of which have increased by over 400 times between 1900 and 2005. In this situation the strengthening of the built environment, adequate risk planning and advancing the business case for the implementation of urban resilience have emerged as critical foci for wider attention. From a post-political perspective, the rise in so-called 'experts' who shape public attitudes to acceptable levels of risk (Beck, 1996) and the rise of governance beyond the state (both participatory governance or transnational networks) have also characterised the emergence of resilience as a key urban policy driver.

Moreover, recent years have seen significant examples of large-scale, low-probability, high-impact disasters, such as Hurricane Katrina in 2005, the 2011 Tohoku earthquake in Japan or the impact of Hurricane Sandy upon New York in 2012, that have starkly illustrated the vulnerability and potential weakness within the design, planning and management of contemporary cities. These events have also highlighted how we might enhance resilience in the future through a consideration of the connectedness between different urban systems, innovation in adaptive responses and enhanced use of community knowledge. Also illuminated by such 'shock' events is a range of underlying socio-economic structures, inequalities and disempowerments characteristic of 'slow burn' situations where persistent vulnerabilities and uneven spatial geographies are uncovered that have been in train for many years. From the perspective of urban and regional planning and other built environment professions, adopting resilience as a modus operandi often, therefore, requires an enhancement of planning and design techniques in order to make cities and associated critical infrastructure more resistant to exogenous shocks *as well as* being acutely aware of endogenous path dependencies which often become apparent over longer time periods.

The remainder of this chapter is divided into three parts. First, we examine the emergence and changing role and remit of urban resilience policies and explore how urban and regional planning, and planning-related professions, are increasingly being asked to contribute to this agenda. Second, we chart the surfacing and progression of different 'styles' of urban resilience over the last decade, highlighting the progression and increased acceptance of the core technical and governing principles of resilience within urban and regional policy. Finally, we illustrate how the urban resilience turn might facilitate more holistic forms of resilient planning.

The resilience turn in urban policy

While resilience discourse has a long evolution, it is only since the turn of the millennium that it has begun to significantly emerge in public policy debates (for a review see Coaffee *et al.,* 2008b) and more recently planning practice (Coaffee and O'Hare, 2008; Davoudi, 2012; Wilkinson, 2012). Most recently, the initially slow adoption of resilience principles and practices in urban and regional planning circles intensified and 'cascaded', in part linked to the flexibility and politicisation of the term. As O'Hare and White (2013) noted in an editorial for a special issue on resilience in *Planning Practice and Research*:

> The passive reception of the term, as well as the considerable ambiguity regarding its articulation and application, has only assisted to *catalyse the cascade of resilience* through a broad variety of policy and practical agendas. Resilience has been heralded as a *prime mobilizing concept upon which a host of strategies may converge to help society and cities better prepare for a range of risks across regional, national and global scales.* (p.275, emphasis added)

The ways in which ideas and practices of urban resilience have emerged within a range of academic and policy debates are highly specific to institutional context and emergent risks faced in particular locations. Initial work within the field of urban and regional planning has noted a number of meta-processes that are commonly brought together by governments, at multiple scales, to pursue resiliency objectives within urban policy and practice, notably: the need for anticipation; holistic hazard management; and integrated governance and/or response.

First, the resilience turn in urban policy and practice has ushered in a greater requirement for foresight and preparedness. In this sense resiliency is proactive and anticipatory, rather than reactive, and as O'Brien and Read (2005) noted, 'the term resilience brings together the components of the disaster cycle – response, recovery, mitigation and preparedness' (see also Chapter 2). Equally, traditional methodologies for assessing risk within the urban context have commonly been replaced by increased consideration of unpredictable and high-consequence 'what if' events as new approaches and models for anticipating an uncertain future have been developed. Resiliency therefore foregrounds risk prevalence, where risk must be extensively planned for. This has simultaneously led to the rise of what some have referred to as 'precautionary governance' where pre-emptive risk management activities are undertaken to map urban vulnerabilities (often with an emphasis on worst-case scenarios), to plan and test for high-impact 'shock' events and to develop and enhance practical and technical expertise across a range of built environment and urban management professionals (notably planning). This seeks to aid both mitigation of and recovery from disruptive challenges as well as making any further adaptations required.

Second, within the urban resilience turn, there is a requirement to consider multiple risks and hazards in a holistic fashion. Traditional regimes of risk management are being reconfigured into what Linkov *et al.* (2014) refer to as 'resilience management'. This goes beyond risk management to address both the interdependencies and the complexities of large integrated infrastructural and service-delivery systems taking a socio-technical approach, and is premised upon the uncertainty of future threats. This encourages the development of urban resilience policy and practices that can respond in a flexible and integrated fashion to multiple risks across a range of socio-economic situations and scales. As Godschalk (2003, p.137) noted:

> Resilient cities are constructed to be strong and flexible rather than brittle and fragile [...] their lifeline systems of roads, utilities and other support facilities are designed to continue functioning in the face of rising water, high winds, shaking ground and terrorist attacks.

While certain risks – be they the occurrence of terror attack, pandemic influenza or of wide-scale flooding – might drive forward the urban resilience agenda at particular points in time, or in specific localities, this should not mean that adequate contingency should not be made for other more likely but less impactful risks. Moreover, a focus upon multiple risks highlights the requirement for additional adaptive capacity and associated resources as well as a change in thinking about systemic optimisation. Specifically there is a pressing need to factor in redundancy that can provide the adaptive capacity (diversity/substitutability) when things go wrong.

Redundancy is a core principle of planning attempts to enhance urban resilience and is seen as:

> the co-existence of diverse options fulfilling the same purpose and ensuring functionality in the event of the failure of one of them [...] Redundancy can also be attained through the identification of synergies amongst seemingly diverse realms or sectors, which in turn prompts the design of buildings, spaces and infrastructure that can be used (or can adapt to being used) in multiple ways. (Caputo *et al.*, 2015, p.13)

Redundancy or substitutability is a crucial aspect that has been ignored in much discussion of resilience in relation to urban and regional planning with planners often failing to incorporate it into city plans. The necessity to adopt a 'vision' which incorporates a 'Plan A' (the perceived optimal path) to create certainty forces the planning community to overlook alternative pathways or incorporate a 'Plan B' into plan making. Path optimisation has often been restricted by planners as alternative paths have been ignored because of the needs for both additional consultation and to maintain market confidence and 'certainty'.

Third, and relatedly, the changing institutionalisation of the resilience response has become paramount in embedding resiliency principles within urban policy and practice. As such:

> a resilient built environment should be designed, located, built, operated and maintained in a way that maximises the ability of built assets, associated support systems (physical and institutional) and the people that reside or work within the built assets, to withstand, recover from, and mitigate for the impacts of extreme natural and human-induced hazards. (Dainty and Bosher, 2008, p.357)

New governance approaches to enhancing urban resilience emphasise joined-up partnership-style approaches to decision making. This is in line with the principles of institutionalist approaches to *Collaborative Planning* (Healey, 1997, 2006), where important aspects of agency are added to the analysis of the functioning of complex systems, and where all relevant stakeholders are acknowledged within planning decision making and learn to build consensus across their differences. Whereas traditional approaches to urban risk have relied upon a narrow range of technically oriented stakeholders, contemporary and future resilience schemas are looking to draw a full range of professional and community groups into decision making at a range of spatial scales; from locally coordinated systems to centralised and sub-national organisations. As the UNISDR (2012b, p.9) noted in their *Making Cities Resilient* campaign:

> These [resilience] issues present mutually dependent challenges, which require *collaborative, integrated strategies, strong governance*, and innovative technological and financial solutions. Nowhere is this more evident than in cities. (emphasis added)

If we conceive the core purpose of urban and regional planning as mediating space and creating places in liaison with a range of stakeholders and communities, then resilient planning can be seen to encompass physical design and strategic spatial intervention, as well as a restructuring of governance and management functions in response to an array of potentially disruptive challenges. This last point requires that urban and regional planners increasingly integrate their activities with a host of other built environment professionals: '*we need to build the goal of the resilient city into the everyday practice of city planners*, engineers, architects, emergency managers, developers and other urban professionals' (Godschalk, 2003, p.142, emphasis added).

Urban and regional planning can contribute to enhancing urban resilience by forging collaboration amongst a range of stakeholders throughout the planning process in order to identify current and future risks and advance potential mitigation solutions. Ensuring these 'solutions' are incorporated at the most appropriate stage in urban development projects and service provision, as well as facilitating the potential of civil society to contribute to its own risk management through community planning activities will require '*a long-term collaborative effort to increase knowledge and awareness about resilient city planning and design*' (ibid., emphasis added).

Emerging styles of urban resilience

In the contemporary city, principles of urban resilience are increasingly being designed into the built environment and embedded within the behaviours and practices of planners and others responsible for construction and management of the urban system. This process of engaging with resilience thinking within the urban and regional planning community has slowly evolved over the last 15 years in a series of overlapping stages or waves which we detail below. In this section we highlight the evolution of resiliency principles in the twenty-first century city, initially channelling the discussion through the lens of disaster, security and emergency planning. Increasingly this has served as a key issue for planners to consider within the design and planning process in itself but also one that has driven a far more overarching development of a range of more locally and community-driven urban resilience policies and practices (Coaffee and O'Hare, 2008).

The genesis of urban resilience planning policy

Although resilience has become the new metaphor employed by many to describe and frame a counter-response to risk, crisis and uncertainty, many of its characteristics are not new and indeed date back to the development of the first cities. Cities have always sought resilience to the uncertainties and stresses they faced. In this sense, resilience has been core to urbanism. Throughout history, cities have been partially or entirely destroyed; a result of natural hazards and deliberate acts of policy as much as war. Cities have vanished, moved, been rebuilt and defended in the face of many threats and events and continue to be sites for both strategic and opportunistic violence (Coaffee *et al.*, 2008b). It is this continuing centrality of cities in twenty-first century life that makes them vulnerable to an array of risks because 'their architectural structures, population concentrations, places of assembly, and interconnected infrastructure systems put them at high risk of floods, earthquakes, hurricanes, and terrorist attacks' (Godschalk, 2003, p.136).

In the current century urban resilience has evolved as a policy and practice in relation to a range of changing socio-political and economic pressures. This has rearticulated the meaning and operational function of urban resilience as it has evolved in particular contexts for embedding 'foresight', robustness and adaptability into a variety of place-making and planning activities. What has been termed resilient planning is increasingly recognised as being context dependent. As Raco and Street (2012, p.1066) highlight: 'discourses of resilience and recovery have taken on path-dependent, concrete forms that reflect the specific politics, contexts and circumstances in which they are located'.

Prior to 2000, the term resilience was seldom heard within urban and regional planning discourse. Although protecting the vulnerability of cities against specific threats often underpinned emergency management regimes, urban planners were seldom included in those discussions. For example, while protecting urban areas from international terrorism or catastrophic disaster had long been a priority in many nation states, this was an agenda that had been almost exclusively delivered by state security services and emergency planners with little impact upon the practice of built environment professionals. This was despite planning ideas from the 1970s and 1980s – for example, of 'defensible space' and crime prevention through environmental design (CPTED) – often being at the core of such implemented strategies of protection and territorial control (Brown, 1985; Coaffee, 2004; Coaffee and O'Hare, 2008). In short, what the twenty-first century urban resilience turn has necessitated is the drawing in of planners to the decision-making nexus for delivering responses to a range of threats, risks and emergencies as a key pillar of the overall strategic development of urban resilience policy. This has required a change in mindset. As highlighted in Chapter 2, resilience has been conventionally understood in equilibrist terms of resisting and recovering from natural hazards and disasters. The term 'resilience', when traditionally used by built environment professionals, often referred to how environments may be calibrated to ensure that potentially devastating stresses can be repelled, resisted or redressed, or, ideally, to embrace the combination of these qualities (Bosher, 2008).

From 2000 onwards, the language and practices of urban resilience, emphasising adaptability, integration and preparedness, have increasingly filtered into the repertoires of planning practice, particularly in the Anglophone world, and are often explicitly linked to emerging social and political concerns and to the broader policy field of emergency or disaster management. This progression has been most advanced in the UK where the concept of resilience has been utilised by a multitude of policy and practice communities across a range of spatial scales. In the UK the emergency response to 'shock' events was historically locally organised, with 'central government quite willing to let local agencies deal with emergencies' (O'Brien and Read 2005, p.353). In 2000, strategically targeted nationwide protests on the transport network regarding the price of fuel led to significant impacts on the national economy. These protests also led to critical questions regarding 'who was in charge' for coordinating the response within the petrochemical industry and emergency services (Coaffee, 2006). Recent rounds of privatisation and reorganisation together with a general hollowing out of the state in previous decades had left a disorganised 'chain of command' without authoritative leadership, indicating that a reform of emergency planning procedures was long overdue (ibid.).

Reform was also prompted by an outbreak of foot and mouth disease and a number of serious flooding incidents in 2000–2001 that highlighted similar organisational failings and, in the case of flooding, the urgent need for enhanced built-in resilience (White and Howe, 2002). The subsequent events of 9/11, and the concern that key sites in and around UK cities would be terrorist targets, accelerated this process and made reform of emergency preparedness a key political priority. At this juncture, the term 'resilience' came to the fore to represent this material and institutional change and was eventually formalised through the 2004 Civil Contingencies Act (CCA). Through the CCA, the UK government attempted to provide a central strategic direction for developing resilience, defined by the UK's Cabinet Office (2003) as 'the ability to handle disruptive challenges that can lead to or result in crisis' (Paragraph 1.1). Subsequently, a range of policy communities, including urban and regional planning, have been drawn into various aspects of preparing for, responding to, mitigating against and recovering from disruptive events including, but not limited to terrorist risk, as well as a host of other policy activities utilising resilience principles.

Similarly, the use of resilience rhetoric in the United States was initially framed in the wake of 9/11. In *The Edge of Disaster* (2007), Stephen Flynn painted a picture of an American nation still unprepared for dealing with a major catastrophe. He argued that terrorism cannot always be prevented and that more effort and resources must be put into preparedness training, infrastructure protection and the building of community and economic resilience. In essence, argued Flynn, resilience should become the 'national motto' as Americans seek to embed protective security and disaster management principles into national organisations and the collective psyche (although it was not until 2007, in the second edition of the National Strategy for Homeland Security, that the term resilience was actually used in security policy). More recently, resilience has been cast wider, focusing upon integrated disaster resilience. In 2012 the US National Academies released a detailed report, *Disaster Resilience: A National Imperative*, where resilience was defined as 'the ability to prepare and plan for, absorb, recover from, and more successfully adapt to adverse events' (National Academies, 2012, p.1). Here it was acknowledged that the term is increasingly used by local, state, and federal governments, community groups, businesses and emergency responders to express the need for collective approaches to reduce the large human and economic losses that communities and the country face each year from disasters, whether infectious disease outbreaks, acts of terrorism, social unrest or financial disasters, in addition to natural hazards. The report placed great emphasis on continual investment in enhancing resilience and providing goals, baseline conditions and performance metrics for national resilience. It also explicitly noted that the 'soundness' of land-use planning, alongside building codes, standards, infrastructure protection and service delivery were seen as key to such enhancement. Moreover, and from a governance perspective, the 'shared responsibility' amongst various parts of government and all parts of the community was highlighted as essential in building greater future resilience.

By contrast to the initial security-driven resilience approach adopted in the UK and US, in mainland Western Europe the focus of urban resilience, and its links to urban and regional planning activity, tended to focus upon the impacts of climate change and inland or coastal flooding, with little emphasis on security concerns (Fünfgeld and McEvoy, 2012). For example, in Germany debates around resilience arose as the result of severe flooding in Dresden in 2002 (Fleischhauer *et al.*, 2009) necessitating the development – from 2004 onwards – of flood protection schemes and new ways of governing in crisis (Hutter *et al.*, 2014). More recent German explorations of resilience in the urban context have, however, begun to focus more upon civil protection and security issues, although often from an overly technical and managerial perspective (National Academies of Science and Engineering, 2014). Similarly, in France, the term resilience entered the urban policy vocabulary as a result of serious reflection over the possible maladaptive design of 1990s flood protection schemes in the wake of the devastation caused by Hurricane Katrina. Likewise in the Netherlands, against a long history of water management, the term resilience was brought forth by policy-making communities concerned with climate change in light of the 'Adaptive Delta Management' (ADM) approaches linked to the Dutch Delta Programme (2008). This programme aimed to ensure flood protection and fresh water supply in an adaptive way until 2100. ADM approaches attempt to ensure that policy makers and decision makers adopt the 'world view' of resilience so that water managers understand that enhancing resilience in increasingly complex and integrated systems requires adaptive capacity and flexibility (Klijn *et al.*, 2015; see also Chapter 6). It is also worth noting that in some European countries there was, until recently, no actual word for resilience in their language. For example, in Italy over recent years the word *resilienza* has entered the vocabulary of urban planners concerned with security and flooding issues. Here *resilienza* means 'resistance of materials to stress' and is largely focused upon technical engineering tasks. By contrast, in Finland a much broader view of urban resilience has been adopted based on multiple stresses affecting urban areas.

Further afield, in Japan there has traditionally been a strong emphasis on connecting disaster management and land-use planning given the everyday risk from natural hazards that the country faces. The national emergency solution is centrally developed with cities being the central coordination and response units in the event of a disaster. However, the term resilience has only recently entered into the lexicon of planning language in the wake of the 2011 triple disaster centred on the region of Tohoku. Debates on the nuances underpinning resilience and the tension between land-use management practices that emphasise equilibrium or evolutionary approaches served to highlight the vacuum in spatial planning between highly technical and social community-led interventions (see Chapter 8 for a detailed analysis). Furthermore, in Australia, the impacts of current weather extremes and the requirement for climate change adaptation has fundamentally shifted the discourse of emergency planning towards an emphasis on resilience. As McEvoy *et al.* (2013, p.287) have highlighted:

> [T]he recognition by Federal Government that responses need to be more holistic, consider all hazards and reach beyond the emergency management community to involve a whole of Government approach is closely intertwined with the rapid emergence of the resilience frame in the Australian context, i.e. from a mindset of protection to one which promotes community preparedness and resilience.

This approach was embodied in the 2011 *National Strategy for Disaster Resilience* (COAG, 2011) which, as McEvoy *et al.* further note, was promoting self-reliance and is:

> shaped by a devolution of responsibility from Federal and State Governments towards households, businesses and communities, although with a recognition that a new focus on 'shared' or 'collective' responsibility will need to be underpinned by enhanced partnership working, a better understanding of risks and impacts (including communication), and the enabling of an adaptive and empowered community. (p.288)

As noted above, since the early 2000s the rolling out of resilience policy and associated practices, and their embedding within systems and processes of urban and regional planning, has developed incrementally and in a context-specific way, reflecting the emergence of different policy priorities. However, from the wide variety of different international experiences we can chart four overlapping stages, or waves, in the evolution of urban resilience and their facilitation of more sophisticated interactions between urban and regional planners and those responsible for related state-level agendas such as national security and emergency planning, economic prosperity, housing, localism, and community development. This journey indicates that there is a transition in the nucleus of resilient planning policy from nationally driven meta-outcomes and primarily technical and engineering considerations which focused upon planning *in* resilience towards a focus upon increasingly collaborative, local and integrated place-based outcomes focusing on planning *for* resilience. This mirrors the transition depicted in Chapter 2 from equilibrium-focused resilience approaches to more evolutionary and transformative approaches. Figure 3.1 schematically highlights the advance of resilience processes over time, noting how its operation has been modified by changing circumstances, technological innovation and a process of learning. The next section unpacks this schema in more detail.

Figure 3.1

The advance of urban resilience practice

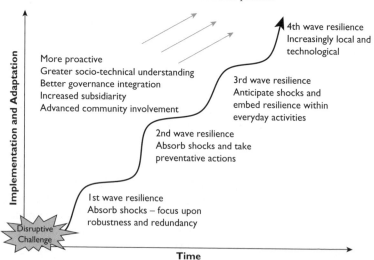

Time

Advancing urban resilience

In many contexts, the initial spatial and governance imprints of urban resilience have been a top-down reaction to large-scale shock events. Such imprints were manifest through technical-, managerial- and engineering-focused solutions which sought to absorb future shock events through the building in of material robustness, or in some case redundancy, to architectural structures and critical infrastructures: those key elements of the national infrastructure which are crucial to the continued delivery of essential services. As Shaw (2012a, p.311) noted, 'more traditional, top-down responses to dealing with "threats" to security, and the dominance of managerial or technical solutions to problems based on disaster or risk reduction strategies' was the most common response to shock events. The physical robustness of designed-in security systems in response to the threat of international terrorism against urban areas perhaps represents the most visible incarnation of first wave resilience. This was exemplified by fortress-like security features such as barriers and crash-rated bollards at high-risk sites (Coaffee, 2004; Benton-Short, 2007) illustrating the engineering focus on shock-absorbing resilience (see also Chapter 7). Other examples of first wave urban resilience often characterised large-scale flood protection schemes dominated by engineering approaches that focused upon interventions that promoted system return to equilibrium after a perturbation. As an example, in the wake of serious flooding in Germany in the early 2000s Hutter *et al.* (2014, p.3) observed how 'technical knowledge mainly based on the natural sciences and civil engineering played a dominant role in flood protection' at the expense of more socially focused efforts.

Whereas first wave resilience was inherently reactive, materially and mitigation focused in nature, over time increased effort was made to focus on the preparedness aspects of the resilience cycle. Here resilience practice began to increasingly interface with the planning system as policy priorities moved beyond the ability to absorb shock to focus on the ability of businesses, governments and communities to absorb shocks and *take preventative actions* (i.e. the socio-economic agility of society). In some contexts this resulted in the development of a multi-level system of resilience governance across national, regional and local levels (e.g. in the UK), action by local governments in developing tailored resilience strategies against a range of risks, and national government attempts to educate citizens in emergency preparedness (Rogers, 2011). Second wave urban resilience was also characterised by attempts to draw in a wider range of relevant stakeholders to the urban resilience effort, notably urban and regional planners. Here urban resilience was increasingly articulated as a collective governance concern requiring a broadening and deepening of the epistemic planning community as a result of the building of new relationships, and the creation of new planning imaginaries in response to emerging risks and vulnerabilities.

Ambient urban risk thus led to a renewed focus upon planning out vulnerabilities and enhancing the responsibility of built environment professionals to consider a range of natural and anthropogenic risks in planning practice. This requirement has often been backed up by bespoke design guidance, building codes and specialist training events to ensure resilience considerations do not get 'forgotten' – or are not an afterthought in the planning process – to avoid causing delays and often additional expense. In the UK, for example, security-driven urban resilience was underpinned by the strategic framework – *Working Together to Protect Crowded Places* – where it was envisaged that a range of key partners including local government, the police, businesses and planning professionals should work holistically to reduce the vulnerability of crowded places to terrorism (Home Office, 2010a; see also Chapter 6).

As the importance of urban resilience has increased, attempts have been made to complement a compliance-based model of urban resilience, where statutory requirements and codes of practice need to be met, with an encouragement to adopt urban resilience thinking as 'best practice' and to embed resilience thinking into established working practices of urban and regional planners. This is indicative of third wave urban resilience: the ability of businesses, governments and communities to anticipate shocks, and to ultimately embed resilience within everyday activities (i.e. the symbiosis of the socio-economic, political and technical aspects of resilience). In the recently released UK National Planning Policy Framework, local planning authorities should, for example:

> work with local advisors and others to ensure that they have and take into account the most up-to-date information about higher risk sites in their area for malicious threats and natural hazards, including steps that can be taken to *reduce vulnerability and increase resilience.* (DCLG (Department for Communities and Local Government), 2012, p.40, emphasis added)

Over time the practices of urban resilience have become much more proactive, flexible, reflexive and integrated as more stakeholders have been given responsibility for delivering resiliency agendas. More critically, though, and as noted in Chapter 2, the wider implication of such collective working is that planners can, in certain situations, feel 'responsibilised' or co-opted into delivering state-driven resilience agendas without adequate funding or training. As Coaffee and O'Hare (2008) have argued, this poses a series of questions for the planning profession related to the role and emerging function of planning. It also elicits a series of questions about whether there is sufficient force (legislation) within the planning system to encourage developers to pay for the embedding of often-costly resilience measures.

The progression of urban resilience, highlighted above, has identified a number of emergent lessons for policy makers that are now being appropriated in different policy spheres and at different spatial scales. Whereas the initial ideas of urban resilience have been largely driven by the need for protection against shock events, environmental and economic change has more recently posed different degrees of risk for urban policy makers. This has led to a swathe of new work in the planning practice literature focused upon the application of resilience principles (see for example, Coaffee, 2010; Albers and Deppisch, 2012; Lewis and Conaty, 2012; Porter and Davoudi 2012). As traditionally understood, and discussed in Chapter 2, resilience, in the guise of emergency management, is premised on a command and control approach from central government, actualised through national-level strategies. Here 'central government [is] able to influence their approach through resource allocation and compliance mechanisms' (Edwards, 2009, p.79) and through the development of specific and general plans. Whereas previously much planning decision making was centred on managing the economic and environmental effects of rapid and uneven economic growth, the global economic downturn has increasingly focused activity upon community-based and localised efforts that might enhance resilience and recovery planning, especially in places deemed to be failing (Raco and Street, 2012). Increasingly, therefore, the focus of urban resilience policy is being directed towards smaller spatial scales and local activities (Coaffee *et al.*, 2008b).

As a result, within many local planning policies there is increased emphasis on responding to major challenges with a long-term view, rethinking risk assessment and mitigation strategies, and giving increased focus to facilitating adaptive human behaviours and developing individual and institutional coping strategies. Notably, principles of resilience have been seen to drive forward locally instigated strategies as part of the international response to the economic crisis that began in 2008 and led to ongoing policy responses as national government and urban leaders try to deliver 'more for less'. In this situation enhancing urban resilience can be severely restricted by available finance. For example, despite being the most at-risk city in the United States for encountering the dire effects of climate change, the City of Miami, Florida, has been unable to implement policies aimed at improving climate resilience due to fiscal retrenchment which has caused staff shortages and limited budgets for planning priorities (Hower, 2015).

Such localised urban resilience approaches are increasingly centred not upon state institutions, but upon networked responses, with governance distributed more widely across key stakeholders and sectors and most notably within local communities (Edwards, 2009). As leading UK policy think tank, the Young Foundation, observes:

> A model of 'resilience', both at the community and individual levels, will potentially help decisions in policy making and local resource prioritisation and enable authorities to develop a *better adaptive capacity to adverse events*. (Young Foundation, 2010, p.1, emphasis added)

By embedding cultural and social processes into the discussion of urban resilience, the balance of much urban policy can be reoriented away from quantitative analysis and increasingly grounded in the everyday realities of citizens and communities that have been invisible or silent in debates in the traditional crisis literature (Durodie and Wessely, 2002). Moreover, and as highlighted in Chapter 2, much of the prior work undertaken on community resilience has been argued to be conservative and structurally deterministic (often based on systems theory), focusing on 'the rules in use' with far too little attention paid to normative factors such as agency, culture, and power/knowledge relations in institutional dynamics and decision-making processes (Cote and Nightingale, 2012). For example, in the context of urban environmental risk, Pelling (2003) has highlighted how the 'adaptive potential' of individuals and communities can be mobilised by institutional modification that 'aims to alter the institutional framework of a city using political influence to create political space for at-risk actors to argue their case' (p.62). Moreover:

> The retreat of the state and expansion of the private sector and civil society in cities worldwide has created an opportunity for

new institutional forms and networks to be created that can enhance a city's ability to deal with vulnerability and environmental hazard. (pp.63–64)

In this sense the community resilience central to urban resilience is seen very much as the participation of citizens in the process of making the state more resilient and in order to help manage threats and 'conditions of uncertainty'. Here the argument is that shared and coordinated action can reduce collective vulnerability. In recent years there has undoubtedly been a 'social turn' in how policy-making communities and civil society groups now utilise concepts of resilience in a positive and transformational way with respect to an emphasis away from 'state variables' to community and local agendas (Brown, 2013). This is reflected not just in greater local empowerment and agency, but also in changing patterns of leadership, social interaction, governance and institutional arrangements in place-making agendas (Folke *et al.*, 2010; Coaffee, 2013b).

The social turn in the resilience literature, and in how its principles have been enacted in urban practice, is also increasingly being reflected in the greater emphasis placed upon new possibilities – learning, innovation (including technological innovation) and novelty – illuminating the way in which resilience approaches have been embraced by civil society groups eager to make a difference in their communities (Hopkins, 2011; Goldstein, 2012). In this context it is the social consequences or 'the ability of communities to withstand external shocks to their social infrastructure' that is of greatest significance and concern (Adger 2000; p.316). More critically through, as Welsh (2014, p.20) notes, such an approach works:

on the normative assumption that communities can and should self-organise to deal with uncertainty, that uncertainty is a given not something with a political dimension, and the role of government is limited to enabling, shaping and supporting, but specifically not to direct or to fund those processes.

Running in parallel to the localist trend in the evolution of urban resilience is the increased importance of digitised technology that presents a number of opportunities to city managers and urban and regional planners to enhance resilience. Through the use of emergent ICT infrastructures, and advanced system monitoring and analytical capabilities, urban managers can better coordinate the information flow between multiple public agencies and utilise a greater amount of data and information more quickly to aid resilience-focused practices – so-called 'smart urban resilience' (Coaffee, 2014). The benefits of urban resilience should go far beyond preparation and response to disaster situations. Resilience planning can add to knowledge as city managers gather and analyse data on a city's vulnerabilities through, for example, incorporating technology and social media into these planning efforts, creating (theoretically at least) an easily available real-time, geo-referenced database to assist with complex challenges. Emblematically, and linking ideas of smart cities with urban resilience, Rio de Janeiro has invested in strategic-level technologies to coordinate and control its various security and disaster management processes in the build-up to the 2016 Olympic Games. Opened in 2010, the IBM-built 'operations centre' now integrates the vast majority of the city's management functions, including security, in what many are hailing as the model for 'smarter city' development (*New York Times*, 2012). The Rio control centre is, however, not unique or the first of its kind. Other countries under arguably greater risk from shock events have advanced not dissimilar operation centres, retrofitting them with new technologies as they emerge. The Tokyo Metropolitan Disaster Prevention Centre that opened in 1991, for example, is the central liaison facility for disaster management organisations for the Tokyo Metropolitan area. This system was further advanced in February 2007 when Japan launched a federal government-funded emergency warning system in order to respond effectively to natural disasters (see Chapter 8) and is demonstrating that with the help of mobile networks, a city authority can reach the majority of its citizens at short notice in the event of a shock event or other emerging crisis.

Towards holistic urban resilience

As demonstrated in this chapter, urban and regional planning has recently been infused with resilience perspectives, frameworks and thinking to the point where it is now seen as critical to planning's future role:

> *Urban planning and design has a key role to play in defining a city's and urban area's resilience.* It can address some of the underlying risk factors linked to natural hazards and related technological and other disasters, and reduce the exposure of people

and assets and their degree of vulnerability in the context of rapid urbanization. (Valdes and Purcell, 2013, emphasis added)

Today, the principles of resilience carry tremendous influence in modifying international urban and regional planning agendas, whether this is dealing with the unique needs and characteristics of places, looking at the short-, medium- and long-term issues, advancing the knowledge, objectives and actions *and* recognising the wide range of stakeholders (who should be) involved in resilient urban and regional planning or, ultimately, 'breaking planning out of its obsession with order, certainty and stasis' (Porter and Davoudi, 2012, p.330).

While the principles of resilience thinking are increasingly influential in reshaping and reframing planning in new and exciting ways, to date there have been few attempts to link macro-level structural changes in society (e.g. national or regional economic restructuring) with micro-level resilience strategies (change in communities). This failure to address the integration of scales demonstrates a separation of disciplines but also a continual tension and distinction between a highly equilibrist and conservative approach to resilience, which focuses on reactive and short-term measures, and a more evolutionary sociocultural and progressive approach focused in the medium-to-long term and with anticipation, adaptation and flexibility as core attributes. The binaries between these two approaches have been highlighted by White and O'Hare (2014, p.11) and are shown in Table 3.1.

Current planning practice, we contend, is in transition between these two meta-approaches that highlight both the regressive and progressive advance of ideas of resilience in urban and regional planning. Here transition is represented as a continuous process of change, from one relatively stable system state to another via a co-evolution of markets, networks, institutions, technologies, policies, individual behaviour and other trends. While a transition can be accelerated by one-time events, such as large disruptions in continuity like 9/11 and Hurricane Katrina, they are not caused by such events in isolation. Slower changes also produce a persistent undercurrent for a fundamental change.

In terms of urban and regional planning approaches there has undoubtedly been a shift in urban resilience from techno-rational approaches towards sociocultural understandings, and from a focus upon standardised and top-down approaches towards diverse and locally integrated methods where there is more than just a 'Plan A'.

Table 3.1   *Aims and foci of equilibrist and evolutionary urban resilience for planning practice*

	Equilibrist	Evolutionary
Aims	Equilibrist	Adaptive
	Existing normality	New normality
	Preserve	Transform
	Stability	Flexibility
Focus	Endogenous	Exogenous
	Short term	Medium-to-long term
	Reactive	Proactive
	Atomised	Abstract
Planning Approaches	Techno-rational	Sociocultural
	Vertical integration	Horizontal integration
	Building focus	Societal focus
	Homogeneity	Heterogeneity
	Deductive	*Inductive*
	Plan A (Optimisation)	*Plan A and B (Redundancy)*

Source: adapted from White and O'Hare, 2014.

Likewise the primary physical focus on the robustness and rigidity of buildings has been reduced in favour of more community-focused efforts. However, these categorisations are not mutually exclusive and the transition towards more transformative practices of urban resilience should be viewed as a continuous journey that helps planners define the problems at hand and develop processes to mitigate emergent and complex issues. This framework will be utilised in our exploration of urban resilience in practice in Chapters 6–9.

Today, urban resilience can be seen as an integrated multi-scalar activity involving a range of activities which shape and manage the built fabric so as to reduce its vulnerability to a range of hazards and threats. It is concerned with both the spatial form and redesign of the built environment as well as the processes that help shape it. However, despite the growing importance of resilience in urban policy and practice there is still an inertia – an implementation gap – when it comes to prioritising resilience, particularly when it comes to collaborative working (Coaffee and Clarke 2015).

That said, as urban resilience policy and practice has evolved, a greater array of stakeholders have been drawn into its network, with planners and other built environment professionals given increasingly prominent roles and greater responsibility. Urban and regional planning is increasingly seen as a remedy to an ever-increasing variety of socio-economic problems, policy priorities and risks facing contemporary society for which resilient responses are required. In many countries the remit of planning professions now includes, either explicitly or implicitly, dealing with climate change, flooding, energy security and counter terrorism, as well as its formative role in balancing the social, economic and environmental impacts of development in all its guises.

What is, however, clear from debates about urban resilience is that planners cannot function in isolation and must be part of a more integrated urban management nexus. This of course means new relationships will have to be formed and operationalised between, for example, planners and the police, and planners and climate scientists. However, this decentralisation of responsibility to meet resiliency objectives advanced by planning professionals at the behest of the state runs alongside a parallel centralisation of power to shape the agenda back towards the state through a constant stream of nationally derived resilience guidance. As noted in Chapter 2, the governance of resilience, and particularly the interactions between citizen and state, is progressively 'responsibilising' and increasingly putting the onus of preventing and preparing for disruptive challenges onto an array of institutions, professions, communities and individuals – notably urban and regional planners – rather than the state, the traditional provider of citizens' security and emergency planning needs.

Resilience is more than a policy buzzword. For many city managers it is becoming a framing device for coping with an uncertain future and, as Doig (2014) from NextCity.org noted, whether we like it or not resilience is 'becoming a way of life – a primary focus for any city that wants to thrive through the next hundred years'. As it has evolved as a policy and practice, it has been suggested that urban resilience has begun to sound less like 'an exercise in doom and gloom' and more a showcase as to how many urban areas are envisioning an uncertain future 'that will demand their agility, flexibility and willingness to transform in accordance with our changing world' (ibid.).

Emerging since 2000 as an international policy rhetoric connected to countering crisis and disaster, urban resilience is now being fully embedded as a policy metaphor for envisioning future place-making activities which planners are increasingly adopting as part of their modus operandi. Urban resilience, rather than being peripheral to urban and regional planning is, in many cases, being mainstreamed into planning policy and practice as more urban areas begin to take the challenge of resilience seriously, committing effort and resource towards strategic implementation of plans to reduce risk and vulnerability against shock events and slow-burn stresses. Through this process, resilience has been blended with sustainability and sustainable development and in some cases is supplanting it as the key rationale for urban and regional planning.

The evolution of urban resilience and its embedding into urban and regional planning agendas is not only leading to fundamental questions about the reimagining of planning in a new era of risk, crisis and uncertainty but also illuminating government priorities and governmentalising tendencies. On one hand this highlights a top-down-driven rhetoric where planners are being steered into taking resilience seriously. On the other hand, it highlights the potential of resilience being acknowledged as the sustenance of a living civil society, through enhanced citizen engagement focused upon localised issues with a view to developing ways in which communities can better cope and thrive in adversity. As Vale highlights in a discussion of *The Politics of Resilient Cities: Whose Resilience and Whose City?* (Vale, 2014), cities produce and reflect underlying socio-economic disparities and planners need to be cognisant of 'uneven resilience' that can threaten the ability of the urban and regional system to function. In short, urban resilience can only function as a progressive practice if it can improve the life prospects of the most disadvantaged groups.

Urban resilience, and its accompanying plans and strategies, can be seen as the union of sustainability and risk, with the former redefined by the latter (Coaffee *et al.*, 2008b). Viewing the development of urban resilience in this way also serves to shine a light on the mistakes of prior practices and how learning from the past in order to adapt in the future is a fundamental prerequisite of urban resilience. In the next chapter we unpack the importance of learning through an analysis of how 'maladaptive' planning practices can be replaced by those that focus upon adaptability and enhancing adaptive capacity within planning processes.

Chapter 4

Urban Resilience as Adaptive or Maladaptive?

Ideas surrounding adaptability and the capacity to respond to risk and perturbation are at the heart of urban resilience. Resilience practices of the epistemic planning community or wider civil society that seek to enhance the adaptability of critical built infrastructure, and to proactively respond to the occurrence or threat of disruptive challenge, often achieve the very opposite effect with poor or suboptimal planning decisions frequently serving to reduce resiliency and increase urban vulnerability. Therefore, rather than urban and regional planning being reimagined, through the lens of resilience, as in pursuit of the adaptability of the built environment, the actions of planners can in many cases be viewed as maladaptive and obdurate to change.

Drawing on a range of international examples, this chapter will illuminate the inherent weaknesses within the design, governance and management of many urban areas that make resilience necessary and which continue to cause concern today due to embedded cultures and practices within urban and regional planning. This chapter proceeds in four main sections. First it will establish the argument that urban and regional planners, when tasked with enhancing resiliency, can learn from the mistakes of the past to illustrate principles for good planning. Second, it presents an analysis of why urban and regional planning can, in many ways, be considered maladaptive, and how ideas of adaptation, adaptability and adaptive capacity are vital in envisioning future planning practices. Third, and drawing from a forensic examination of prior disruptive events, it presents nine 'design weaknesses' within the planning process that are commonly used examples of *in situ* maladaptation. Finally, it highlights how urban and regional planning can modify its everyday working practices and procedures in order to better implement appropriate urban resilience measures.

Learning from the fracture-critical past

Learning the lessons from previous disruptive challenges has become a key feature of urban resilience narratives. For example, in *The Resilient City: How Modern Cities Recover from Disaster*, Vale and Campanella noted that:

> By studying historical examples, we can learn the pressing questions that have been asked in the past as cities and their residents struggled to rebuild ... How has the symbolic power of the built environment been used as a magnet for attack and as a signal for recovery? What does each particular process of recovery reveal about the balance of power in the society seeking to rebuild? Whose vision for the future gets built, and why? (2005, p.9)

Notwithstanding the importance of local and historical context in mediating how knowledge can be transferred and adopted from one location to another, increasing emphasis is now placed upon what urban and regional planners can learn from the recognition of prior incidents as well as how good practice can be appropriately adopted. Put simply, why is it in hindsight that planners are often seen to make poor decisions that increase, rather than reduce, risk to local communities? The need to evaluate and learn from earlier incidents as a means to promote greater resilience, but also to affect the cultural norms and the process of change, is highly important but not unprecedented. This historiographic approach echoes Peter Hall's *Great Planning Disasters* (1980) in which he studied the 'pathology of planning' and attempted to examine past planning failures, as a means to make better-informed decisions in the future. It also has parallels within Zolli and Healy's (2013) wide-ranging study of resilience that constructed a range of 'parables' based on real-world examples to advance simple principles and wider lessons for resilience practice. Fisher (2012) in his book on fracture-critical design also argued that disasters are caused *by* 'design errors', and thus the key to a more resilient built environment is to learn from these earlier incidents and practise experience:

> What distinguishes many of the disasters we have faced recently is that they have stemmed largely from design errors, from mistakes of our making. As such, they remain within our control, for if we have designed our way into these disasters, we can design our way out of them. But we first have to understand the nature of our

errors so that we don't simply repeat them, as we have been doing over and over in recent years. (p.xi)

Fisher refers to the collapse of the I-35W Bridge in Minnesota in 2007, which killed 13 people and injured more than 150 (Fisher, 2012, p.14), as illustrative of what he refers to as 'fracture-critical design' 'in which structures have so little redundancy and so much interconnectedness and misguided efficiency that they fail completely if any one part does not perform as required' (ibid, p.ii). Fisher expands on this by suggesting that the civic and social collapse of New Orleans in the wake of Hurricane Katrina provided a wider example of fracture-critical design (see Chapter 7), noting that built environment professionals such as planners, architects and urban designers have been unwilling to reflect on the limitations and failures of previous developments, speculating that this is perhaps because their reputation is so critical or to avoid litigation. This absence of *a priori* evaluation limits the ability to learn from the past in order to inform current and future behaviour and indicates a need for greater reflexivity (see Chapter 10) amongst planning communities that learns from both good and bad (*maladaptive*) practice. From a more technical engineering perspective, Woods and Branlat (2011, p.131) have also argued that patterns of failure within non-linear complex systems, such as cities, arise due to a set of 'basic regularities' in how the system is (un)able to adapt to handling new challenges or stress. This involves complex interconnections between the disruptive challenge event, technical elements of the system and associated social processes:

> The patterns [of failure] all involve the dynamic interactions between the system in question and the events that occur in the environment. The patterns also involve interactions among people in different roles each trying to prepare for and handle the events that occur within the scope of their roles. The patterns apply to systems across different scales – individuals, groups, organisations. (ibid.)

Learning these lessons from the past and embedding them within the culture of an epistemic community of practice is seldom easy. As Donahue and Tuohy (2006) have noted in a review of emergency response operations:

> [T]he term 'lessons learned' may be a misnomer. Anecdotal evidence suggests mistakes are repeated incident after incident. It

appears that while identifying lessons is relatively straightforward, true learning is much harder – lessons tend to be isolated and perishable, rather than generalized and institutionalized. (p.1)

Maladaptive planning

Fisher's concept of 'fracture-critical design' could be viewed as representing one aspect of a wider phenomenon of what might be termed maladaptation: broadly understood to mean a process that is 'inappropriate', no longer 'fit for purpose' or which increases vulnerability (Barnett and O'Neill, 2010; Supkoff, 2012). Such maladaptation can occur at different scales and magnitudes and over different timeframes; sometimes occurring as a result of well-meaning adaptation strategies. There are, as the UN-Habitat (2011) *Report on Global Settlements* observed:

> actions and investments that increase rather than reduce risk and vulnerability to the impacts of climate change and these are termed maladaptation [...] *Removing maladaptations and the factors that underpin them are often among the first tasks to be addressed before new adaptations.* (p.35, emphasis added)

The most popular definition of maladaptation from the Inter-governmental Panel on Climate Change (IPCC, 2001) refers to any changes in: 'natural or human systems that inadvertently increase vulnerability to climatic stimuli; an adaptation that does not succeed in reducing vulnerability but increases it instead' and reflects a growth in practice-based literature on maladaptation and planning mostly linked to issues of climate change. A recent Royal Society (2015) publication – *Resilience to Extreme Weather* – also noted a number of different ways in which maladaptation could be framed. First, if mitigation features, such as large-scale engineering interventions, have a low likelihood of failure but catastrophic consequences when failure occurs. For example, when overtopped dykes in New Orleans trapped floodwater in the city they could be considered maladaptive (p.70) and there needs to be a back-up substitutable system, or adaptive approach (a Plan B). Second, in the realm of governance 'poorly co-ordinated sectors can not only fail to build resilience, but can also undermine each other's objectives, potentially increasing vulnerability and leading to maladaptation' (p.77). Third, the Royal Society note that not properly accounting for the multi-scalar nature of resilience can be problematic:

> [E]xperience from past events suggests that building resilience at one level (e.g. neighbourhood) can risk undermining it at another (e.g. regional or national) [...] [and] should take account of risks that are not immediately visible at the local level, and should prevent local actions that compromise larger-scale resilience. *Failure to do this can result in maladaptation.* (p.80, emphasis added)

For example, where flood defences upstream in one neighbourhood affect downstream conditions and have unintended consequences or displacement effects, this could be considered a governance approach that is maladaptive and lacking multi-scalar methods of assessment. Similarly, other ways of viewing maladaptation have tended to focus upon institutional considerations and see maladaptation as a failure to change and learn (including locked-in approaches). For example, Barnett and O'Neill (2010, p.211) see maladaptation as 'action taken ostensibly to avoid or reduce vulnerability to climate change that impacts adversely on, or increases the vulnerability of other systems, sectors or social groups'. Moreover, Brown (2012), in an analysis of climate change policy discourses of resilience, argued that adaptation attempts overwhelmingly to support the status quo and promote 'business as usual' (see also Brown, 2013). In most cases the resilience discourse thus appears to be focused upon an equilibrium-based approach to recovery efforts rather than an evolutionary approach which fundamentally changes established modes of action or outcomes. As Jerneck and Olsson argued (2008), incremental rather than transformational change is most likely with, in many cases, support for adaptation and the continuance of practices that in the longer term will be unsustainable.

The practices of insurance are also important in mediating how contemporary urban society deals with its risk and embeds resilience, often in ways that might be considered maladaptive. In many cases the distribution and control of risk is intimately linked to the provision of insurance – 'an attempt to make the incalculable calculable' (Beck 1994, p.181) – where the insurance industry can limit or withdraw cover on particular risks: 'It is the private insurance companies which operate or mark the frontier barrier of risk society.' (Beck 1996, p.31) In an earlier passage that offers more detail,

Beck (1992b) drew a distinction between actual risks and threats within such a society, relating this to insurance:

> Is there an operational criterion for distinguishing between risks and threats? The economy itself reveals the boundary line of what is tolerable with economic precision, through the refusal of private insurance. Where the logic of private insurance disengages, where the economic risks of insurance appear too large or too unpredictable for insurance concerns the boundary that separates 'predictable' risks from uncontrollable threats has obviously been breached again and again in large and small ways. (p.103)

From a more institutional perspective, insurance provides one way that risk is 'rendered calculable and governable' (Lupton, 1999, p.87). Giddens (1991) also showed how the strategy of objective statistical risk assessment and an attempt to predict or 'colonise the future' has been built into contemporary institutions:

> Insurance, for example, has from early on been linked not only to the risks involved in capitalist markets, but to the potential futures of a wide range of individual and collective attributes. Futures calculations on the part of insurance companies is itself a risky endeavour, but it is possible to limit some key aspects of risk in most practical contexts of action [...] and such companies typically attempt to exclude aspects or forms of risk which do not conform to the calculation of large-sample probabilities. (p.29)

In relation to flood resilience, O'Hare *et al.* (2015) have highlighted how insurance fosters what they term a 'cycle of maladaptation' whereby insurance promotes rapid recovery but does not encourage adaptability (i.e., moving to a new path) and this in turn increases exposure. Here insurance (or government handouts, in the case of state-backed insurance) often enables recovery through policies that encourage restoration or like-for-like replacement – a business-as-usual or equilibrium approach – that can be seen to be tackling the symptoms rather than the cause (see Chapter 8 for an example of this in the case of post-Fukushima planning responses). This does not concord with fostering new resilience cultures based on innovation and adaptation. Moreover, where insurance coverage is guaranteed, it can create a false sense of security and actually decrease incentives for individual households to take resiliency actions (IPCC, 2012). In a further example, van den Honert and McAneney (2011) have noted how in the aftermath of bushfires in Victoria, Australia, which occurred in 2009 state handouts of $50,000 to homeowners whose principal property was destroyed encouraged victims to build back in the same way and in the same location. This, they note, 'is an example of government generosity not encouraging risk-reducing behaviour' (p.1168).

The emerging field of resilience engineering has also advanced ideas of maladaptation through highlighting a number of patterns by which adaptive systems break down. Although framed around increasing the 'robustness' of a system to recover to equilibrium, such 'patterns of maladaptation' highlight similar design and process challenges (Woods and Branlat, 2011). The *first* pattern highlighted focuses upon conditions that mean a system's capacity to adapt becomes exhausted, illuminating a lack of redundancy to cope with a situation of cascading network collapse. The resilience of complex networks to failure, particularly in urban settings where such networks are spatially proximate, has become increasingly important given the interconnectedness and interdependencies between multi-scale and multifunctional systems ranging from the Internet and electrical transmission grids to social and economic networks. Such non-linear complex adaptive systems have also been referred to as robust yet fragile (RYF) systems (Carlson and Doyle, 2000), that while designed to cope with anticipated challenges through compensatory systems, slack or redundancy, are susceptible to unexpected threats. As Zolli and Healy (2013 p.28) noted, the paradox of such systems makes the properties of resilience both an advantage and disadvantage: 'as complexity of that compensatory system grows, it becomes a source of fragility itself – approaching a tipping point where even small disturbances, if they occur in the right place, can bring the system to its knees'. Such network assemblages have been shown to be particularly susceptible to nodal failure or overloading causing increased susceptibility to 'cascade failure' within and between a range of infrastructural systems. In short 'in a RYF system, the possibility of black swans – low probability but high impact events – is engineered in' (ibid.).

The second broad pattern of maladaptation highlighted in resilience engineering is 'working at cross purposes' – the inability to coordinate effectively the governance of resilience, horizontally within an organisation, and at different scales. Working in rigid organisational silos is a classic example of this. For example,

Coaffee and Bosher (2008) suggested that urban and regional planners and personnel working in strategic emergency service provision in the UK seldom work together, in spite of the obvious benefits of doing so. Such evidence of silo working demonstrates how interrelated facets of urban resilience are, in practice, not considered holistically. The third pattern of maladaptation noted by Woods and Branlat refers to getting stuck in 'outdated behaviours' (2011, p.130), and highlights an inability to change organisational practices. The concept is also impacted by locked-in path dependency and institutional inertia. Pike *et al.* (2010) also highlighted work within economic geography that analyses the importance of 'lock-in' for urban and regional areas 'whereby economic, social and institutional outlooks, relationships and configurations in place ossify over time, relying upon previous growth paths and inhibiting adaptive behaviours' (p.6), further noting that 'how places interpret and address lock-ins is central to the geographically differentiated adaptation and adaptability *explaining resilience*' (ibid., emphasis added).

These patterns from urban history and from resilience engineering illuminate how understanding maladaptation is an increasingly important variable in urban resilience. When we talk about maladaptation within the context of urban resilience we are, in essence, highlighting sub-optimal decision making that leads to an increase in vulnerability and a reduction in adaptive capacity or willingness to adapt. Research on maladaptation within urban and regional planning repeatedly highlights the importance of ongoing change; more often it reflects a failure or inability to adapt policy or practice in response to changing circumstances, further reinforcing the need to see urban and regional planning – the design and governance of the built environment – as part of a continual process, rather than a one-off action.

These understandings of maladaptation reinforce the importance of challenging existing practices of urban and regional planning at a range of scales, but also the potential benefits of promoting wider adaptation and adaptive capacity building within the planning profession. Ultimately, any urban resilience action will need to be proportionate and based upon risk management/mitigation principles, and thus resilience adaptation efforts must be balanced against the scale of maladaptation and potential vulnerability so that urban and regional planners, and the planning system, can better adapt to changing circumstances by modifying behaviour, actions or plans according to current and future need.

Adaptation, adaptability and adaptive capacity

Resilience can be viewed as 'as the capacity to adapt to stress from hazards and the ability to recover quickly from their impacts' (Timmerman, 1981, p.5) with Gunderson and Holling (2002) famously noting that 'adaptive management' was necessary to enhance resilience in interconnected systems. Resilience can also be seen as a response to maladaptation, delivered through the enhancement of adaptive capacity (sometimes referred to as adaptability) into the built environment, associated governance systems and a variety of place-making and localist planning activities (Coaffee and Clarke, 2015) although as Galderisi and Ferrara (2012) note, adaptive capacity encapsulates not only efforts to be more flexible within different circumstances, but also captures how adaptive measures are more contextual, site specific and relevant at a local level. In short, urban systems that are 'best able to adapt to new circumstances, vulnerabilities and hazards, will be the most resilient' (Coaffee, 2013b, p.2).

The conceptualisation of adaptation and adaptability here is important and relates to a distinction between equilibrium models of resilience which focus upon bouncing back to a pre-existing state following a perturbation and more evolutionary approaches which have a focus upon longer term transformation and bouncing forwards, with change being seen as a prerequisite of resilience (Folke *et al.*, 2010). Urban and regional systems are therefore viewed as being in a constant state of flux and are always evolving. Pike *et al.* (2010) provide a useful distinction between adaptation and adaptability, relating them to different timescales of action and interactions between key 'agents' of resilience. They define adaptation as 'a movement towards a pre-conceived path in the short run, characterized by strong and tight couplings between social agents in place' (p.4). This definition highlights the reactive nature and short-term thinking that often drives policy making in urban and regional planning and where transforming urban governance becomes difficult and is often bound up by path dependencies. By contrast, adaptability is defined as 'the dynamic capacity to effect and unfold multiple evolutionary trajectories, through loose and weak couplings between social agents in place, which enhance the overall responsiveness of the system to unforeseen changes' (ibid.). From the perspective of governance, Walker *et al.* (2004, p.5) have noted that adaptability can be seen as 'the capacity of actors in a system to influence resilience'.

These definitions illuminate the proactive, flexible and responsive properties of resilience that help explain 'the geographically uneven resilience of places' (Pike *et al.*, 2010, p.4) and why some localities can respond better than others to unforeseen events and stresses. Of relevance here is the design of urban space and public realm which is crucial to the adaptability of cities and to deliver a vibrant urbanism that is supple and capable of reorganising when there is a change of social or economic function (Corner, 2004).

A number of authors have also referred to 'adaptive resilience' as a key property of successful urban and regional systems. Martin (2012, p.5), for example, referred to adaptive resilience in a regional economic context as the 'ability of a system to undergo anticipatory or reactionary reorganization of form and/or function so as to minimize impact of a destabilizing shock'. By contrast Healey (2012, p.26) linked adaptive resilience to the invigoration of community planning or Japan's *Machizukuri* approach that was stimulated by the Kobe earthquake in 1995 and illustrates how civil society can contribute to 'resilient governance capacity' (see also Chapter 8). This echoes Pelling's (2003) work in the context of urban environmental risk, where he argued that the 'adaptive potential' of individuals and communities is related to social networks that may be mobilised to reframe local governance.

Similarly, resilience has also been promoted through the analytical framework of 'adaptive governance' which highlights the need to engage in co-productive efforts and decision making with different networks of formal and informal institutions (Carp, 2012) and which through approaches that are collaborative, flexible and learning-based rely on networks of people and organisations at multiple levels (see also Walker and Salt, 2012; Boyd and Juhola, 2015). Wilkinson (2011, p.4) has used this understanding of adaptive governance to promote more resilient urban planning approaches, where 'adaptive capacity' allows for uncertainty, change and new forms of practice to be integrated in governing-linked social–ecological systems (see also Boyd and Folke, 2012).

The notion of *adaptive capacity* is also increasingly recognised as critical to wider understandings of urban resilience, being viewed as 'the ability to adapt to changed circumstances while fulfilling one's core purpose [seen as] – an essential skill in an age of unforeseeable disruption and volatility' (Zolli and Healy, 2013). Moreover, Jones *et al.* (2010) noted that:

> adaptive capacity denotes the ability of a system to adjust, modify or change its characteristics or actions to moderate potential damage, take advantage of opportunities or cope with the consequences of shock or stress. (p.2)

Writing on the governance of urban resilience Wagenaar and Wilkinson (2015, p.1271) further highlight that 'in order to deal with complex non-linear dynamics facing irreducible uncertainty, resilience approaches to governance argue for *generating adaptive capacity*' (emphasis added). Adaptive capacity is thus, perhaps, the core concept in ideas of urban resilience as it is fundamentally related to the resources that a system requires to adapt and learn, and how particular individuals or groups can mobilise these resources effectively to mitigate the impact of known risks or unknown disruptive challenges. In this sense, ideas of adaptive capacity echo work in urban and regional planning linked to building institutional capacity through collaboration so as to improve the qualities of places. Such an institutionalist reading shifts the focus in urban planning away from the materiality of building places and towards how better and more deliberative governing arrangements might be fostered (Healey, 1998; Coaffee and Healey, 2003) to bolster *collaborative planning* approaches which emphasise:

> the importance of building new policy discourses about the qualities of places, developing collaboration among stakeholders in policy development as well as delivery, widening stakeholder involvement beyond traditional power elites, recognising different forms of local knowledge, and building rich social networks as a resource of institutional capital through which new initiatives can be taken rapidly and legitimately. (Healey, 1998, p.1531)

Here key questions are asked about the appropriate governance capacity to deliver such improvements, with analysis highlighting that local policy cultures are key mediating variables with differing degrees of integration, connectivity and ability to mobilise readily (mobilisation capacity) in order to capture opportunities, improve local conditions and increase institutional capacity. In an almost identical way, adaptive capacity is often seen as a quality of local urban systems which can be 'enhanced through collaborative problem-solving, social learning and engaging a diversity of stakeholders and knowledge practices' (Goldstein *et al.*, 2015, p.1287). At broader spatial scales the idea of adaptive capacity also has a particular resonance with resilience against climate change, with the 2014 Intergovernmental Report on Climate Change (IPCC, 2014) using the concept to represent the ability to adapt to the impacts and requirements of a changing climate. Where such adaptation is not forthcoming the term 'adaptation deficit' is often used to illuminate where there is the lack of adaptive capacity to enhanced resilience and is strongly related to appropriate strongly related institutional and governance provision to ensure adaptation (UN-Habitat, 2011). Such adaptation deficits can also indicate evidence of the propensity towards maladaptation in planning and governance processes. Unpacking and enhancing the adaptive capacity of governance institutions, planning communities and civil society, and envisioning how this might be utilised as part of developing a new 'urban resilience' is a pressing research agenda in urban and regional policy (Bull-Kamanga *et al.*, 2003; Pelling and High, 2005; Coaffee *et al.*, 2008b) and one that is increasingly being informed by learning from past incidents of maladaptation.

Learning from planning and design weaknesses

Learning from earlier incidents and utilising new forms of risk assessment to target context specific adaptive measures is vital for urban resilience. Disruptive incidents occur due to failures or lapses in the combined physical, communicative and management systems that are in play in urban areas at critical moments of risk (Fisher, 2012). In order to enhance urban resilience, and in particular to better understand how urban and regional planners can improve the design and management of urban spaces, it is necessary to analyse a body of examples from a range of different incidents, in order to draw out common features or characteristics that contributed to, or detracted from, the outcome of the incident or subsequent resilience response. In our work we have surveyed hundreds of past urban incidents, with a main focus on critical features of the material built environment and on the governance of response. In addition we have also analysed the material specificities of changes brought about by new risk challenges and attempts to enhance urban resilience through a detailed audit of the physical and social landscape changes enacted. In combination, this analysis has provided empirical evidence relating to a range of vulnerabilities for different types of disruptive challenges (e.g. terrorist attack, flooding, earthquakes, industrial accidents and crowd management) that can be used to inform the (re)design of more resilient urban spaces. This work is critical to establishing a framework for resilient planning and design, which can be defined as:

> a holistic activity involving a range of activities which shape and manage the built fabric so as to reduce its vulnerability to a range

of hazards and threats. It is concerned with both the spatial form and redesign of the built environment as well as the processes that help shape it. (Coaffee *et al.*, 2012, p.2)

From this work we have drawn out a series of maladaptation properties – common planning and design weaknesses – which can be used to identify potential adaptive measures for the design and governance of urban areas and to make them more resilient. The identification and appropriate analysis of earlier incidents can help to overcome the limitations of stakeholders' lack of knowledge and lack of experience in dealing with these issues (Coaffee and Clarke, 2015). Our 'incident database' identified three broad areas for consideration for urban and regional planners:

- *Design and construction* – the design, material and construction used, the employment of comprehensive modelling of known or suspected threats and risks and the inclusion of design measures to mitigate against these risks.
- *Governance* – the establishment of frameworks within which urban spaces are shaped which include planning policies, construction codes and guidance and the establishment of procedures for its design, construction and use.
- *Management* – the use of the space and the way in which is it monitored, managed and maintained so as to minimise the risk of incidents occurring.

These considerations represent different points in the process of planning, but also how the manifestation of weaknesses in them can occur in different ways. Intersecting with these three broad areas of consideration were nine categories of planning and design weakness which are illustrated below with corresponding examples. During any disruptive event it is likely that more than one weakness will be present. For clarity the examples focus upon what we consider to be the most pertinent planning and design weakness evident in a particular incident.

First, *land-use planning weakness* can arise as a result of failures in planning policy and procedures that see inappropriate or incompatible land uses develop, often as a result of inadequate consideration of potential risks and vulnerabilities. This might include, the lack of appropriate building codes or the enactment of resilience interventions in one part of a city that inadvertently impact upon another part. For example, the flooding which occurred in Carlisle in the north of England in 2005 illustrates both a basic failure to address the potential exposure of new residential development within areas of the floodplain but also a more serious failure arising from locating critical infrastructure in areas particularly vulnerable to flooding. In total, three lives were lost, over 1,700 homes were flooded and critical emergency infrastructure was badly affected. Carlisle's location adjacent to a river has always made it liable to flood but this was compounded by planning and development decisions made prior to the flooding which approved expansion of the town but failed to address this vulnerability. In addition, the loss of floodplain capacity contributed to more severe flooding elsewhere. Moreover the town's critical emergency infrastructure was also located in this area and was severely impacted, drastically hampering emergency response efforts. Notably, the area's police and fire and rescue services as well as its telecommunications facilities were located close to the river, with no special protection against flooding. Post-event adaptation strategies have subsequently seen many of the town's residential suburbs now surrounded by new flood defences, while the town centre received greater protection in the form of flood walls, embankments and a pumping station, to protect local infrastructure including roads and medical facilities. Finally, Cumbria's police and fire services were moved out of Carlisle to a new, less vulnerable location. Completed in 2009 and costing over £20 million from the UK Environment Agency, the Carlisle flood alleviation scheme provides a 1 in 200 year flood defence approach appropriate to the residential, historical and industrial locations along the two environmentally sensitive rivers (Environment Agency, 2007). The scheme has greatly reduced the risk of flooding and, according to the UK's Landscape Institute (2011), has 'created new areas of high quality public realm, encouraging development along the river, strengthening and enhancing the sustainable transport network and ultimately turning the city's focus back towards the river'. However, in December 2015 unprecedented rainfall in the Carlisle area saw the flood defences overtopped leaving thousands of homes and businesses devastated. While it would appear that the previously installed flood protection barriers helped to delay the floodwaters and gave people time to prepare, they were simply unable to cope with the scale of the floodwaters. In response to calls to move beyond the usual rhetoric of flood defence and embrace flood resilience, the government subsequently established the Cumbrian Floods Partnership group to look at how defences can be improved in the communities worst hit, and a National

Flood Resilience Review to ensure the UK has the best possible plans in place for flood prevention and protection nationwide.

These adaptations demonstrate the necessary resilient response, based upon embedding realistic risk assessment into land-use planning decision making. Typically land-use planning weaknesses involve the poor siting of activity (as noted above and in many other flooding examples) and the advancement of the built environment in ways that inadvertently enhance risk. For example, there has been concern among urban and regional planners that increasing urbanisation is enhancing the risk from river flooding, and in particular flash flooding, caused by increased run-off and reduced absorbency (White, 2008). Nirupama and Simonovic (2007) also highlighted that between 1974 and 2000 there has been a considerably elevated risk from floods due to heavy urbanisation in the watershed of the Upper Thames River, near the City of London, Ontario, Canada. The lack of enforceable building codes is another area where failure of planning becomes evident. For example, in the Caribbean, Chmutina and Bosher (2014) have highlighted that the lack of building codes and complacency towards natural hazards in Barbados have significantly increased disaster risk and weakened urban resilience.

Second, *architectural and industrial design weaknesses* occur as a result of design and construction failures of built environment elements. This includes inadequate consideration of the processes taking place within urban areas, or where the built elements impede the effectiveness of resiliency functions. For example, the design of Mississippi River Gulf Outlet canal, which linked the city of New Orleans to the shipping lanes of the Gulf of Mexico, was shown to have acted as a funnel for the 2005 Hurricane Katrina storm surge, accelerating water speeds, increasing the height of floodwaters and subsequently leading to more damage within the city (Olshansky and Johnson, 2010; see also Chapter 7). In relation to security risks we can also highlight the design of the Glasgow Airport terminal buildings as maladaptive as it failed to include measures to address hostile vehicles or vehicle-borne explosives. Following an attack in 2007 – when terrorists were able to drive a jeep loaded with propane canisters into the glass doors of the Glasgow International Airport terminal and set it ablaze – over £4 million has been spent on additional security adaptations including redesigning the access to the terminal building and the installation of hostile vehicle mitigation barriers and CCTV (Coaffee and O'Hare, 2008; see also Chapter 6). These examples highlight the need for ongoing considerations of both risk and the suitability of the material built environment for current and future needs.

Third, *site management and monitoring weaknesses* develop as a result of management failures or inadequate monitoring. This includes instances where the lack of management and monitoring is the cause of a weakness, or has contributed to a weakness, including consideration of ongoing works to the built environment and their impact on the contained processes and functions. It also involves a failure to adequately monitor building regulations in the construction and post-construction period. This refers to legal requirements to ensure the safety, health and welfare of people in and around a building which need to be periodically monitored. Examples of this weakness are especially pertinent in the context of crowd management and large-scale public events. For instance, a crowd crush which killed 21 people and injured 500 at the 2010 Duisburg Love Parade (Germany) occurred when over 1.4 million people were allowed into a site that had been prepared to accommodate just 400,000. In particular, access and egress points were inadequate and the event lacked crowd management strategies or practice. The incident highlights how site management is not only about on-the-day activities, but also involves the preparation and testing of emergency and evacuation plans which are increasingly being designed into how event facilities are planned using the skills of a range of urban stakeholders, including planners. In a further example, Alsnih and Stopher (2004) argued from an Australian perspective that effective emergency planning and management should successfully combine the skills and knowledge of law enforcement agencies and transport planners as well as those of emergency planning professionals.

The poor monitoring of building regulations has also been a direct cause of, or significantly contributed to, the impact of many disasters. In recent times one of the most prominent examples of this occurred in Dhaka, Bangladesh in 2013 when a huge garment factory collapse occurred, killing over 200 people. Although mired in a human tragedy of sweatshop labour, this incident also highlighted a violation of building regulations and an inability of local government to monitor such regulations effectively (BBC, 2013). Unfortunately this is a very common occurrence, particularly in less developed counties. For instance, in Kenya, despite specific building and planning regulations, a significant number of building collapses continue to occur, leading to calls for more rigorous enforcement:

> With this kind of a pattern, national safety and security is at stake and will worsen if urban planning is not prioritised, especially in

the era of devolution. A critical assessment of the past indicates that inadequate enforcement of urban planning regulations and standards has impacted on the safety and security of citizens in different parts of the country and unless drastic non knee-jerk reactions are prescribed, then such disasters will continue claiming lives in the country. (Ougo, 2015)

Fourth, *structural weaknesses* which have occurred as a result of a structural failure – due to lack of structural integrity or insufficient robustness – can also be seen as maladaptive. Typically this relates to elements of the built environment that have been inadequately designed or constructed. There are many examples we can draw on to illuminate this weakness, particularly linked to seismic risk. In May 1960 the twentieth century's largest earthquake hit Valdivia in southern Chile (a magnitude 9.5 event) causing massive structural damage and triggering tsunamis in coastal areas. The combined death toll was around 5,000 with two million Chileans being made homeless as the majority of the homes in affected areas lacked structural robustness. In the wake of this earthquake the government initiated country-wide modernisation of building construction, designing housing to withstand the shaking produced by seismic events. A subsequent large-scale quake in northern Chile in 2014 (a magnitude 8.2 event) left only six dead and damaged only 2,500 homes, testimony to the programme of building work that was implemented (Franklin, 2014).

Other areas have not been so lucky. For example, the Spanish town of Lorca suffered massive damage to buildings and infrastructure, nine deaths and many more injuries from falling rubble when, on 11 May 2011, a moderate 5.1 magnitude earthquake struck. Although only a moderate event, this incident highlighted a widespread lack of structural robustness, inadequate building codes and failures to act on the area's vulnerability to earthquakes. Many argued that not only should buildings have withstood the event, but that pre-existing structural problems could be the only explanation of why so many collapsed. More specifically, there had been a widespread failure to make ongoing structural repairs following earlier events, or more general structural improvements necessary within an area of heightened seismic risk (Romão *et al.*, 2013). A further example can be drawn from the 2015 Nepalese earthquake that killed many thousands of people. In the wake of this devastating event much of the commentary focused upon the poor quality of building construction. For example, *The Guardian* newspaper, in an article entitled 'Nepal earthquake: a disaster that shows quakes don't kill people, buildings do', noted that:

> Around three-quarters of all deaths in earthquakes are due to building collapse. Low-cost and informal buildings are most likely to fail, meaning that earthquakes disproportionately affect the poorest in the community, and usually leave them even poorer. (Cross, 2015)

In Nepal's case, and in many others, rapid urbanisation is out-stripping a government's ability to enforce standards. In essence this highlights to the international community the need to embed resilience into long-term planning rather than just response efforts (Ravilious, 2015).

Fifth, *materials' weaknesses* often exacerbate the impact of a disruptive event and occur as a result of inadequate performance or specification of construction materials within the built environment, particularly to a given vulnerability. This weakness is well illustrated by the June 1996 Manchester bombing, at the time the largest peacetime bomb ever detonated in Great Britain, where the use of insufficiently robust materials, in this case glass, greatly amplified the impact of the explosion. While the area was successfully evacuated before the blast, there was considerable destruction of property and many injuries caused by shattered glass from glass-fronted shops. Subsequent to this attack, reconstruction plans demonstrated a number of adaptations to ensure that the problems highlighted by the event were addressed. These included the designing of 'stand-off' areas between publicly accessible roads and high-profile buildings using security bollards, and the extensive use of bomb-proof glazing, commonly utilised in other locations deemed at risk from terrorist attacks (Coaffee, 2003).

A different example of material maladaptation was evident during the Brisbane floods in 2011 as the result of the use of widespread non-permeable pavements which reduced natural infiltration of water and increased surface water run-off, placing greater demands on established storm water infrastructure (Brisbane City Council, 2011; see also van den Honert and McAneney, 2011). In response, and continuing on from a range of water management plans produced since 1999, Brisbane have rolled out a water sensitive urban design strategy which is seeking to enhance the permeability of the built environment (Brisbane City Council, 2011) and Water*Smart* and Flood*Smart* future strategies to ensure an integrated resilience approach planning to flood risk (Brisbane City Council, 2013b; see also Chapter 6).

Sixth, *maintenance weaknesses* arise as a result of inadequate maintenance to built environment elements and processes. This includes both routine maintenance and the reactive repair of defects within the site, buildings or to equipment vital to the site's successful functioning. The failure of routine site maintenance can be exemplified by a massive fire at the Kings Cross Underground Station, London, in November 1987 that led to the deaths of 31 people and injured more than 60 (Department of Transport, 1988). The post-event investigation found that a discarded match had ignited a large pile of debris beneath the escalators, consisting of grease, discarded tickets, sweet wrappers, fluff from clothing and both human and rat hair, that not been cleaned since the escalator was constructed in the 1940s. The event was the catalyst for new legislation: the Fire Precautions (Sub-surface Railway Stations) Regulations 1989, and led to a variety of adaptations, including the replacement of wooden escalators, installation of sprinklers and smoke alarms, and rigorous staff fire training with the appropriate emergency services.

In the built environment, historic buildings and critical infrastructure require periodic maintenance to ensure structural integrity, although often this does not occur. For example, during the 2009 L'Aquila earthquake many historic buildings which had not been properly maintained collapsed despite the moderate nature of the earthquake (Akinci *et al.*, 2010). Similarly, the devastating 2005 floods in the Indian state of Maharashtra, which led to the deaths of over 1,500 people, were found by investigators to have been exacerbated by inadequate maintenance of the region's drains and sewers (Gupta, 2007).

Seventh, *hazard mitigation weakness* occurs as a result of inadequate hazard mitigation procedures and is typically a result of deficiencies within the risk assessment process. This weakness is well illustrated by the impact of 'Superstorm Sandy' upon New York in 2012 where a failure to address underlying vulnerabilities was exposed by a storm surge which overwhelmed the city's mitigation measures. The city's scant flood walls and defences were overwhelmed, flooding streets, tunnels, subway lines and, most notably, the city's main energy plants at Battery Park, which led to widespread electricity blackouts. The flood walls protecting the city's power plants were also found to be insufficient to deal with this 1 in 100 year storm event. This loss of power caused a cascading failure of more critical infrastructure as local hospitals lost power and much of the city lost water supply. In this case the policy response can be seen as maladaptive as earlier city risk assessment had highlighted the vulnerability of New York's infrastructure to flooding yet policy makers had delayed action. As we will highlight in Chapter 10, in the wake of Hurricane Sandy New York has seen a host of initiatives to boost the city's resilience to these types of event, including changes to building codes and major initiatives to secure the long-term future of the city, which prioritise mitigation around critical infrastructure (Hurricane Sandy Rebuilding Task Force, 2013; see also Chapter 1).

Another example of a hazard mitigation weakness was illuminated during a catastrophic state-wide flooding episode in Queensland, Australia, in 2011 where inadequate flood defences, and the lack of a state-wide strategic hazard mitigation plan, greatly increased the scale and impact of the incident. In the wake of this event, in 2015 the state of Queensland set up a permanent disaster recovery agency – the first permanent resilience arrangement in Australia – to deal with a future of more extreme floods and cyclones as a result of climate change. The Queensland Reconstruction Authority was originally established on a temporary basis to deal with the 2011 floods (Robertson, 2015).

The eighth weakness we can identify is in terms of inadequate *emergency response*, and, in particular, where the emergency response (or lack thereof) has caused, exacerbated or contributed to the impact of an incident. This can be illustrated by the circumstances surrounding the 7/7 public transport bombings in London which killed 52 people and injured over 700, where confusion over communication between responders and front-line staff hampered relief efforts, having a significant impact on the post-incident care of survivors (House of Commons, 2006a). In the immediate aftermath of this incident mobile networks were overloaded leading to a failure to deploy the right numbers of ambulances to the right locations, a lack of necessary equipment and supplies at the scenes and delays in getting some of the injured to hospital. A number of mitigation measures were put forward by the coroner at the conclusion of the inquest into the deaths during the incident, including improved training, communications and regular exercises between transport groups, emergency services and other relevant stakeholders, such as strategic planners.

The importance of having an up-to-date, tested and readily available contingency or emergency plan in place was also demonstrated during the UK's Buncefield Oil Depot explosion in 2005 where emergency information and procedures were not available to the blue light services because they were located within the affected site/buildings and were consequently destroyed. This incident was also compounded by another planning and design weakness which saw residential developments and a school located close to the oil storage plant and where local stakeholders, including residents and businesses, were unaware of the potential explosion risk or what to do in the event of such an explosion (see Health and Safety Executive, 2011).

Ninth, *stakeholder involvement weaknesses* can also be identified as a result of inadequate engagement with appropriate stakeholders. In particular, this often occurs where the design and construction of the built environment has commenced without key stakeholder inputs. For example, the impact of the flooding of New Orleans in 2005, following a storm surge driven by Hurricane Katrina, was compounded by the inability of approximately 100,000 area residents to leave the city due to the lack of transportation, money or external family support, and exacerbated by the inadequacy of the regional evacuation plan. The impact of Hurricane Katrina on the city highlighted the unpreparedness and lack of coordination by and between local, state and national government stakeholders (Farazmand, 2007; Moynihan, 2009). Critically, residents hadn't been involved or made aware of evacuation plans in the event of such an occurrence. Furthermore, the city proved to be 'fracture critical', with a total failure of critical facilities and emergency response, leaving many residents stranded in flooded areas (see Chapter 6 for a detailed account).

Another stakeholder involvement weakness example was shown following the devastating Haitian Earthquake in 2010 where there was a lack of decentralised administration and funding which hampered the ability to implement effective emergency response programmes (see, for example, Pelling, 2011). In this case, and in others, importance should have been placed on getting the most appropriate stakeholder engagement at the right time in the emergency response cycle, as well as the planning and development cycle, so that urban resilience measures are most effective. Stakeholder engagement weaknesses can also occur where the design and construction of the built environment has commenced without key stakeholder inputs. For example, many authors have drawn attention to the reluctance of developers and planners to engage with specialist security stakeholders until their development is a *fait accompli*, meaning that in many cases expensive and less effective retrofitted security solutions have had to be installed (Coaffee and Bosher, 2008; see also Chapter 7).

Table 4.1 provides a summary of the nine urban planning weaknesses highlighted above. As a counterpoint we have also provided examples of resilient responses that might accompany the identification of weaknesses.

Table 4.1   *Overview of weaknesses and resilient responses*

Weakness	Description	Examples
Land-use planning issues:	Where a weakness has arisen as a result of failures in planning policy and procedure that see inappropriate or incompatible land uses develop, or inadequate consideration of potential risks and vulnerabilities.	The allocation of land for housing development is unsuitable as the chosen site is risk prone (e.g. a floodplain). **Resilient response:** *Undertake appropriate risk assessment and do not allocate risk-prone sites for development.*
Architectural and industrial design issues:	Where a weakness has occurred as a result of design and construction failures of built environment elements.	Where arrangement and siting of architectural elements designed to add security is lacking or is inappropriately located. **Resilient response:** *The careful siting of risk-reducing architectural features appropriate to context and risk.*
Site management and monitoring:	Where a weakness has developed as a result of management failures or inadequate monitoring.	Where access to an event is not adequately controlled or building regulations are not monitored. **Resilient response:** *Installation of robust procedures to manage crowd flow or monitor building regulations.*

Structural issues:	Where weaknesses have occurred as a result of a structural failure, due to lack of structural integrity or insufficient robustness.	Where a building collapses as a result of inadequate structural coherence. **Resilient response:** *Improved building code and inspection procedures during construction.*
Materials issues:	Where weaknesses have occurred as a result of inadequate performance or specification of construction materials, within the built environment.	Inappropriate building materials have been used which magnify the impacts of hazards. **Resilient response:** *Use appropriate building materials in vulnerable locations.*
Maintenance:	Where a weakness has arisen as a result of inadequate maintenance to built environment elements and processes.	The lack of robust maintenance enhances risk. **Resilient response:** *Ensure a robust maintenance programme is implemented to reduce risk.*
Hazard mitigation:	Where a weakness has arisen as a result of inadequate hazard mitigation or risk assessment procedures.	Resiliency measures which are insufficient to deal with the magnitude of a major event. **Resilient response:** *Undertake periodic risk assessment and instigate appropriate risk mitigation measures in a timely fashion.*

Emergency response:	Where weaknesses have occurred as a result of a failure in the emergency response (or lack thereof).	Poor communication between responder services leads to confusion in response to a major incident. **Resilient response:** *Improve emergency planning of communication procedure for emergency responders and incorporate into planning exercises.*
Stakeholder involvement:	Where a weakness has occurred as a result of inadequate engagement with appropriate stakeholders.	Important stakeholders have not been consulted on the resilience measures. **Resilient response:** *Include all relevant stakeholders at the right time in planning urban resilience.*

Key lessons in planning for resilience

Urban resilience is ultimately about dealing with change through adaptation and learning and within a transdisciplinary environment where all the aspects of design, governance and management are hybridised: 'the essence of resilience is an ability to change as circumstances change, to adapt and, crucially, to transform rather than continuing to do the same thing faster and better' (Goldstein *et al.*, 2015, p.1287). This raises a number of key questions about the appropriateness and unintended consequences of resilience interventions and plans. *First*, how can issues of equity and social justice (Beilin and Wilkinson, 2015) become key facets of urban resilience strategies amidst a post-political landscape that attempts to marginalise alternative voices? Moreover, the related issue is then raised of spatial justice and the differential impact of urban resilience policy across different scales and trade-offs within scales. As Leichenko (2011, p.166) has highlighted:

> [S]ome recent studies identify situations where promotion of resilience for some locations may come at the expense of others or enhancement of resilience at one scale, such as the level of the community, may reduce resilience at another scale, such as the household or individual.

Other studies raise questions about the relationship between resilience and poverty and recommend more attention to the issues of power and inequality that arise with application of resilience approaches (see also Adger *et al.*, 2005; Pike *et al.*, 2010).

The *second* key question raised by the implementation of urban resilience policy relates to cost. Making the business case for resilience is often a difficult task, especially when risks are not fully known and when funds are limited. Increasingly, developers are now focusing on the advantages of adopting a resilience strategy to protect their properties, but also to create value for their developments. For example, the Urban Land Institute's (2015) report *Returns on Resilience: The Business Case*, focused upon financial risks to real estate posed by climate change and highlighted how developers and owners are increasingly investing in new infrastructure and technologies, innovative design and construction methods and other resilience strategies 'to enhance the adoption of so-called triple-bottom-line principles, where environmental sustainability and social equity are pursued in tandem with strong financial returns' (Pyati, 2015). One mechanism that has been suggested is to think about synergising urban resilience efforts in, for example, climate change adaptation and security. As Coaffee and Bosher (2008, p.81) noted:

> [E]xamples of synergies between security and sustainability might include developing landscaping systems that are both 'green' and can conform to crime prevention through environmental design principles, for example, ponds and strategically planted trees acting as physical barriers instead of expanses of concrete and rows of steel bollards. It is also possible that such ponds and landscaping features could be used as part of sustainable urban drainage systems (SudS) that are designed to reduce the occurrence and impact of flooding in urban areas.

Moreover, in their 2011 White Paper *Financing the Resilient City*, Local Governments for Sustainability (ICLEI) highlighted that 'the challenge is to match local demand for resilience with the supply of finance' (p.4) and 'for local-level officials to develop a demand-led approach to leveraging the right finance in invest in the resilience upgrading of vulnerable urban areas'. This all combines to illustrate that enhancing 'the capacity of *planning processes* for identifying vulnerabilities and risks, and linking the related risk mitigation solutions with priority performance enhancements in relevant areas or systems' is seen as vital (ibid.).

Third, while the development of cities has enhanced vulnerability, how can innovation be fostered that can promote greater resiliency? As Leichenko (2011, p.166) notes, 'cities are sites of social, political, economic and technical innovation. This innovation potential can be drawn upon to develop and implement strategies that promote resilience'. She further notes the potential of new governance configurations to promote resilience that is not constrained by prior institutional inertia and the often-embedded 'cultures' of professionals which may mitigate against more collaborative and participatory working practices.

The push for urban resilience is, in essence, 'a response to existential or material vulnerability, insecurity and, ultimately, change' (Coaffee *et al.*, 2008b, p.1). In this chapter we have illuminated planning and design weaknesses that, from a historical perspective, have tended to reoccur, presenting barriers or maladaptive processes that have exposed a larger number of people than previously to risk and hindered the crafting of truly adaptive polices where risk is considered, assumed and shared and where implementing urban resilience becomes part of the everyday practices of urban and regional planners. In Chapters 6–9 we will present a series of vignettes illuminating how such urban resilience strategies are being increasingly adopted in response to different types and scale of risk. However, before we detail such operational strategies of urban resilience we turn our attention to the growth of urban resilience assessment tools, highlighting their utility as well as their limitations of use for everyday planning practice. Here particular emphasis is placed upon how measuring urban resilience can, on the one hand, facilitate strategic and holistic planning processes while, on the other hand, professionalising aspects of planning; providing planning consultancy opportunities while potentially disempowering local planners.

Chapter 5

Assessing City Resilience

The discussion we have engaged with in this book concerning what urban resilience is and what it does is further complicated by questions of how to measure and assess its qualities. In recent years, and across numerous disciplines, many indices have been developed which seek to standardise methods of assessing the properties of resilience. However, as Prior and Hagmann observe (see also Hinkel, 2011):

> [I]n general, these measures employ different definitions of resilience, they are constructed using dissimilar constituents (indicators or variables), they are utilised for different purposes – and as a result they ultimately measure different things. Even a basic exploration of what might constitute a measure (or index) of resilience, for example, reveals the difficulty in establishing a measure that is both accurate and 'fit for purpose'. (Prior and Hagmann, 2013, p.4)

Within the context of urban and regional planning practice and an ongoing view of the need for urban resilience processes to ideally be both multi-scalar and multi-dimensional, advancing such a 'fit for purpose' assessment framework for city resilience is premised upon thinking and acting strategically and spatially, and in so doing, drawing a wide range of related stakeholders into a collective and collaborative effort. While the governance of cities has altered dramatically over the post-war period, recent austerity impacts within the public sector stretch the resilience of public and private services and infrastructure, and lead to urban resilience assessment processes that increasingly seek value for money.

City managers and urban and regional planners are increasingly tasked with developing an understanding of how exposed communities and assets are to risks and their capacity to cope with shock events. In doing so they need to engage with a wide range of stakeholders and intelligence to reframe planning efforts for resilience purposes. Capturing key resilience performance indicators in an ongoing holistic way to address current and future planning challenges is by no means an easy task. The expansion of urban areas as a result of continued urbanisation and their increased exposure to multiple shocks and stress has increased the complexity of urban planning decision making and placed a greater burden on the delivery and maintenance of key services and infrastructures. Within this context this chapter proceeds in four parts. First we contextualise the need for urban resilience assessment through a framing of urban and regional planning as a complex and strategic activity involving the integration of planning stakeholders across spatial scales. Second, the chapter provides a description of resilience assessment frameworks developed specifically for addressing disaster risk reduction (DRR) at the urban and regional scale before going on to look at indicator sets used to assess the economic and social resilience of cities. Third, we critique some of the commonly used and emerging indices and frameworks arguing that the overly strategic and techno-rational assessment of resilience that has become *de rigueur* results in a tendency towards prescriptive top-down and professionalised assessment methodologies (often driven by neoliberal imperatives). Fourth, we conclude the chapter by providing a summary of key issues arising and the implications for urban managers (including planners) for delivering cost-effective public services while dealing with increased complexity arising from urban expansion and systems interaction. This, we argue, includes an urgent requirement to understand and implement an *integrated and holistic* resilience programme, or agenda, but to do so using more tacit, qualitative judgements in their proper spatial context in order to help unpack the precise resilience mechanisms and qualities of urban systems and communities.

Urban complexity and resilience needs

In line with advances in the strategic and multi-scale nature of modern-day planning, urban resilience provides a workable framework for reducing multiple risks, integrating service delivery and embedding these principles within urban planning practice and, more broadly, urban governance. In her work on urban complexity and strategic spatial planning, Patsy Healey (2007) highlights how the evolution of planning practice has embraced ideas of vertical and horizontal integration across a variety of spatial configurations and, like emerging ideas of urban resilience, has shifted from traditional notions of scale and territory as a fixed, stable bounded container to a more diverse set of arrangements where networked relations are continually rescaled and renegotiated (Chapter 2). As Healey noted, her concern in planning is with the mobilisation of resources and political action through:

> strategies that treat the territory of the urban not just as a container in which things happen, but as a complex mixture of nodes and networks, places and flows, in which multiple relations, activities and values, co-exist, interact, combine, conflict, oppress and generate creative synergy. (p.1)

This, she continues, is a 'material and imaginative effort to make some "sense" of the complexity of urban life. The planning project, infused with this understanding of socio-spatial dynamics, becomes a governance project focused on managing the dilemmas of coexistence in shared spaces' (p.3).

In response to this complex challenge, a range of, often contradictory, planning initiatives have emerged, frequently centred upon local partnership modes of governance involving public, private and civil society stakeholders, (see, for example, Wilkinson and Appelbee, 1999) as well as a rescaling of governance towards increasingly multi-level and localised modes of action (see, for example, Brenner, 2004). Combined, such attempts to advance holistic and multiscalar governance, as Healey (2007) further noted, can be viewed as an attempt to break down silo mentality and 'create linkages between policy fields as they impact upon the places and connectivities of urban areas, expressed in the search for policy integration and joined-up government' (Healey, 2007, p.5). More recent work on so-called 'new spatial planning' (see, for example, Haughton *et al.*, 2010) underscores this focus on integration and holism where planning is seen as a process that is continually reinventing itself as a means to become more responsive and adaptable, and as a form of meta-governance – the governance of governance. This involves attempts to integrate a range of relational processes utilising more 'fluid' scales and 'fuzzy boundaries' which don't align with existing planning or political jurisdictions, and allow practitioners to break away from territorial tensions, pre-existing working patterns and traditional silos. In terms of urban resilience, the focus here translates to imagining place-making activities which can better reflect the real geographies of problems and vulnerabilities and in finding ways that policy makers can address them using urban resilience interventions.

At the local level, increased urban complexity, rescaling and, more recently, austerity have resulted in a call for a different type of place leadership to coordinate efforts (see for, example, Gibney *et al.*, 2009; Collinge and Gibney, 2010; Trickett and Lee, 2010), requiring a greater understanding of inter- and intra-urban system interactions. For example, in the UK, public policy mechanisms such as *Total Place* (DCLG, 2010) have been deployed in an attempt to break down the problem of place leadership through integrating data and knowledge of public service expenditure at the local level so as to deliver cost effectiveness in the context of austerity. Here, such approaches are implicitly aimed at delivering more resilient communities, underscored by the tenor of normative language used to describe coordinated programme aims to integrate services at the local level, to address the health, well-being and employment needs of vulnerable groups and build 'stronger', 'safer' communities with greater institutional capacity. Total Place provides an example of the type of innovative, transformative 'resilient' intervention that aims to mobilise professionals responsible for local place leadership, to transpose and integrate their thinking, which has wider implications for planning policy and urban resilience.

While integration of public services has been a key goal of recent planning and public sector initiatives such as Total Place, the measurement of resilience and the outcomes arising from changes affecting the resilience of cities requires the balancing of evidence of risks from natural and man-made hazards with evidence on the characteristics of urban actors and agents to create the conditions to withstand shocks and associated stresses. This gap between exposure and ability to withstand or adapt to risks has important implications for how urban resilience is operationalised and understood at the local level. While in many cases national guidance exists on the identification of risks and appropriate governance responses, there is no consistent or agreed framework or method of assessment at the national or international level to measure differential exposure of urban areas and/or communities to risks or their ability to mitigate them. As the Rockefeller Foundation notes in the context of measuring city resilience, 'there is no single framework available at the moment that enables resilience to be measured holistically and comprehensively at a city level' (Rockefeller Foundation, 2014d, p.1). While there is no agreed international measurement approach for urban resilience, there is broad agreement on *why* we need to measure it. Prior and Hagmann (2013, pp.4–5) highlighted five key reasons. First, *to characterise resilience* in context and to articulate it key constituents; second, *to raise awareness* and assist (urban) managers to identify entities whose resilience is lower than some predetermined threshold; third and relatedly, *to allocate resources for resilience* in a transparent manner; fourth, *to build resilience* in order to better manage disruptive challenges and to gauge the impact of mitigation measures; and fifth, *to monitor policy performance* and to assess the effectiveness of resilience-building policy through comparison of policy goals and targets against outcomes. To this list we might also add a sixth reason to measure resilience – *learning and advocacy* – that can be advanced through comparison within and between urban areas faced with resilience challenges, creating a shared knowledge community.

Within this context of attempts to assess urban resilience the remainder of the chapter considers a number of emerging frameworks, methods and indices for measuring resilience at the city and sub-city level. This includes indices advanced by academics and resilience assessment frameworks commissioned by global NGOs, as well as methodologies designed to measure resilience and developed by city authorities, independent think tanks and research foundations. Our approach here is informed by previous work we have developed on measuring deprivation and understanding risk of housing market failure (see Chapter 9) while also drawing on research related to the technical construction of indices and on the use of single and combined indicator sets (Lee *et al.*, 1995, Lee, 1999; Lee and Nevin, 2003). We further frame the analysis of these approaches within a realist context-mechanism-outcome evaluation approach in order to understand how useful these indicators, indices and frameworks are for decision makers in relation to the *context* in which they are deployed, and the *mechanisms* that are deemed most influential in delivering resilient *outcomes* (see Pawson and Tilley, 1997).

Assessing cities' preparedness for disaster

The ability of cities to respond to natural shock events and to improve disaster risk reduction (DRR) is emphasised in a number of resilience indices and frameworks developed by global organisations such as the World Bank and the United Nations Office for Disaster Risk Reduction under their International Strategy for Disaster Reduction (UNISDR). The UNISDR runs concurrently with the Hyogo Framework for Action (HFA) 2005–2015: *Building the Resilience of Nations and Communities to Disasters*, endorsed by the UN General Assembly after the 2005 World Disaster Reduction Conference held in Kobe, and which promotes the decentralisation of authority and resources to enhance local-level disaster risk reduction (the HFA was replaced by a new framework, agreed in Sendai in March 2015; see Chapter 10 for more details). The HFA was premised on a number of core principles that also feed through into UNISDR resilient cities campaigns. The building of institutional capacity to ensure risk identification, assessment and monitoring are core components of this approach, as is the building of a culture of safety through understanding and awareness, knowledge transfer, innovation and education. Ultimately the gathering of environmental, social and economic measures *to reduce underlying risk factors* and implement appropriate land-use planning policies is aimed at minimising the damage caused by natural hazards through an 'ethic of prevention' (UNISDR, 2015b). When this ethic is corrupted by human error and poor planning decisions, communities are exposed and can be vulnerable to natural hazards (e.g. earthquakes, floods, droughts and cyclones). As UNISDR notes, urban and regional planning therefore plays a key role in mediating risk highlighting the following planning aspects that make a city resilient:

> Sound development practice with good regulations, well-maintained infrastructure, capable emergency management and solid institutions, which develop participatory urban plans, provide building permits, and manage water resources and solid waste, help to build up cities' resilience over time. Political processes and decision-making that have addressed particular needs, or reduced risks, as the city was constructed will provide safe, good quality living conditions for everyone and protect the most vulnerable. This type of 'accumulated resilience' makes the city function on a daily basis. (UNISDR, 2012b, p.11)

Having a clear understanding of the risks local authorities face is seen as key to assessing the resilience of cities and for planning meaningful responses to disasters and shock events. UNISDR (2012a) has identified a number of significant risk drivers which have influenced the selection of criteria for assessing the ability of cities to absorb shocks including:

- *demographic* factors such as urban population growth and density especially in hazard-prone areas;
- *centralisation* or *concentrated resources* that reduce the flexibility of local actors to respond to disasters;

- *weak local governance* resulting in insufficient participation by local communities in urban planning;
- *inadequate water resource management* to respond to floods;
- *declining ecosystems* resulting from over development;
- *decaying infrastructure and buildings* that provide the conditions for hazards during disaster;
- *uncoordinated emergency services* that reduce the capacity for a swift response;
- *impact of climate change* exacerbating natural hazards. (see UNISDR, 2012a, p.8)

DRR resilience frameworks have focused on *natural hazards* and recovery from *disasters*, but frameworks for the urban governance of resilience are emerging which assess the capacity to absorb other types of shock (see Chapter 3), using the 'ethic of prevention' at the core of DRR approaches, to mitigate anthropogenic and socio-economic shocks. Alongside traditional engineering and technical mitigation approaches to tackle natural hazards and disasters, what is therefore emerging within urban resilience assessment frameworks is the strengthening of information systems and formalisation of governance mechanisms to assess capacity to absorb shocks in different contexts.

Such formalisation and prescription for assessing city resilience is evidenced by a number of UNISDR-commissioned reports as well as the launching of a global campaign on *Making Cities Resilient,* including a 'Disaster Resilience Scorecard for Cities' to measure the preparedness of cities to cope with shocks (see, UNISDR, 2012a, 2012b, 2014a and 2014b). Publications such as *How to Make Cities More Resilient: A Handbook For Local Government Leaders* (UNISDR, 2012a) aim to support public policy decision making and organisation for disaster risk reduction and resilience activities, and create a set of standardised tools and approaches for use in the business of resilience making. In this approach, local priorities are self-assessed by municipalities using a *Local Government Self-Assessment Tool for Disaster Resilience* scorecard (UNISDR, 2014b) which assesses cities' and municipal authorities' preparedness for disaster against ten criteria:

1. organisation and coordinated disaster response across spatial scales;
2. budgeting and incentivising risk reduction across stakeholders;
3. data management and maintenance of hazards and vulnerabilities;

4. investment in the maintenance of critical infrastructure to reduce risk;
5. assessment safety and hazard risk of schools and health facilities;
6. enforcement of building regulations to comply with risk assessment;
7. education programmes and training in schools and local communities;
8. protection of ecosystems and environmental buffers;
9. early warning systems and cooperation within cities and regions; and;
10. existence of comprehensive post-event recovery plans for victims.

The UNISDR-approved scorecard facilitates the setting of local baselines and the identification of gaps by local authorities grading each of their ten 'essentials' against 82 separate indicators measuring the degree of resilience (UNISDR, 2012a, p.25) necessitating systematic adoption of resilience codes of governance practice to provide such level of detail.

Similarly, the World Bank approach to urban resilience (*Building Urban Resilience: Principles, Tools, and Practice*, Jha *et al.*, 2013) contains all of the 'essential' elements that are featured in the UNISDR scorecard with a number of subtle variations on indicators and the process of assessment. In addition to *infrastructural* and *institutional* resilience which is central to the UNISDR approach, the World Bank includes *social* and *economic* resilience indicators and assesses these categories of resilience against *locational, structural, operational* and *fiscal* conditions (Jha *et al.*, 2013, p.19). For example, *infrastructural* resilience, measured against locational, structural, operational and fiscal conditions, measures the vulnerability of the built environment and the provision of key transport and buildings that can support populations during any emergency. This will include the provision of open space for temporary shelter accommodating displaced populations and critical infrastructure for response and recovery. Specific indicators cited in the World Bank approach include the mileage of arterial routes as a proxy for the ability to evacuate an affected area quickly. Meanwhile, economic resilience is included to assess the diversity and health of the economy and its capacity to respond following shock through measurement of the degree of support for resilience training within the business community, the rate and type of employment, the ratio of large to small firms and the location of firms and their exposure to risks or hazards (Jha *et al.*, 2013, p.19).

Assessing urban and city resilience

The World Bank and UNISDR approach form a basis for the measurement of different aspects of resilience, capturing a number of measures of risk and the adaptive capacity of cities and communities to respond to shock events. Building on this, the Rockefeller Foundation, together with Arup (the British multinational engineering and planning professional services consultancy), have developed a comprehensive framework of resilience that is, to date, one of the more advanced approaches to urban and city resilience, highlighting the requirement for integrated and holistic approaches. The Rockefeller Foundation argues that urban resilience is a set of cross-sectoral activities that cannot be approached in silos: 'the definition of resilience demands a cross-sector perspective […] shrewd cities can capture multiple social, economic and physical resilience benefits from individual actions' (Rockefeller Foundation, 2014c, p.100). The Rockefeller *City Resilience Index* (Rockefeller Foundation, 2014d) echoes the structure of DRR frameworks of UNISDR and World Bank and is organised around four categories (People, Place, Organisation and Knowledge), 12 broad indicators of resilience qualities and 150 variables (see Table 5.1).

Table 5.1 *Rockefeller Foundation/Arup City Resilience Index framework*

Category	Indicator	Description
People – Health & Well-being	Minimal human vulnerability	Extent to which basic needs are met
	Diverse livelihoods and employment	Degree of access to finance, ability to accrue savings, skills training, business support and social welfare
	Adequate safeguards to human life and health	Integrated health facilities and services, and responsive emergency services
Place – Infrastructure & Environment	Reduced physical exposure and vulnerability	Environmental stewardship; appropriate infrastructure; effective land-use planning; and enforcement of planning regulations.

	Continuity of critical services	Diverse provision and active management; maintenance of ecosystems and infrastructure; and contingency planning.
	Reliable communications and mobility	Diverse and affordable multimodal transport systems and information and communication technology (ICT) networks; and contingency planning.
Organisation – Economy & Society	Collective identity and mutual support	Observed as active community engagement, strong social networks and social integration.
	Social stability and security	Including law enforcement, crime prevention, justice, and emergency management.
	Availability of financial resources and contingency funds	Observed as sound financial management, diverse revenue streams, the ability to attract business investment, adequate investment, and emergency funds.
Knowledge – Leadership & Strategy	Effective leadership and management	Involving government, business and civil society, and indicated by trusted individuals; multi-stakeholder consultation; and evidence-based decision making.
	Empowered stakeholders	Education for all, and access to up-to-date information and knowledge to enable people and organisations to take appropriate action.
	Integrated development planning	The presence of a city vision; an integrated development strategy; and plans that are regularly reviewed and updated by cross-departmental working groups.

Source: adapted from Rockefeller Foundation, 2014a, p.7.

From an extensive review of the academic, policy and practice literature on resilience, three typologies or qualities of resilient systems have been identified by the Rockefeller Foundation: *asset-based* characteristics (e.g., hazard-proofed infrastructure); *practices or process*-based characteristics (e.g., community involvement in planning) and *attributes* (e.g., flexibility and adaptability) (Rockefeller Foundation, 2014b, p.21). These are assessed against eight qualities that underpin these typologies across the urban system:

- *Accepting* – of uncertainty with foresight incorporated in system design.
- *Reflective* – evidence of learning from previous events.
- *Adaptive* – tacit and corporate knowledge used.
- *Robust* – systems can withstand loss of functionality.
- *Resourceful* – spare capacity is available when systems fail.
- *Integrated* – information is shared across sectors.
- *Diverse* – assets are distributed across the city to ensure that risk is not concentrated.
- *Inclusive* – marginalised communities are included in resilience vulnerability measurement and plans (see Rockefeller Foundation, 2014b, pp.22–23).

Testing the applicability of their resilience indicators in six cities (Concepción, Chile; Cali, Colombia; Cape Town, South Africa; New Orleans, USA; Semarang, Indonesia; and Surat, India), Rockefeller and Arup established that the same principles of leadership and planning applied to both 'shock cities' (i.e. cities experiencing hurricanes, earthquakes etc.) and 'stress cities' (those suffering from the effects of climate change such as droughts and water shortage). How cities work with different stakeholder groups in planning and prioritising resilience themes was crucial, irrespective of the type of threat, highlighting 'the importance of understanding resilience from different stakeholder perspectives, as no individual group will fully reflect the priorities of all' (Rockefeller Foundation, 2014c, p.97). They further note that measures that assessed the role of city leadership and coordination of decision making were recognised as vital by all six case studies with a 'strong emphasis on *factors related to urban planning*, information and knowledge management, and capacity and coordination' (Rockefeller Foundation, 2014c, p.98, emphasis added) and that 'social and strategic factors are considered more crucial for urban resilience than the physical factors' (Rockefeller Foundation, 2014c, p.99). While this may be true, it may also reflect the dominance of a DRR resilience framework that has prevailed and a concomitant need to focus on planning and governance processes that lead to greater social and economic resilience rather than simply focusing on a city's physical resilience aspects.

Building on this perspective, and in an attempt to fill a gap in the resilience measurement literature that is littered with inconsistent indicators, the work of Cutter *et al.* (2008) and Burton (2014) emphasises the importance of community resilience. Their respective indices draw heavily on the DRR model of resilience in identifying exposure to risks but also develop measures of the capacity to absorb these at the local and municipal level. Burton's is the most developed and tested academic model of resilience drawing on a Disaster Resilience of Place (DROP) model. This utilises proxy measures of a community's ability to absorb shocks and includes social, economic, infrastructural, institutional and environmental aspects of resilience. The 98 variables across six domains measure characteristics of communities and households that make them vulnerable to shock events or inherently resilient (Burton, 2014, p.69). The construction of indices of this nature require them to have some relative criteria for measurement across time and space; therefore they need to be consistently available from open or publicly available sources and scalable so that methods of standardisation and comparison can be carried out. The resilience domains, variables and a sample of some of the core indicators used in Burton's community resilience index is shown in Table 5.2.

Table 5.2   *Community resilience domains and indicators*

Resilience domain	Sub-domain	Example indicators
Social	Social capacity	% population that is not a minority
		% population that doesn't speak English as a second language
	Community health/ well-being	Community services (recreational facilities, parks, historic sites, libraries, museums) per 1,000 population
	Equity	Ratio % college degree to % no high school diploma
		Ratio % minority to % nonminority population

Economic	Economic/ livelihood stability	% home ownership % female labour force participation
	Economic diversity	Ratio of large to small businesses
	Resource equity	Doctors and medical professionals per 1,000 population
	Infrastructure exposure	Density of commercial infrastructure
Institutional	Hazard mitigation planning	% population covered by a recent hazard mitigation plan
	Preparedness	% workforce employed in emergency services (firefighting, law enforcement, protection)
	Development	% land cover change to urban areas over a given period
Infrastructure	Housing type	% housing not built during specific building code periods
	Response and recovery	% housing that is vacant rental units
	Access and evacuation	Number of rail and arterial miles
	Infrastructure exposure	% building infrastructure not in flood and storm surge inundation zones
Community capital	Social capital	Religious organisations per 1,000 population Arts, entertainment, and recreation centres per 1,000 population
	Creative class	% workforce employed in professional occupations Research and development firms per 1,000 population
	Cultural resources	National sites of historic importance per square mile
	Sense of place	% population that is not an international migrant

Environmental systems	Risk and exposure	% land area not in an inundation zone
	Sustainability	% land area under protected status
	Protective resources	% land area that consists of windbreaks and environmental plantings
	Hazard event frequency	Frequency of loss-causing weather events

Source: adapted from Burton, 2014, pp.72–73.

The DROP model has both positive and negative attributes. Prior and Hagmann (2013) argued that, unlike many previous models from the disaster literature, where resilience models are often focused on engineered systems, the DROP model serves to explicitly focus upon social and organisation factors. There is also an attempt made to map resilience over time in an attempt:

> to capture the dynamic nature of these processes/concepts [and allow] the model to better account for some of the challenges or frustrations that have plagued resilience and vulnerability measurement: multiple or gradual onset events, place specificity and context/circumstance, spatial and temporal dynamics of vulnerability and resilience and the perceptions or attitudes of those people affected. (ibid., p.10)

While the DROP model provides a useful framework in which to compare community resilience between geographic locations its application in practice does present technical and logistical difficulties, and is very resource intensive (especially if scaling up to larger geographical areas).

The resilience indexes discussed thus far have been heavily informed by a DRR perspective. In many industrialised and post-industrialised city contexts it is, however, the social and economic factors that have had more relevance to the planning of urban and regional areas especially since the economic recession and financial crisis of 2007–2008 and associated social impacts. That crisis promulgated serious efforts by a number of key agencies and stakeholders to measure social and economic resilience of urban and regional systems in order to illuminate impacts and to target ever-reducing public sector resources to areas in most need. To exemplify this we now highlight a number of UK approaches: indices by BBC/Experian (2010a and 2010b), the Centre for Local Economic Strategies (CLES), the Young Foundation and a resilience index produced by Birmingham City Council as an example of efforts at measuring resilience locally by a large metropolitan local authority in the UK.

The Experian index of resilience was designed to measure the exposure of local authorities to public sector cuts and was commissioned by the BBC (British Broadcasting Corporation). The index, based on four domains of *Business, Community, People* and *Place* and underpinned by 31 indicators, ranked local authority districts according to how far their local economy was exposed to recession and withdrawal of public sector investment (see Table 5.3).

Table 5.3   *Experian/BBC economic resilience indicators*

	Indicator (weighting %)	Description
Business (50%)	Vulnerable sectors	% employed in particularly vulnerable sectors given the economic climate in 2009–2010, e.g. engineering and vehicles, construction, metals, minerals and chemicals and other, mainly public, services (weighting: 8%)
	Resilient sectors	% employed in resilient sectors faring well despite tough economic times, e.g. agriculture, forestry and fishing, banking and insurance (8%); % high growth (knowledge) sectors (15%)
	Business structure	Days beyond terms (time taken to pay suppliers) (5%); business density – businesses per 1000 people of working age (15%); highly exporting SICs (6%); adaptive companies – based on balance sheet information this variable shows the number of firms that have shown signs of distress in the past but have recovered (5%); foreign-owned business (5%)
	Business start-up	The number of businesses that had started up since 2008 (5%)
	Insolvency rate	The number of businesses that had gone out of business in the previous nine months (10%)
	Self employed	The % of the working-age population that was self-employed (5%)

Community (17%)	% long-term unemployed	The proportion of households that were vulnerable to long term unemployment (10%); % vulnerable to decline in disposable income – combines information from the ONS Expenditure and Food Survey (EFS)
	Claimant count	The rate of people claiming benefits, based on May 2010 figures
	Social cohesion	Survey responses to the question 'Do neighbours look out for each other?'
	Deprivation	Life expectancy at birth female and male; % Lower Super Output Areas (LSOAs) amongst 10% most deprived nationally
People (17%)	Working age population	The percentage of the local population that is of working age and therefore able to contribute to the local economy
	Professionals	% employed as corporate manages, senior officials, production managers, functional managers, office managers, financial managers, managers in agricultural services
	Low-skilled workers	% employed in elementary occupations: e.g., cleaners and helpers, agricultural labourers, other labourers, food preparation assistants, street and related sales and services workers, refuse workers) (16%); NVQ4+ (17%); low qualifications
	Earnings	Annual gross pay (mean) per annum
Place (17%)	Crime rates	Total number of incidents recorded by police per 10,000 population
	House prices	Median house price based on land registry data (2010 Q1)
	School achievement	Performance of schools
	Green space	The proportion of land classified as green space by the department for communities and local government; previously developed land; ERV commercial office space (Experian/BBC, 2010)

Source: adapted from BBC/Experian, 2010a and 2010b methodology. Docs/papers accessed 15 January 2015 and 7 April 2015.

Experian's partnership with the BBC produced a highly publicised economic resilience index which heavily focused on the weaknesses of the seemingly least resilient city of Middlesbrough – ranked bottom out of a total of 364 local authorities in England. But the results also demonstrated a consistently broad spatial pattern of exposure to economic recession and austerity; the 25 most resilient local authorities were all located in the south of England and London while the 25 least resilient authorities were located in the north and Midlands regions. This confirmed a structural and longstanding 'north-south divide' in England and continuing weakness of declining industrial heartlands with an overexposure of cities in the north and Midlands to public sector investment and jobs.

Birmingham (the UK's largest single tier metropolitan authority) was ranked 234 (the second to bottom quartile on the Experian index) while the neighbouring local authority of Sandwell ranked as one of the least resilient (360) thus highlighting the importance of scale and the problems of intra-regional dependence when measuring economic and social resilience. Since 2010 the city of Birmingham has produced its own internal ranking of resilience at small-area level, basing its approach on four resilience domains underpinned by a range of indicators sourced from the public and private sector:

- *Social support networks* – the presence of strong networks of family, friends and wider community networks to offer practical and emotional support; perceptions measured from the city's Annual Opinion Survey.
- *Education* – average qualification level of adult population.
- *Finance* – the availability or otherwise of a financial cushion to support the individual/household; average household income from the Annual Survey of Hours and Earnings data.
- *Mental health* – the existing quality of mental health experienced by the individual at the point of becoming unemployed affects their subsequent resilience (NHS data).

The Birmingham resilience index maps the extent to which known 'resilience factors' were present in the local population at administrative ward level (approximately 12,000 to 15,000 households). A *Social Impact Index* maps the extent to which known and measurable social consequences are present in wards across the city and includes changes in crime and anti-social behaviour, homelessness applications, court judgements for insolvency of individuals,

Figure 5.1

Social impact factors and resilience of wards in Birmingham

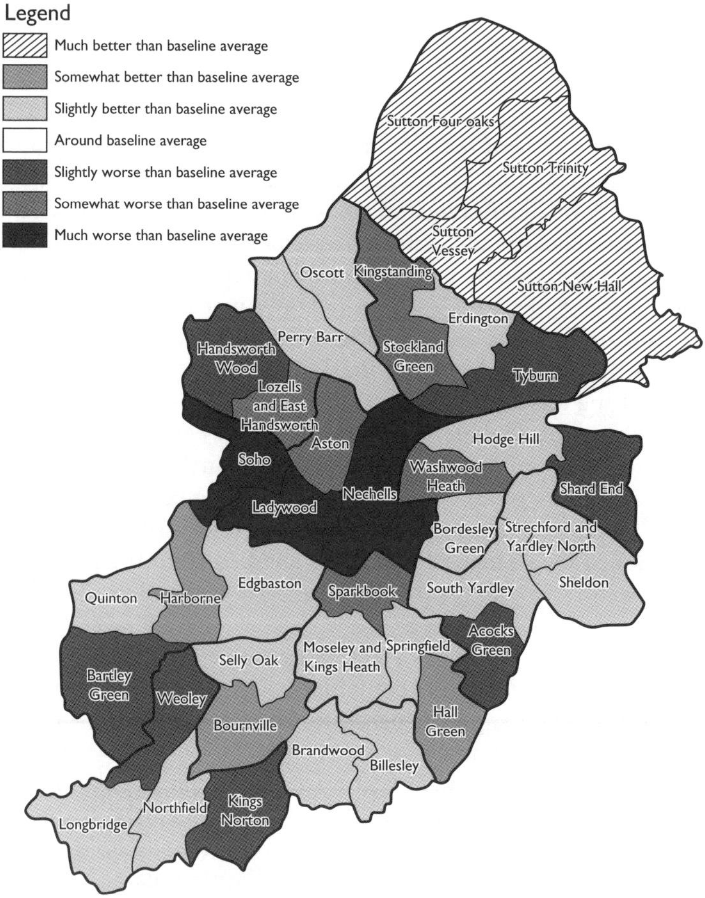

Source: Birmingham City Council, 2015.

households excluded from access to credit and households in receipt of welfare benefits. This is illustrated in Figure 5.1. This index enabled the city to analyse the gap between resilience and the impact of recession and allowed more informed decisions to be made about resource allocation.

In contrast to the quantitative, indicator-based methods of mapping resilience developed by Experian and Birmingham City Council, the Young Foundation (Mguni and Bacon, 2010) and the

Centre for Local Economic Strategies, UK (CLES) (see McInroy and Longlands, 2010) have adopted a more asset-based qualitative approach to resilience and well-being at the local level. The Young Foundation's Wellbeing and Resilience Measure (WARM) (Mguni and Bacon, 2010) attempts to measure life satisfaction and map this against assets and vulnerabilities to inform decision making at the very local level. A range of datasets available in the public domain are utilised in WARM to measure the state of a locality in relation to its *systems and structures* (unemployment, governance etc.), *support mechanisms* (family, networks and support services) and *individual assets and needs* (health, income, life satisfaction) using an approach 'designed to be owned and managed from the bottom up and not from the top down' (Mguni and Bacon, 2010, p.5). CLES meanwhile have adopted a different approach in the measurement of resilience by capturing the inter-relationship between the local economy (commercial–public–social) and how this maps on to the wider relationship with *health and well-being* (e.g., quality of life), *environment* (climate change and mitigation and adaptation strategies), *local identity, history and context* and the relationship of these elements to *national and local governance*. A four-point scale for creating resilient places (Table 5.4) – where resilience is seen as the polar opposite of brittleness – is underpinned by a set of questions which seek to understand the key factors that enable some areas to respond effectively to threats

Table 5.4 *CLES local economic resilience framework*

Resilient status	Description
Resilient	• Robust relationships between the different spheres of the local economy have been developed in bold and innovative ways
	• Area very well prepared to deal with economic, social and environmental change and opportunities and evidence that they have responded effectively in the past – track record
	• High levels of readiness and response
	• Evidence of being able to recover and take advantage swiftly
	• High levels of learning

Stable	• Sound relationships between the different spheres of the local economy
	• Adequate communication between the sectors
	• More creative collaboration is required in order to strengthen local economic resilience
	• Poor evidence of being able to recover or take advantage
	• Poor learning
Vulnerable	• Significantly under-developed relationships
	• Relationships may be precarious
	• Limited evidence of the sectors coming together
	• Some evidence of recovery or taking advantage
	• Good learning
Brittle	• No relationship between elements
	• Tension and conflict
	• Area not faced up to challenges of local identity and culture
	• Poor ability to withstand future shocks or take advantage of opportunities

Source: McInroy and Longlands, 2010, p.20.

and opportunities while other areas facing similar challenges fail to take advantage, falter and decline:

- What makes some more able to withstand economic blows and come out the other side while others are hit hard and unable to recover?
- How important are readiness, response, recovery and learning in the development of resilience for a locality?
- How does this play out in economic development strategies and delivery? (McInroy and Longlands, 2010, p.15)

The CLES model of social and economic resilience is predicated on a need to shift the economic base and meet the new paradigm challenge of austerity and the restructuring of local economies. CLES challenges prevailing economic models, arguing that a paradigmatic shift in delivering urban resilience exists due to conflicts in economic, social and environmental goals being pursued as part of the regeneration and economic development strategies of cities. The key resilience features underpinning local economic resilience and emerging from this perspective are different from those constructed from a DRR perspective advanced by global organisations, NGOs and multinationals such as UNISDR or Experian (from a national economic resilience perspective). CLES recognises the 'importance of connections and relationships' (McInroy and Longlands, 2010, p.11) and of bouncing forwards, and is critical of economic resilience measures that simply measure gross domestic product (GDP) and commercial economic strength. It argues that economic resilience is not simply about commercial activity (economic wealth creation by business) but includes the public and social economy (activities funded through the public purse or voluntary and not-for-profit activities). Understanding the relationships between the commercial, public and social economy is therefore seen as vital to ensuring local urban resilience.

Understanding the assessment of urban resilience: Reflections on methods and techniques

There is evidence of a growing global industry engaged in the assessment of urban resilience. There is also a set of core ideas emerging that provide a relatively consistent group of largely quantitative approaches for cities to develop their resilience strategies and assess how prepared or exposed they are to varying threats. While quantitative indicators provide an important tool for decision makers by reducing complexity in measuring progress and setting priorities, many technical and conceptual issues remain unresolved. As Cutter *et al.* (2008) noted:

> Important criteria for indicator selection include validity, sensitivity, robustness, reproducibility, scope, availability, affordability, simplicity, and relevance [...] the most important of these is validity which speaks to the question of whether the indicator is representative of the resilience dimension of interest. (p.603)

Many of the existing indices exhibit significant shortcomings in terms of robustness (Gall, 2007). A number of criticisms and problems also emerge in relation to the aggregation of data to different scales (Luers *et al.*, 2003). As Prior and Hagmann (2013, pp.293–294) highlight, existing assessment frameworks serve to simplify an inherently complex resilience process, often as a result of time and resource pressures, and thus often only 'measure' relative urban resilience (for example one neighbourhood versus another) rather than the risks faced and capacity to cope in any one area (absolute resilience). Moreover the current assessment processes, given their bias towards quantitative indicators and to parameterisation, often use arbitrary indicators and associated weighing to create an amalgam of several core indicators. This too is a complicated and time-consuming task and assumes an 'in-depth knowledge of the way particular behaviours, structures, policies, etc. contribute to the resilience of the entity under examination' (ibid.). It also assumes appropriate data is readily available and consistent across a defined geographical area. Overall, Prior and Hagmann argue for greater importance to be placed upon context, scale and risk specificity in any measurement of resilience.

Therefore, in summary, the limitations and issues in terms of how local measures have different meanings dependent on *context*; what precision there is in relation to the *mechanism* of resilience captured in the relationships between risk and capacity to absorb shocks within resilience frameworks; and what types of *outcomes* are measured or illuminated by current approaches to measurement.

The importance of context in assessing urban resilience

The wide variety of methods and measures used to assess urban resilience come from very different contexts and starting positions. The measurement of urban resilience is highly influenced by disaster (DRR) frameworks with a heavy emphasis placed on physical and technical (engineering) aspects of resilience and which draw on case studies from cities in developing regions and/or those subject to natural hazards. For cities in industrial and post-industrial contexts a number of indicators used in these approaches may not be relevant or are subject to variations in meaning according to the spatial context.

The most advanced frameworks – the Rockefeller Foundation and in the work by Cutter *et al.* (2008) and Burton (2014) on community resilience – use extensive literature reviews to justify inclusion of specific indicators. However, evidence is drawn from a variety of contexts and may not be universally relevant to the measurement of city resilience; there is also evidence of overlapping categories based on subjective criteria. For example, indicators measuring the density of urban population are used negatively to imply that there is greater risk associated with high-density population (see for example, % *population living in high-intensity urban areas* in Burton, 2014). In areas subject to flooding and with high levels of segregation and poor infrastructure this may be an appropriate indicator, such as in the case of New Orleans and Hurricane Katrina to which Burton and others have applied their analysis. In other contexts, such as the Netherlands and the UK, the prevailing policy emphasis has been on social integration and mixed communities with encouragement of brownfield land development policies to increase population densities in urban areas. Social segregation in these contexts is less intense than in the United States and the greater intensity of land use in cities results in a different set of outcomes when comparing different planning and welfare regimes. While policies on social mix may not necessarily translate into greater social interaction, the point being emphasised here is that indicators can be interpreted in contradictory ways that are either negative or positive for city, or for community resilience, depending on local (demographic, morphological, economic) and national (political economy and welfare regime) context.

Some of the indicators used in the frameworks assessed here, for example, reflect significant differences in the nexus between social welfare and the wider political economy and highlight inherent differences in welfare regimes and views on the role of business in enhancing urban resilience. The DROP index includes a measure of the ratio of large to small businesses: while this may indicate a high degree of corporate and external investment it does not promote the local economic development of cities and may be contrary to other fundamental goals of resilience within economic and social systems such as redundancy and diversity; a dependence on a handful of corporations arguably does not provide the novelty, diversity and embedded capital that provides the adaptive capacity to evolve when things go wrong. The indicators and indices developed by Burton and colleagues contrast with the indices developed by CLES. Whereas Burton uses the ratio of large to small firms as a measure of resilience, CLES takes an opposite view and sees greater resilience and strength in diversity of small firms. This, it argues, leads to the circulation of money in the local economy and to investment in a greater number of social exchanges through a richer, more diverse local economy.

Similarly, the role that minority groups play in resilience at an individual or aggregated spatial scale is more nuanced than advanced in the indices reviewed here, perhaps reflecting a North American and DRR contextual bias. In Burton's contribution to these debates *migration, minority status* and *failure to speak English* are all seen as negative attributes. But minority status and migration can be viewed in different ways. On the basis that we might consider that the most resilient communities have experienced prior shocks we might also consider that diverse communities with high migration rates are more resilient as they have had to negotiate different systems in order to arrive in their host country/community. The much touted resilience of the Vietnamese community in New Orleans in the aftermath of Hurricane Katrina in 2005 provides a good example of such qualities (see Chapter 7 for further details). Clearly these are relative positions and depend on the nature of the hazard and the degree of relative or absolute loss. These issues point to the problems of associating a single indicator such as migration with a negative score on resilience capability.

The inclusion of *% population that doesn't speak English as a second language* in the Burton index may be of more relevance in the context of communities that are exposed to economic and social stresses (e.g., unemployment, public sector austerity measures etc.) but even here there are caveats related to the operation of the welfare state and to support systems in highly concentrated urban areas. In a similar vein, the inclusion of welfare-based indicators such as *doctors and medical professionals per 1,000 population* depends very much on the welfare state regime context and access to public medical assistance. Cutter *et al.* (2008) and Burton (2014) write in the context of natural hazards in the southern states of the US where access to medical professionals is highly dependent on race and social class. While the issues of class and race are relevant to all contexts, the availability and quantity of care, accessibility and the extent to which it is universally available are also highly relevant.

Accessibility to welfare may be dependent on age, especially in post-industrial cities where the baby boomer generation generally have a greater equity or stakehold in established welfare entitlements compared to younger age cohorts. In the majority of resilience frameworks reviewed here, older age is used as a negative proxy, a factor undermining resilience and largely justified from a DRR perspective on the basis that older people have lower ability to evacuate in the event of a disaster. Conversely, older residents might well bring local or tacit knowledge to decision-making processes which cannot easily be assembled into an index of resilience but which is an important product of 'historical experience of [place] and not merely a hunch' (Corburn, 2003, p.421) and can help to refine resilience strategies (see Chapter 8 for further details). Tacit knowledge is therefore a key component of the adaptive capacity of communities and their ability to adjust to change within resilient urban systems. However, the tension between viewing chronological age as a burden as opposed to an asset within resilient systems highlights the problems of reductionism in index construction, the formalisation of frameworks and the tendency to centralisation and a 'one size fits all' approach to resilience assessment.

This reductionism leads to problematic assumptions about relationships between variables. For example, intuitively one would expect there to be a strong negative correlation between resilience and deprivation. The more resilient a community or neighbourhood is, the less deprived or the more affluent it will be. Again, while it is pernicious to assign resilience and responsibility to the individual or household, the nature of the relationship between poverty and resilience require greater thought in order to design effective policy solutions in relation to urban resilience. Béné *et al.* (2012) point to research on households affected by Hurricane Mitch which hit Honduras in 1998, in which it was found that households affected by the hurricane increased according to wealth, leading the researchers to observe that this 'contradicts the notion that poorer households are more vulnerable to shocks' (Carter *et al.*, 2007, p.842, cited in Béné *et al.*, 2012, p.10). As we have noted above, poorer and migrant households display a degree of resilience to their personal circumstances but this has the potential of falling into a trap of *responsibilising* the poor for exogenous events. The research by Béné *et al.* may demonstrate evidence of bias as it depended on analysis of loss from the hurricane measured four to five years after the event and captured through survey questionnaires. This does not prove that the poor are more or less resilient than the rich but only that the wealthy have more to lose and therefore more to invest in chasing down their losses. Nevertheless, there is a conundrum, which perhaps underscores some of the critiques of the resilience discourse, especially the *responsibilising* of the poor: is there an attempt to position the most resilient communities and households as those that have experienced shocks or hardship and have made it through the other side? For the urban and regional planner wanting to develop a city or community resilience measure suitable to local context it is important to consider alternative interpretations of indicators dependent on local context and their ramifications for policy.

Mechanisms of resilience: How is resilience enacted?

While interviews and research evidence are used to justify the inclusion of particular indicators in many of the frameworks and indices, it is the precise mechanism and relationship to context and outcome (CMO) (Pawson and Tilley, 1997) that is often absent from quantitative and aggregated assessments of resilience. The utilisation of aggregated data and indices mapped against the risk or outcome of hazards and shocks fails to overcome this. Linking context and mechanisms to outcomes has proven particularly difficult in assessing community resilience, illustrated in some of the assumptions of community resources, poverty and resilience used in the frameworks reviewed in this chapter. One of the problems of measuring resilience of communities based on the fixed physical assets that they possess is the problem of scale: the degree to which resources are shared or accessed across urban areas. The precise location of facilities and their use is not accounted for so the measurement of, for example, *community facilities and services* in many indices may be susceptible to ecological fallacy (making incorrect conclusions about individuals based only on analyses of group data) depending on the scale at which the variables are sampled and measured.

In an effort to address some of these issues, Burton (2014) provides the most comprehensive attempt at measuring community resilience and some of the best examples that demonstrate the difficulties of reconciling resilience contexts and mechanisms. To assess community resilience Burton compared his index scores against visual inspections of photographs taken at 131 sites affected by Hurricane Katrina between October 2005 and October 2010. Over this five year period 5,764 photographs were utilised and a score of 0–100 given to categories of reconstruction (100 = full recovery; 75 = rebuilding exterior or interior; 50 = demolition and clearance; 25 = clean-up and partial clearance; 0 = no visible recovery). Before-and-after photographs of the storm damage in New Orleans arising from Hurricane Katrina were inspected and measurements made of the rebuilding and renewal process from visual inspection of photographs; a logit regression model was used to identify a range of key variables accounting for the observed changes at the observed sites. Burton claims:

> [I]n the community capital subcomponent the presence of (1) art, entertainment, and recreation centers; (2) religious organizations; (3) social advocacy organizations; and (4) professional service occupations were found statistically significant by the regression models. Here, the ability to recover is a function of

innovation, community involvement, and personal community support. (Burton, 2014, p.79)

While the database cataloguing the changes on site appeared to be robust, there was, however, no evidence of ongoing assessment of the *changes* in the communities that had been affected. The efforts to match changes on the ground with baseline indicators of 'inherent resilience' illustrates the difficulties faced by researchers in assembling evidence that measures the precise mechanisms of *absorption*, *adaptation* and *rebound*. The approach lacks the dynamism and longitudinal monitoring required to measure the relationship between rebuilding and the indicators of community resilience assembled (see Table 5.2). For example, it is unclear what mechanism affected change at the sites damaged by Katrina and whether the observed changes were a result of conditions described by the indicators assembled before the hurricane or a result of subsequent rearrangement of social and economic relationships and a reassignment of land after the hurricane.

Recurrent across the frameworks reviewed are other methodological weaknesses such as a systematic failure to reconcile the *degree* of risk and a measurement of the absolute *exposure of* urban areas based on an assessment of the mechanisms to mitigate loss. All quantitative indices of community and city resilience are relative – therefore there has to be a bottom or top of an index and the degree of exposure or weighting of capacity to absorb shocks is missing. A related issue surfaces in the failure to standardise indicators to reflect the absolute and relative degree of resilience (or lack of it). Burton's maps tend to misrepresent community resilience levels due to this lack of standardisation (Burton, 2014, pp.81–82) which raises issues not only of scale, but also of the choice of indicators which may distort the mapping of resilience and the location of vulnerable or exposed communities. In some cases the double or triple counting of indicators (e.g. multiple measurements that capture language, migration, transient populations etc.) will skew geographic results resulting in some communities being overlooked.

This can have the effect of conflating scale and spatial autocorrelation: 'a measure of the degree to which a set of spatial features and their associated data values tend to be clustered together in space [...] or dispersed' (Environmental Systems Research Institute, 2015). For some key variables such as the relationship between commercial activity and crime levels, spatial autocorrelation can confuse mechanisms and outcomes as both crime and commercial activity are spatially correlated with specific parts of the city and are used in a range of resilience measures. Weighting of indices or individual indicators to reflect the relative importance of hazards and risks or the mitigating qualities of an area's population or resources are either absent or arbitrarily applied. Assumptions that underpin the Experian index concerning the relationship between resilience and key indicators such as house prices, for example, are not explained and equal weights are assigned. Weighting is as much dependent on spatial scale adopted as it is the choice of variables. However, indicators underpinning the business domain in the BBC/Experian index were weighted at 50%, 'reflecting its overall importance to short-term resilience' (BBC/Experian, 2010a), while *People*, *Community* and *Place* were weighted equally with no theoretical or practical justification for the allocation of importance across indicators.

These examples illustrate the problems associated with making conclusions about individuals or places based on analyses of aggregated data across space (ecological fallacy) reflecting inconsistency in spatial and temporal resolution and a failure to identify the precise *mechanism* of resilience at these different scales. This is not to criticise the authors in their attempt to reconcile the measurement of resilience and assess outcomes. However, it is important to highlight problems of moving from the 'theory of change' (what affects resilience?) to the precise mechanism of how this change occurred (what works and how?) (Pawson and Tilley, 1997). In the introduction to this chapter we noted that assessing the resilience of cities requires a balance to be struck in evidencing natural and man-made hazards with evidence on the characteristics of individuals, households and agents to withstand shocks and associated stresses. This requires a slightly different approach to that developed in resilience assessments, indices and associated frameworks produced to date.

Outcomes: Neoliberalism and the resilience industry

The rise of private security firms that exploited public anxieties and publicly available funds to profit from disaster in the aftermath of events that followed 9/11 hastened opportunities for profiteering and explain the drive for more techno-rational approaches and control of information to standardise and assess city resilience. Naomi Klein (2007) in her critically acclaimed *The Shock Doctrine: The Rise of Disaster Capitalism*, highlighted how humanitarian relief, reconstruction and the provision of security in a post-war or post-disaster zone must be rationalised to maximise it as a profit-making opportunity 'not to be missed' by corporate interests. In a similar vein, indexes of resilience also provide a basis for business to profit through the development of IT and management consultancy.

In reviewing the frameworks developed academically, by NGOs such as UN or the World Bank and by large foundations such as Rockefeller, it is clear that development of these measures implicates significant resource investment locally in adopting resilience practices and standards being advanced. For example, in order to get the top rating on the UNISDR resilience scorecard, cities need to have carried out a skills inventory in the previous 12 months. This should provide details of all key skills and experience that is available in 'required quantities for all organizations relevant to city disaster resilience' (UNISDR, 2014b, p.11). UNISDR advise that skills will include: 'land use planning, energy, environmental, water and structural engineering, logistics, debris disposal, healthcare, law and order, project planning and management' (ibid.). As demanding as the skills inventory is the requirement for cities and municipal authorities to gather information on the likelihood of residents being contacted immediately after a shock event as an indicative measure of social cohesion ('social connectedness and neighbourhood cohesion'). Cities are rated highly if they can demonstrate that sufficient volunteers are 'available from grass-roots organizations to give "reasonable confidence" that 100% of residents will be contacted within 12 hours of an event' (UNISDR, 2014b, p.10). To ensure that cities do not rely on unduly subjective qualitative measures inherent in judgements of 'reasonable confidence' UNISDR recommends that cities include 'a history of people in each neighbourhood meaningfully helping each other after previous events' or an inventory that assesses the 'fabric of community organizations in general, even if not focused on disaster resilience in the first instance' (ibid.). All of these efforts at measuring a community's capacity to respond implicate a high degree of organisation and multi-systems governance to monitor and measure these elements.

The development of these measures also points to more economically rational and strategic developments in the *professionalisation* of resilience processes: the UNISDR scorecard for cities (ten sections, includes 82 measures and is 56 pages long) implies considerable commitment and resources for initial completion, notwithstanding that this will become a periodic exercise as urban resilience is seen as something to work towards, with the scorecard expected to highlight improvements through a new public management framing and requiring a high degree of professionalisation and information management. The processes arising from such detailed assessment serve to continually professionalise and demand new forms of governance of cities that support the needs of business exploitation, for example, IBM and AECOM both helped develop the Disaster Resilience Scorecard used in the UNISDR *Making Cities Resilient* campaign. The preface to their scorecard is explicit in how it can be used as:

> a tool for cities to demonstrate their attractiveness for inbound economic investment; as a basis for insurers to assess the level of risk inherent in cities, to allow them to adjust premiums for the well-prepared or possibly write policies where none exist today [and] as the basis around which private companies such as IBM, AECOM or any other company that so desires may create supporting software or services that they will sell for a profit. (UNISDR 2014a)

Similarly, the Rockefeller 100 Resilient Cities (100RC) initiative promotes a view of resilience which addresses both sudden shocks (such as natural disasters) and what it describes as 'the stresses that weaken the fabric of a city on a day to day or cyclical basis' (Rockefeller Foundation, 2013) and include in this 'high unemployment; an overtaxed or inefficient public transportation system; endemic violence; or chronic food and water shortages' (ibid.) that affect the business environment of cities and business profitability. Meanwhile, the senior management team of the 100RC initiative is occupied by the ex-deputy global head of Operational Risk Management (ORM) at Deutsche Bank and the ex-public finance banker at Morgan Stanley, Lehman Brothers and Barclays in San Francisco and New York. Notwithstanding the attention (and resources) that the 100RC campaign has given to the need for urban resilience, the resilience framework of 100RC is informed by a particular business perspective and constructed in a way that maximises the potential for forward business development in the resilience arena. The cities in the 100RC network are provided with 'the resources necessary to develop a roadmap to resilience along four main pathways' (ibid.). Services offered to those participating in the programme include 'expert support for development of a robust resilience strategy' and access to solutions, service providers, and partners from the Rockefeller network to help develop and implement resilience strategies. This techno-rational state of resilience assessment is also illuminated starkly by the 100RC Chief Resilience Officer concept (see Chapter 1), and at an everyday level by the training and skill set development required by planners, or other local officials to undertake the urban resilience assessment process. Support in the form of financial and logistical guidance for establishing chief resilience officers in each of the participating cities in 100RC is provided by Rockefeller to develop a single point of contact in participating cities to coordinate resilience strategies.

These developments demonstrate how urban resilience is leading to new avenues for the privatisation of services and the shaping of public policy discourse. The development of public–private partnerships in delivering core services such as the administration of IT systems and routinised services such as welfare benefit administration is well documented. This new strand of privatisation finds the private sector developing quasi-academic perspectives on city challenges and resilience and then providing the knowledge capacity and expertise, as well as advising on the procurement and financing of posts within the public sector that will be paid for by the public purse, to reinforce vested interests in urban resilience thinking. As Raco and Street (2012, p.1067) have noted in relation to the links between neoliberalism and the privatisation of resilience policy, the current avalanche of resilience assessment frameworks and policy discourses represent a 'speeding-up of international policy transfer models under neoliberalism [...] in which relatively simple policy rationalities are rapidly disseminated and adopted through the work of international agencies, an expanding knowledge-transfer industry and national and local government networks'.

More positively, the approaches to the assessment of urban resilience we have outlined in this chapter undoubtedly have a significant advocacy function – a core feature of the planning profession since Davidoff's seminal article in 1965 – representing a departure from post-war rational planning and focused upon the participation of the different interest groups involved in the planning process itself. Resilience assessment serves to illuminate issues of concern as well as promote multi-stakeholder responses. As Johnson and Blackburn (2012, p.30) noted with regard to the UNISDR *Making Cities Resilient* campaign, 'the campaign promotes resilience-building in cities through many mechanisms, including raising awareness of DRR among local governments through high-profile events, providing tools, technical assistance and training to local authorities and facilitating city-to-city support networks and learning opportunities'. Specifically they saw such advocacy as important in initiating local conversations about how to join up resilience approaches as well as stimulating, and then mainstreaming, new innovative approaches to planning to enhance resilience.

How do we better assess urban resilience?

The importance placed upon local response has led to an explosion of interest and efforts to measure the resilience of cities, and their communities, in the midst of shock and stress events. This has often taken the form of assessing vulnerability and the resources cities and their communities have to cope with these vulnerabilities. In globalised urban resilience assessment there are emerging attempts to reconfigure how assessment is undertaken. Notably, in April 2014 at the seventh annual World Urban Forum (WUF7) hosted in Medellín, Colombia, many of the NGOs and organisations involved in the assessment of urban resilience came together to sign the 'Medellín Collaboration on Urban Resilience', with the goal of empowering cities by:

> facilitating the flow of knowledge and financial resources necessary to help [them] become more resilient to disruptions related to climate change, disasters caused by natural hazards, and other systemic shocks and stresses, including the socio-economic challenges associated with rapid urbanization. (UN-Habitat Press Release, 2014)

The collaboration includes: UN Office for Disaster Risk Reduction (UNISDR), UN-Habitat, the Rockefeller Foundation, the 100 Resilient Cities Acceleration Initiative, C40 Cities Climate Leadership Group, the World Bank, the Global Facility for Disaster Reduction and Recovery (GFDRR), ICLEI – Local Governments for Sustainability – and the Inter-American Development Bank. Amongst the agreements made was a commitment to the primary objective of '*fostering harmonization of the approaches*' for assessment (UN-Habitat Press Release, 2014, emphasis added) and to link local efforts and communities with national strategies and commitments. To date this has been advanced through a proposal to develop an International Standard in Sustainable and Resilient Cities (ISO 37120) based on 100 indicators to measure quality of life and city performance that is being implemented by the Toronto-based World Council on City Data (UNISDR Press Release, 2015). Perhaps worryingly, such an approach privileges a prescriptive blueprint or one-size-fits-all model of assessment, implicitly tied to furthering growth and development, and embedding local need within a broader national context. Such assessments increasingly place great emphasis on local regimes of planning as a key variable in city resilience building. For example, as one of its ten essential criteria for making resilient cities, the UNISDR (2012a, p.41) highlighted that land-use planning should 'apply and enforce realistic, risk-compliant building regulations and land use planning principles'. Paradoxically, though, the complex and intensive timescales and resources required to undertake current urban resilience assessment might well be having the effect of forcing local governments to look beyond planning as a mechanism to integrate resiliency activities. Here appointing external consultants to undertake increasingly prescriptive approaches to measuring urban resilience is ever more common which may also serve to remove important contextual knowledge, held by local planners, from the assessment process.

This potential loss of local contingency is not unprecedented. Historically, in urban and regional planning, the local context or nature of exposure at the local scale has often been overlooked as the centralist planner was perceived, until recently, 'to be insensitive to cultural, historical, landscape, ecological contexts' (Van Assche, 2007, p.106). Increasingly though, this is beginning to change. Over the past quarter century sensitivity to local context has become ever more important to understanding the theory and practice of urban and regional planning (Healey, 1997; Flyvbjerg, 1998, Allmendinger, 2002; Hillier, 2002). Similarly, while the assessment of resilience has been heavily influenced by centralised, techno-rational and quantitative approaches to risk assessment often associated with material aspects of resilience, there has been a recent shift towards approaches that promote more holistic approaches to the development of assessment frameworks and indices.

The challenges of constructing techniques of measurement for resilience lie in its multifaceted nature, and beg the question of resilience *of what* and *to what* raised by a number of authors (see Cutter *et al.*, 2008; Davoudi, 2012). While existing assessment 'tools' provide a broad and scalable baseline measure of resilience that might be of interest to policy makers, and indeed further illuminate the requirements of urban resilience, they are currently developed at a level of abstraction that does not fully account for context. Largely they typify an equilibrist, engineering-based model of urban resilience, though with a pre-eminence of techno-rational framing and quantitative measurement they do provide a degree of certainty, seen by many as a desire of urban and regional planning systems (Tewdwr-Jones, 1999). As White and O'Hare (2014, p.942) note in relation to evolving notions of resilience within planning, the desire for certainty means the complex sociocultural world of the city creates undue and undesired messiness and as such:

> facilitates the domination of engineering agendas overemphasising *responses* to peril, and relegating efforts to reduce their sociocultural drivers [...] This view links with a techno-rational form of planning which is familiar and comfortable for policy makers. Moreover, the reliance on long-held quantitative modelling and evidence-based approaches in spatial planning also predisposes engineered outcomes.

It is therefore an issue of the combinatorial, dynamic and evolutionary nature of urban resilience that requires measurement – a task perhaps better undertaken through a mixed-method approach involving quantitative and qualitative measures to study communities in situ – and to combine this with a generalised framework or index of urban resilience that provides a relative aggregated picture of exposure to shock and stressful events. For example, Cutter *et al.* (2008) argued that it is often difficult to 'quantify resilience in absolute terms without any external reference with which to validate the calculations' (p.603). They suggested that 'baseline indicators provide the first "broad brush" of the patterns of disaster resilience within and between places and the underlying factors contributing to it' and that:

> a second step is a more detailed analysis within jurisdictions to assess place-specific capacities in each of these areas (social, economic, institutional, infrastructure, community) and the development of fine-tuned and local appropriate mechanisms for enhancing disaster resilience. (Cutter *et al.*, 2010, p.18)

In short, assessing the management of resilience in the city requires a qualitative in-depth understanding of communities alongside longitudinal analysis to track vulnerable groups exposed to risk, linking the interaction of people to hazards across time and space to ensure spatial justice. As the UN-Habitat (2014, p.2) dialogue note *Raising Standards of Urban Resilience* highlights, it is imperative to advance tools and methodologies aimed at providing a measurement of urban resilience to contribute to the advancement of equitable urban development. All of the assessments reviewed in this chapter are static, cross-sectional measures of resilience in that they measure a baseline at one point in time and correlate this against change that has occurred. A context–mechanism–outcome approach demands that the precise mechanism that has resulted in a changed set of outcomes relates to the population affected by the shock and the response to the shock.

Mirroring the evolution of urban resilience in policy and practice (Chapter 3), the explosion of interest in measuring urban resilience and the demand for holistic, and increasingly complex local resilience responses is occurring, although this is being advanced alongside the diminishing of resources for local communities, a withdrawal of the state and, many argue, the *responsibilising* of citizens through localism initiatives to make them increasingly responsible for their own resilience. These processes serve to locate the solution to exogenous problems of austerity and a shrinking state locally and the interest in targeting those areas that are most vulnerable and least resilient is used to maximise public investment. However, it remains unclear what makes a community or locality resilient and how these factors interact across scales. While there have been some attempts at measuring the impact, absorption and adaptation to shock events, questions remain as to whether techno-rational approaches to assessment embed normative assumptions that engender governance mechanisms that only permit communities to bounce back to a pre-shock state rather than advancing more evolutionary 'bounce forward' pathways.

Attempts to integrate public services through initiatives, such as the UK's Total Place programme (DCLG, 2010), have started with the premise of improving the efficiency and coordination of public resources in the context of austerity and financial constraints but are also used to justify delivering resilience at the local scale (see for example, Mguni and Bacon, 2010). While conceived in an era of austerity, such attempts chime with the ambitions of other initiatives that localise sustainability and resilience such as the Transition movement which aims to prepare for a 'leaner future, more self-reliant, and prioritizing the local over the imported' (Hopkins, 2008, p.55). The inherent problems related to equity, inequality and the ability for self-determination built into such initiatives are also implicit in resilience frameworks in that their ambition is for communities to be increasingly responsible for their own environment; their perspective is towards a trajectory of self-determination requiring a techno-rational understanding of assets, risks and exposure to underpin localised responsibility for resilience – it restricts outcomes to adaptation along existing paths rather than fostering adaptability to new possibilities for communities.

The methods and measurement and the transference of an equilibrium-based model of resilience from the natural and physical sciences therefore remain problematic for socio-technical systems such as urban and regional planning (see Chapter 2). This has been challenged from a planning perspective (Coaffee *et al.*, 2008b; Davoudi and Porter, 2012; Shaw 2012a; White and O'Hare, 2014) with questions raised concerning the kind of equilibrium that should be established, and by whom, and calls for new models of evolutionary urban resilience which can take account of new urban dynamics and urban tensions (Flint and Raco, 2012) and the different trajectories that planning needs to take into account in its decision-making processes rather than a single, often path-dependent, equilibrium. Alongside this, our understanding of the mechanisms of how communities remain resilient is still under-specified while the 'development of standards that are meaningful for measuring resilience remains a challenge' (Burton, 2014, p.67). Managing hazards and the capacity of communities to increase their self-reliance requires an understanding of the exposure of risk as well as a more granular understanding of what events affect particular communities most and their capacity to cope and adjust to risk, absorb shock and transform in resilient ways (Keck and Sakdapolrak, 2013).

Existing resilience assessment approaches therefore need modifying to enable recognition of capacities and capabilities in addition to physical risks. They need to avoid silo thinking, capture the perspectives of a range of urban stakeholders, better represent interrelationships between different aspects of resilience and capture the multiple scales at which resilience can be encapsulated – from individual, community/neighbourhood to city and regional level (adapted from Rockefeller Foundation, 2014c, p.102). Furthermore, measuring the resilience of urban areas requires significant investment in information management to capture exposure to risks as well as measures of the ability of different actors and agencies (not least of communities and households) to withstand various shocks. While evidence on both exposure and ability to absorb shocks can be assembled, as we have observed, problems arise in attributing cause and effect across time and space within urban and regional systems.

In the next four chapters (Part III) such issues will be explored empirically by way of a series of examples illustrating the different approaches to resilience principles deployed in international planning practice.

Chapter 6

Adaptive Resilience to Climate Change and Extreme Weather Events

Urban resilience has gained notable prominence as a result of the global threat of climate change that has localised consequences, particularly flooding, that must be mitigated and managed if catastrophic social and environmental effects are to be avoided, especially in our ever-expanding cities (Stern, 2006; IPCC, 2014). As Scott (2013, p.103) highlighted, 'recent years have been marked by increased flood risk vulnerability caused by intensive urbanisation processes, shifting agricultural practices, out-dated urban drainage systems and fragmented policy responses'. As further noted (cited in Reuters, 2015) by a senior figure in the UK Environment Agency, responding to the devastation wrought by Storm Frank that hit the UK in late 2015: 'We are moving from known extremes to unknown extremes ... we will need to have a complete rethink [and] move from not just providing better defences ... but looking at increasing resilience.'

Urban and regional planners thus have a key role to play in enhancing urban resilience and mitigating the impacts of, and adaptation to, climate change. This might include a range of adaptive water management techniques, engaging in sustainable design, planning development away from areas at risk such as coastal plains and flood-liable areas (Howe and White, 2004; McEvoy *et al.*, 2006; White, 2010), adjusting zoning arrangements and altering building codes and standards to facilitate adaptation (UN-Habitat, 2011). While most of these efforts have traditionally focused upon incremental and short-term mitigation measures, increasingly, in the twenty-first century, issues of adaptation and adaptability have come to the fore as the international community seeks a framework of long-term transformative action to

135

cope with what the Royal Society (UK) highlighted as *Resilience to Extreme Weather*:

> Climate change will affect the frequency and severity of extreme weather in the future. If emissions of greenhouse gases continue at the current rate, extreme weather is likely to pose an increasing threat to people. Yet even if emission rates are reduced, societies will still need to adapt to climatic changes caused by past emissions. *Both mitigation of climate change and adaptation are therefore vital*. (Royal Society, 2014, p.2, emphasis added)

While mitigation was often seen as a climate science challenge to reduce the impact of greenhouse gas emissions, the alternative pathway of adaptation is more concerned with the implementation of, for example, planning or urban design interventions to reduce vulnerability within a complex socio-political and economic landscape (Roberts, 2010). Subsequently, this has created a new enlarged multidisciplinary epistemic community focused on the urban and regional planning challenges presented by climate change. The increased emphasis and prevalence of adaptation approaches can broadly be broken down into managerial and developmental perspectives (Manuel-Navarrete *et al.*, 2011); the former being more concerned with expert-led assessment of risk and responses while the latter is focused upon how the vulnerable and poor can become more resilient. As we will unpack in this chapter, it is at this juncture that the discourse of resilience has entered the debate as a translation term that can simultaneously reflect the desire to mitigate *and* adapt to the impacts of climate change in myriad ways.

Climate change adaptation has become an important public policy domain since the Intergovernmental Panel on Climate Change (IPCC) scientists published findings in 2007 highlighting the possible, likely impacts of alteration in the Earth's climate and the key role of urban and regional planning within the endeavour of mitigating these. This has not proved an easy task to implement. As Fünfgeld and McEvoy (2012) have highlighted, developing approaches to deal with the likely impact of climate change requires thinking and acting in new ways and with new collaborators, and the creation of new epistemic communities:

> Climate change adaptation poses challenges of a different kind for decision-makers. It requires navigating a raft of information generated at different scales, and involving a diverse range of actors in translating these into adaptation options that are

socially and politically acceptable despite significant degrees of uncertainty. (p.325)

As we noted in Chapter 4, there is a conceptual as well as a practical difference between adaptation and adaptability, with the former often being seen as 'a movement towards a pre-conceived path in the short run' (Pike *et al.*, 2010, p.63) and the latter being a longer term approach which advances in a flexible way towards multiple different pathways of action. Thus in many ways, climate change adaptation in its current guise can be viewed as reactive and equilibrist, and as Brown (2012) illuminated in a discourse analysis of existing climate change policy, adaptation approaches tend to be incremental and support the status quo, focusing upon recovery to a stable position rather than fundamentally changing established modes of action. Such a stasis approach does not encourage innovation within urban and regional planning of the kind that is arguably needed to tackle this complex and long-term problem. Rather, what is required is the mainstreaming of future-looking resilience techniques and strategies that focus upon embedding adaptability into everyday planning processes (see for example Smit and Wandel, 2006).

Until recently, climate change adaptation was most notably aligned to urban and regional planning through the discourse of sustainability or sustainable development; seen by Rydin (2010) as the most important planning policy goal of our time. Increasingly, though, the discourse of resilience is now emerging as the key rhetoric for dealing with the impact of a changing climate, and particularly those impacts that are urban in orientation. However, as Fünfgeld and McEvoy (2012, p.325) have noted, the fuzziness of the resilience discourse and the inconsistent ways in which it is deployed in planning practice 'impede the process of efficient planning for climate change adaptation across disciplinary and departmental boundaries'.

Internationally a range of influential policies focusing on climate change adaptation have emerged, from national governments to NGOs attesting to the importance placed upon the mobilisation of resilience ideas to cope with the issues presented by climate change. Notable international publications and work programmes include: the UN-Habitat *Cities and Climate Change Initiative* (from 2008); the World Bank primer on *Climate Resilient Cities* (Prasad *et al.*, 2009); the Asian Cities Climate Change Resilience Network (launched by the Rockefeller Foundation in 2008); and more generic approaches to urban resilience which have a significant climate change adaptation component such as the UNISDR's *Making*

Cities Resilient campaign (2010), the UN-Habitat (2011) *Cities and Climate Change: Global Report on Human Settlements*, the United Nations report on *Resilient People: Resilient Planet* (2012), the Rockefeller *100 Resilient Cities Campaign* launched in 2014; and international urban capacity-building programmes such as the United Nations' (2014a) *Resilient Cities Acceleration Initiative* focused upon climate change adaptation and the associated *Compact of Mayors* (2014b) – an agreement by city networks to 'undertake a transparent and supportive approach to reduce city-level emissions, to reduce vulnerability and to enhance resilience to climate change, in a consistent and complimentary manner to national level climate protection efforts' (United Nations, 2014b, p.2). However, in all these publication narratives and action programmes, resilience is deployed in a loose way, often highlighting the principles of stability and equilibrium associated with social–ecological systems (SES) and engineering resilience and traditional risk management approaches (see also Chapter 2), that seek 'a tangible adaptation outcome, such as a community, a place, or physical infrastructure being "more adapted" to climate variability and change' (Fünfgeld and McEvoy, 2012, p.325). The governance of such processes is also inherently traditional, adopting a vertical command and control structure rather than the horizontally integrated approach favoured in so-called evolutionary urban resilience. This current conservative orthodoxy can be summed up by the fourth IPCC (2007) scientific report which defined resilience as: 'the ability of a social or ecological system to absorb disturbances while retaining the same basic structure and ways of functioning, the capacity for self-organisation, and the capacity to adapt to stress and change' (p.86). This definition has many of the same framings as disaster risk reduction (DRR) approaches with a focus upon understanding and assessing risk and its mitigation (as best exemplified by the UNISDR approach and the broader Hyogo Framework for Action – see Chapter 5).

Framing climate change adaptation

In response to such an equilibrist urban resilience reading of the initial climate change adaptation agenda, others have suggested how we might move from a dominant narrative of adaptation to 'resilience and beyond' (Bulkeley and Tuts, 2013, p.652). This mirrors our more general framing of urban resilience in Chapters 2 and 3 where we argued that the practice of resilience is 'on the move' from a equilibrist understanding towards an evolutionary understanding, where there is more emphasis upon a social-technical approach, in which the location of action is devolved, anticipation and preparedness are stressed and where responsibility is distributed. Moreover, as UN-Habitat (2011, p.4) noted, there is much uncertainty and unpredictability associated with framing climate change at this time:

> most of the mechanisms within the international climate change framework are addressed primarily to national governments and do not indicate a clear process by which local governments, stakeholders and actors may participate. Despite these challenges, the current multilevel climate change framework does offer opportunities for local action at the city level. The crux of the challenge is that actors at all levels need to move within short time frames to guarantee long-term and wide-ranging global interests, which can seem remote and unpredictable at best.

In terms of providing a conceptual framing for climate change adaptation and urban resilience, Chelleri *et al.* (2015) proposed three (slightly overlapping) stages of climate change resilience – recovery, adaptation, transformation – related to short-, medium- and long-term time scales. Here the recovery perspective is mainly related to system shocks (endogenous and exogenous) and seen through the lens of engineering resilience with a focus upon bouncing back. The second perspective – adaptation – is seen 'as the processes of adjustment to actual or expected changes and its consequences, disregarding system boundaries by moving thresholds in order to make the system persist within the same regime' (p.7). A third perspective refers to structural transformation in the longer term as a result of nearing dangerous thresholds, or tipping points, resulting in 'the alteration of fundamental attributes of the system, which will allow it to enter a new regime' (p.8).

From a more institutionalist perspective Pelling (2011) in *Adaptation to Climate Change: From Resilience to Transformation* also suggests three overlapping levels where resilience thinking can be embedded within climate change adaptation – resilience, transitional adaptation and transformation. His concern here was predominantly with governance – a less visible cause of vulnerability – rather than materialist concerns such as protective infrastructure. In the first level, resilience is considered as a type of equilibrist adaptation that seeks stability through incremental change and requires modification of existing governance frameworks. Two additional levels of adaptation are considered that go beyond traditional accounts of resilience that see adaptation as a narrow defensive task. First, transitional adaptation that 'arise[s] when adaptations, or efforts to build adaptive capacity, intervene in relationships between individual political actors and the institutional architecture that structures governance regimes' (p.82). Second, transformational adaptation where the potential exists to shift 'the balance of political or cultural power in a society' (p.84) and bring about more radical local change as a result of moving from a coping response involving existing ways of working towards responses which seek to differentially frame practices and governance. Pelling's progressive framing of adaptation and resilience within the context of climate change highlights the intensely political nature of the challenges of adjusting to a changing climate, often with existing path dependencies and associated impacts upon development visions, governance structures, and coping strategies (Manuel-Navarrete *et al.*, 2011, p.250). Similarly, the 2014 report by IPCC, *Climate Change 2014 Impacts, Adaptation, and Vulnerability: Summary for Policymakers* has a modified definition of resilience which is more focused towards ideas of learning and transformation, or:

> The capacity of social, economic, and environmental systems to cope with a hazardous event or trend or disturbance, responding or reorganizing in ways that maintain their essential function, identity, and structure, while also maintaining the capacity for adaptation, learning, and transformation. (IPCC, 2014, p.5)

Here transformation' reflects strengthened, altered or aligned paradigms, goals or values moving towards promoting adaptation with the language of 'adaptive capacity' used to represent the ability to adapt to the impacts and changing requirements of climate change. In a similar vein, and specifically in relation to urban and regional planning, Bulkeley and Tuts (2013, p.655) have highlighted the key responsibilities of planners in facilitating transformative adaptive resilience that involves different ways of engaging with citizens and other stakeholders and multi-level 'holistic' thinking:

> While an 'incremental' approach to climate-change adaptation does not require fundamental changes in local government planning, management and governance systems, a more 'radical' or transformative approach to climate-change adaptation will require fundamental changes in these systems. This in turn suggests that if cities are to take adaptation to climate

change seriously, *a fundamental rethink of urban planning* [...] *is required.* (emphasis added)

In line with this framing of climate change adaptation and urban resilience, this chapter will proceed in four main sections which will illuminate the role of urban and regional planning towards this goal. First we will focus upon narratives that highlight recovery from extreme weather events and the processes put in place to mitigate the impacts. Here we will use the example of Hurricane Katrina in 2005, and the resulting storm surge, which devastated large parts of Gulf Coast of the United States, most notably affecting New Orleans, to highlight the limitations of a mitigation-focused approach where a protective system of levees failed leaving approximately 80% of the city flooded in one of the worst urban disasters in US history. We will also highlight the more transformative and adaptive resilience approach that has subsequently emerged. Second, and drawing from examples of the Adaptive Delta Management (ADM) programme in the Netherlands, and a range of approaches to 'living with water' that have been advanced in Brisbane, Australia, we highlight how a range of adaptation and transformation strategies are emerging which work with, rather than against, nature, and involve consensual dialogues at multiple scales and across multiple stakeholder groups, including local communities. Third, we focus upon the increasing movement in the less-developed world towards climate-resilient development. Here, urban resilience is seen as the main means by which vulnerability can be reduced and ongoing development climate-proofed. We use the example of Jamaica to exemplify this approach and highlight how climate-resilient development aims are feeding into the national development plan. The fourth and final section will reflect upon the collective ways in which transnational agencies, city leaders and urban communities are attempting to progressively mitigate and adapt to climate change through the narrative of resilience and to address political questions as to how to create governance institutions to address these challenges in a collective and socially just way (Biermann, 2014).

Recovering from and mitigating climate change

In its 2014 publication *Resilience to Extreme Weather Events*, the Royal Society noted that 'weather-related disasters act on short timeframes and often have significant consequences, including triggering societal demand for new roles and actions for government to protect its citizens and in regulating risk' (pp.4–5). This was never truer than in the aftermath of Hurricane Katrina which struck on 29 August 2005, leaving a devastating impact on the US city of New Orleans. Hurricane Katrina was, at the time, the costliest and most devastating 'natural' disaster in US history. The hurricane and subsequent floods cost nearly 2,000 lives and caused property damage along the Gulf coast from central Florida to Texas estimated at the time at $108 billion, much of this due to a storm surge. The most significant death and destruction occurred in New Orleans where the levee system flooded leaving 80% of the city under water. The subsequent recovery and rebuilding programme has illuminated the maladaptive nature of historical flood defences as well as facilitating a larger discussion about the sociospatial implications of urban and regional planning interventions that are seeking to enhance future urban resilience in innovative and adaptive ways.

In their forensic account of the complex and contested politics of planning in post-disaster New Orleans, Olshansky and Johnson (2010) illuminated attempts to recover and build afresh, and to embed resilience principles into emerging planning projects and returning communities. As their title, *Clear as Mud: Planning for the Rebuilding of New Orleans*, suggests, this has been a far from easy process and has been beset by complex macro and micro planning issues played out across multiple scales and involving multiple agencies and funding arrangements. *Clear as Mud* is also a tale of failure and maladaptation. As we noted in Chapter 4, the protection failures in New Orleans were at the time considered the worst civil engineering disaster in US history and led to a lawsuit, under the Flood Control Act of 1965, against the US Army Corps of Engineers who were responsible for constructing and maintaining the levee system that failed. This Act was devised in the aftermath of Hurricane Betsy when Congress gave control of the flood protection to the US Army Corps of Engineers and instructed them to build a flood protection system to protect the southern part of Louisiana from the worst possible storm imaginable. While Katrina was a catastrophic event it was, as Olshansky and Johnson noted, 'decades in the making' and exacerbated by significant and underestimated place vulnerabilities (p.8) and a range of planning maladaptations. This local geographical and institutional context is worth detailing as it highlights how path-dependent trajectories can be 'locked in' and urban resilience severely compromised.

A recycling of mitigation and design failure

New Orleans was first settled in the early 1700s on land which itself had been created by centuries of silt deposits from flooding events. As Olshansky and Johnson (2010) noted, its place vulnerability was initially limited as development was restricted to higher ground. In the early twentieth century significant urbanisation led to pressures on existing settled land resulting in lower lying areas around the Mississippi Delta being built upon. By 1960 only 48% of the city's population lived above sea level (compared to 90% in 1919). New Orleans was always a risky place to locate a city. As Wilbanks and Kates (2010) reported, it has experienced 27 major floods in the last three centuries. In terms of flood protection, from 1879 when the US Congress created the Mississippi River Commission, the US Army Corps of Engineers had been largely responsible for constructing and maintaining a system of levees. More advanced flood defences were not built in New Orleans until after the Great Mississippi Flood of 1927, under the Flood Control Act of 1928 when 'after a major flooding along the Mississippi River [...] and extensive and intricate system of levees, floodwalls, pumping stations and drainage canals was constructed along the entirety of the river' (Olshansky and Johnson, 2010, p.8). At the time this engineering effort by the US Army Corps of Engineers was the world's longest system of levees and floodways.

The 1927 flood inundated 27,000 square miles of land around the Mississippi River despite a misplaced confidence amongst the engineering fraternity that the levees would not be breached:

> The Corps built the levee system to confine the river. They represented man's power over nature [...] In the spring of 1927, the U.S. Army Corps of Engineers assured the public that the levees would hold. The Corps had built them, after all. But as had been the case at the mouth of the river, the Corps overestimated its own prowess and underestimated the power of the river. (Ambrose, 2001)

Socially, the 1927 flood also displaced many thousands of low-income, largely African American residents, and was a significant factor in accelerating the great migration of African Americans to northern US cities (Hornbeck and Naidu, 2014).

The aftermath of Hurricane Betsy in 1965, as previously noted, also saw the 'hardening' of the levee system by the US Army Corps of Engineers who were authorised to construct over 350 miles of levees and flood walls to cope with a 'standard project hurricane'. Such protective measures served to encourage new development in low-lying areas increasing the exposure of 17,000 households (Wilbanks and Kates, 2010). By 2005, this engineering-focused protective system was still incomplete, having been delayed by political wrangling:

> [T]he complex construction and maintenance arrangement between the Corps of Engineers and the multitude of local levee boards resulted in reductions in design standards and construction quality, as well as ongoing maintenance problems, which all contributed to the systems failure in Katrina. (Olshansky and Johnson, 2010, pp.10–11)

Other factors, such as increased building on the Mississippi River Delta plain, the tapping of underground aquifers (which led to ground subsidence and meant that recently built levees were lower than they were designed to be) and the erosion of freshwater marshes (which naturally dampen storm surge waves) as a result of saltwater intrusion caused by oil and gas exploration on the Gulf of Mexico, also contributed to the devastation wrought by Hurricane Katarina (ibid., p.11).

Overall, the development of the levee system had 'provided the city with a false sense of security' (ibid.) which was reinforced by national risk management policies which allowed thousands of dwellings to be built in vulnerable areas with only minimal protection (but eligible for flood insurance). This represented a failure of urban and regional planning and, as Fischer (2012, pp.98–99) noted: 'this was no "natural" disaster [...] while no one designed the New Orleans levee system to cause such catastrophic damage, we did not design it to ensure it did not happen either'. As Olshansky and Johnson (2010) further highlighted, prior to Hurricane Katrina 'the State of Louisiana required neither local comprehensive plans nor the adoption and enforcement of building codes' (p.12), and although the City of New Orleans did have a master plan, building regulations and a building safety department to aid compliance with flood insurance requirements, enforcement of such stipulations and good practice was ad hoc at best.

The vulnerability and subsequent impacts of Hurricane Katrina were also related to a range of socio-economic factors – slow-burn issues – that are illuminated by shock events. As became readily apparent after the storm hit, there were large concentrations of socially vulnerable residents (largely African American low-income communities, many without a car) which 'created tremendous logistical challenges for mass evacuation, short- and long-term sheltering, and other means of disaster response and recovery' (ibid., p.13). This lack of social resilience was coupled with a predominance of poor services, and badly maintained and fragmented infrastructure ownership – a result of decades of financial hardship faced by the city as a result of population decline and, as a result, a reduced tax base.

A failure of anticipation and governance

Resilience is increasingly premised upon accurate risk assessment and the foresighting of future danger. In the case of Hurricane Katrina, the risks and vulnerabilities were apparent and well known. A range of high-level workshops (including one in March 2005 at the National Academies of Science), scenario exercises (including one centred on New Orleans – called Hurricane Pam – run in 2004) and simulated modelling had made clear that New Orleans would be severely affected if a significant hurricane hit – its levees' protection system would likely fail, the entire city would be flooded for many weeks or months, and a large proportion of the population would have to be evacuated to other US regions. As one expert noted *before* Hurricane Katrina:

> New Orleans was holding its breath waiting to see if the worst case scenario happens instead of investing in coastal wetlands restoration and the types of long-term mitigation that would restore region's deteriorating environment. (cited by Olshansky and Johnson, 2010, pp.17–18)

Anticipating disaster, as we highlighted in Chapter 2, is an inherently political process, bound up with questions of agency and responsibility, tensions between national and local government, and fear of overreacting in a disproportionate way. It is also framed through a specific spatial and temporal context. In the case of Hurricane Karina there were a series of other factors that contributed to the failure of anticipation and governance. First, the restructuring of the Federal Emergency Management Agency (FEMA) that had occurred in the post-9/11 reorganisation of emergency management with the creation of the Department of Homeland Security and the establishment of a new all-hazards national response system. This gave FEMA less power and responsibility for integrating various emergency functions and federal response plans, and shifted some of their function away from natural disasters and towards counter terrorism. Concomitantly, this change of emphasis saw experienced operatives leave and added many military personnel to the FEMA staff who had little knowledge of natural disaster planning (ibid., p.16). Olshansky and Johnson also highlight that a reduced federal budget for new levee construction, and maintenance of existing hurricane protection systems, left many fearful that a large-scale hurricane would devastate New Orleans. In the late 1990s and early 2000s the US Army Corps of Engineers alongside the Environmental Protection Agency unsuccessfully sought significant Federal funds for wetland restoration to act as a hurricane impact buffer. One senator prophetically noted in 2005, just before Hurricane Katrina hit, that 'it's not a question of if; it's a question of when. Instead of spending millions now, we are going to spend billions later' (cited in ibid., p.20).

Planning recovery and resilience

The role of urban and regional planners, and representative bodies such as the American Planning Association, in recovery efforts in the wake of Hurricane Katrina must be set within the highly complex and highly charged post-disaster planning effort fraught with a range of multi-level governance and funding challenges. As Rodin (2015) documented, even at a very basic organisational level Greater New Orleans had five parishes and the city was divided into 13 planning districts, 17 wards and 72 neighbourhoods, thus making city-wide integration and strategic thinking very difficult. For example, she notes (p.249) how the *Bring Back New Orleans Commission*, the body that was initially responsible for pulling the planning process together, was unable to secure adequate funding for its planning intentions resulting in 49 neighbourhoods developing their own plans with little integration between them. Rodin also highlighted that this failure in the planning process led to the Rockefeller Foundation being asked by the Louisiana Recovery Authority to assist this process and help develop a plan for long-term city resilience (ibid.; see also Chapter 5).

From the perspective of urban resilience a number of core principles are evident within the future-looking planning processes that have sought to reduce vulnerabilities of place and enhance resiliency in New Orleans. These have focused upon not only the technical and engineering efforts used previously in attempts to mitigate the impact of hurricanes but increasingly upon adaptation and nature-driven responses.

Planning efforts in New Orleans in the post-Katrina era have been both reactive and aspirational, typifying a post-disaster response. This, in the case of New Orleans, as in many other cases, was played out as a series of tensions between rapid restoration and longer term sustainable and equitable change, most notably in a pressure to abandon large swathes of the city to water or to 'build back better'. In New Orleans' case, within the context of racial mistrust, attempts at rapid restorative projects were often accused of a lack of deliberation and community engagement as well as actually enhancing vulnerabilities. As has been highlighted, in New Orleans 'the city's hasty issuance of thousands of building permits in the months following the flood has reduced the chances of rebuilding large numbers of structures in ways that reduce their vulnerability to flooding' (Olshansky and Johnson, p.219).

As we have already seen in this chapter, the history of flood protection in New Orleans is littered with false promises of security and maladaptive, ad hoc and incremental design. Combined with the city's patterns of urbanisation which saw vulnerability from flooding highly correlate with socio-economic disadvantage and race, 'post-Katrina' represented an opportunity to not only build enhanced urban resilience through long-term planning strategies, but to rebuild the community with questions of social and spatial justice at the forefront. Improvements have undoubtedly occurred in the plan-making process, in community planning and in emergency planning and preparedness. A myriad of local plans has been replaced by a legally binding master plan 'to forestall ad hoc planning decisions by the city council' (ibid., p.21) and governance transparency has significantly improved with enhanced citizen participation and neighbourhood planning projects.

In the immediate aftermath of Hurricane Katrina, the US Corps of Engineers notably embarked upon yet more hurricane protection work, this time utilising a variety of wetland conservation and restoration actions signalling a shift in flood defence strategies from an over emphasis on levees and floodgates to the incorporation of more natural buffer solutions. A traditionally mitigation-only approach now embraces significant elements of adaptation. While New Orleans undoubtedly has the most comprehensive flood protection measures of any coastal community in the United States, it was slow to fully embrace a comprehensive and multi-level flood-resilience programme of measures. However, from 2010 it has developed a comprehensive, integrated and sustainable water management strategy which was finalised in 2013 as the *Greater New Orleans Urban Water Plan* (City of New Orleans, 2013); a long-term vision for urban water management and the first regional urban water plan in the United States. The Urban Water Plan is essentially a resiliency planning study that aims to develop sustainable strategies for managing the water resources. The specific actions of the plan provide a roadmap for mitigating flood risk, limiting subsidence, and improving the quality of water, and the plan is divided into three temporal phases:

- Near term (2013–2020): implementation of 'smart retrofits', interventions to reshape legacy infrastructure or ongoing projects to incorporate water management strategies.
- Medium term (2020–2030): improving water flows and connectivity within the scale of the actual project.
- Long term (2030–2065): diffusing Urban Water Plan's strategies throughout Southeast Louisiana.

The general principles behind the plan follow the innovative 'slow, store and use, and drain' model popular in the Netherlands (see next section); an approach which seeks to slow down the water (rather than pumping it away as quickly as possible) by using bioretention and infiltration strategies, such as rain gardens, which store it naturally. It is also expected that such an approach will reduce property and infrastructure damages and associated insurance premiums, and is expected to have a positive impact on property values. As an advisor to the Urban Water Plan noted:

> With the Urban Water Plan, Greater New Orleans can directly address these challenges and make better use of its water assets, while bringing innovations in engineering, planning, and design to other coastal regions where robust water infrastructure is critical to survival and economic prosperity. (Greater New Orleans Urban Water Plan, 2013)

The Urban Water Plan has recently received the American Planning Association's 2015 National Planning Excellence Award for Environmental Planning, an accolade that celebrates efforts to create greener communities and improve environmental quality. Finally, we should remember that Hurricane Katrina is also a story of forced mobility. It tore apart the social fabric of the city with thousands of residents evacuated to other US states (as they were after the great flood of 1927), many of which have not returned:

> Many residents of the inundated neighborhoods who fled to the Superdome and Convention Center were subsequently evacuated to places far from New Orleans [and] one of the first comprehensive surveys of the New Orleans evacuee population, conducted in early October, 2005 determined that 39% of evacuees mostly poor and Black, did not intend to return. If a city's capacity to rebound rests largely upon its citizenry, then it is a bad day indeed if the citizens go missing. (Campanella, 2006, p.144)

There were, however, some inspirational stories of community resilience that have emerged in the wake of Hurricane Katrina, perhaps most notably from the Vietnamese community. This is an example used by a recent US National Academies report – *Disaster Resilience: A National Imperative* (2012) to illuminate how disadvantaged ethnic groups cut off from mainstream society, and with a collective experience of immigrating to the US, still have strong internal ties that protect against some disaster impacts (p.101). It also highlights the importance of understanding culture in disaster recovery efforts. For example, some 40,000 Vietnamese lived in relative isolation in New Orleans before Katrina and saw the storm as an opportunity to rebuild their community to be even stronger. Before the storm they established community evacuation plans, coordinated through the local Catholic Church, and after the storm the community worked together, drawing on collective skills to rebuild the area (ibid., p.102).

The longer term efforts of the Vietnamese community in the wake of Hurricane Katrina were highlighted by the *New York Times* on its tenth anniversary (Vanlandingham, 2015). Here particular focus was placed on Village de l'Est, in the eastern corner of the city, that was extensively flooded, where 'there are now bustling restaurants, tidy homes with well-tended lawns and brisk street traffic. Much of the surrounding area, by contrast, still seems to be struggling' (ibid.). Available evidence also supported the impression that the Vietnamese communities were more resilient than others in New Orleans with psychologists finding a much higher rate of return for Vietnamese–Americans than that for blacks and whites, and much less post-traumatic stress. The tenth anniversary of Hurricane Katrina was also used by the city authorities to launch its overarching plan for urban resilience – *Resilient New Orleans* – a policy agenda that calls for 41 actions in three broad areas: environment, city services, and social and economic equity and which focuses on a long-term 2050 vision (City of New Orleans, 2015). This strategic policy is the centrepiece of the city's participation in the Rockefeller Foundation's *100 Resilient Cities* initiative (from 2014) where the core resilience challenge is articulated thus (ibid.):

> Our environment is changing. Climate change is accelerating it.

> Equity is critical to resilience.

> We must plan in the face of uncertainty.

Planning for long-term climate change adaptation

As highlighted above, in the post-Katrina recovery period the authorities in New Orleans drew inspiration from the Dutch in developing plans to live with water more effectively and develop city- and region-wide plans for flood resilience. Many countries and cities are now advancing such plans and embedding principles of 'water' or 'blue' planning into everyday planning policies and practices with the aim of enhancing resilience through innovative adaptation of deltas.

The Dutch Adaptive Delta Management approach

The Netherlands has a long and celebrated history of flood protection but has become increasing concerned about climate change and floods in other European countries. Launched in September 2008 and officially adopted in February 2010, the nationwide Delta Programme seeks to maintain the Netherlands as a safe and attractive country, today and in the future. The Delta Programme is a nationwide venture that brings together central government, provincial and municipal authorities and water boards. Also involved are civil society organisations, the business community and organisations with specialised water expertise. Within the Delta Programme a philosophy known as Adaptive Delta Management (ADM) has been prominently used in an attempt to make urban and regional planning more climate-resilient and more water-robust. The Dutch Delta Programme has formulated ADM as a 'phased decision-making [process] that takes uncertain long-term developments into account explicitly ... in with transparency towards society [and that] encourages an integrated and flexible approach to land and water management' (Delta Alliance, 2014, p.2). ADM is the long-term vision (up to 100 years) which engages with local communities, has support across many government departments, and is embedded in urban and regional planning practice. While ADM is directed towards safety and socio-economic targets and at the same time flexible in how and when to implement management interventions, short-term decisions should also be sustainable or resilient in the longer term. This requires ADM to be more 'anticipative' of future conditions as already planned actions are unlikely to be sufficient to deal with the future challenges of climate change and stop tipping points being reached.

As we highlighted in Chapter 2 and 3, urban resilience requires redundancy, diversity of approach, and more than just a Plan A. In the ADM approach 'adaptation pathways' are developed as alternatives for the traditional 'end-point' scenarios, to support robust decision making and the coherent monitoring and evaluation of responses. As the Delta Alliance further highlights, ADM plans to minimise the impacts of path dependency where policy action is limited by prior decisions:

> [T]he history of deltas shows developments which, once started, cannot easily be changed or adapted to new conditions. Learning from the past and knowing that we cannot predict the future this leads us to the ambition to avoid such lock-ins. One way to do this is to use adaptation pathways. (ibid., p.3)

The formation of adaptation pathways is linked to the acknowledgement of uncertainty in climate change and thus bases much of its thinking on a scenario matrix which looks at the linkages between climate change and socio-economic development. These scenarios are shown in Figure 6.1.

Reflecting upon how the generation of such scenario-driven adaptation pathways seeks to make urban and regional planning more resilient, Restemeyer *et al.* (2014) observe how:

> scenarios are used to anticipate the future. The pathways help to select measures, as they not only depict actions for the short and the long term, but also give an overview [of] which measures may form an appropriate set of measures [...] It also leaves room for emergent policy processes and outcomes, because it clearly shows that the policy actions depend on how the future unfolds.

Figure 6.1

The four delta scenarios (Delta Programme, 2011, p.14)

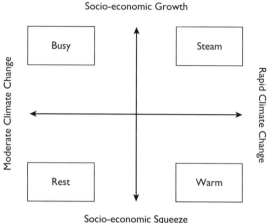

From an urban and regional planning perspective, this approach relies on the process of reflexivity and on a sound *ex-ante* policy analysis that encompasses a future outlook to enable appropriate adaptation to current and emerging trends. This will involve 'establishing whether a policy transition is required, an assessment of alternative flood risk management strategies, and their planning-in anticipation without running the risk of regret of doing too little too late or too much too early' (Klijn *et al.*, 2015 p.845). Moreover, ADM calls for 'new approaches, especially because of uncertainties about long-term future developments [and] [...] entails reconsideration of the underlying principles and of the application of portfolios of technical measures versus spatial planning and other policy instruments' (ibid.). ADM is premised on finding robust yet flexible solutions both now and in the future, and as with the planning system in general, good governance is required. The Delta Alliance (2014, p.10) has argued that this can be captured in a cyclical process that mirrors planning processes (Figure 6.2).

The national ADM programme is regionalised through nine subprogrammes, including the regional sub-programme for the highly urbanised region of Rotterdam where 80% of the land is below sea level. In practice, ADM is well integrated in Rotterdam where the municipal water strategy is coordinated with that of the Delta Programme, both highlighting the need for a multifaceted response

Figure 6.2

Adaptive Delta Management and the planning cycle

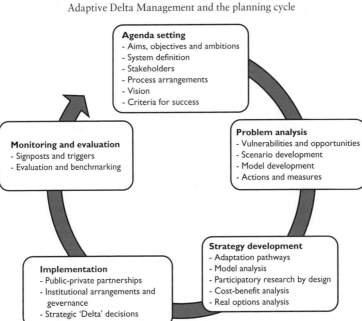

Agenda setting
- Aims, objectives and ambitions
- System definition
- Stakeholders
- Process arrangements
- Vision
- Criteria for success

Problem analysis
- Vulnerabilities and opportunities
- Scenario development
- Model development
- Actions and measures

Monitoring and evaluation
- Signposts and triggers
- Evaluation and benchmarking

Strategy development
- Adaptation pathways
- Model analysis
- Participatory research by design
- Cost-benefit analysis
- Real options analysis

Implementation
- Public-private partnerships
- Institutional arrangements and gevernance
- Strategic 'Delta' decisions

that can buffer unexpected water levels in a multitude of ways, thus enhancing resilience and reducing risks. In both plans water is viewed as 'as a resource, with new urban and building typologies using floods as an opportunity for innovation. Water squares, floating gardens and waterways are identified as new urban features' (Caputo *et al.*, 2015, p.7). Caputo *et al.* (ibid.) further highlight the ways in which innovation is brought into the planning process, for example by turning flood mitigation measures into distinctive urban realm design features, and through public education programmes which allow local residents to learn to live with an acceptable level of water risk. Water planning in Rotterdam has also been given a significant boost in recent years by its inclusion, as with New Orleans, on the Rockefeller *100 Resilient Cities* partnership (see Chapter 5) where the focus of the municipality is very much upon integrated water management and innovative climate adaptation to restrict the impact of flood events:

Rotterdam's efforts are still being undertaken with an eye towards the flood of 1953, which killed almost 2,000 people and caused widespread property damage. It was an event that under-scored the destructive power of the sea, and spurred the modern flood management industry in the country. In 2007, this Dutch city announced its ambition to become 100% climate-proof by 2025 – able to continue functioning economically and socially with minimal disturbance under any extreme weather situation. (Rockefeller Foundation, n.d.)

The proactive Dutch ADM programme is in its infancy but its adaptive, pragmatic, flexible and anticipatory philosophy has seen the approach utilised around the world, notably in Bangladesh, Indonesia and Vietnam (see, for example, Planning Commission General Economic Department, 2014) but also in New Orleans where the *Dutch Dialogues* – a series of US–Dutch workshops – helped shape the post-Katrina comprehensive water management strategy (Meyer *et al.*, 2009).

Design-led resilience for flood risk

As we highlighted in Chapter 4, flooding is an increasing problem in the City of Brisbane, Australia, the impacts of which have been enhanced by urbanisation and maladaptive urban design (Brisbane City Council, 2011a; see also van den Honert and McAneney, 2011). In response, and flowing on from a range of water manage-ment plans produced since 1999, Brisbane City Council has devel-oped a water sensitive urban design strategy (WSUD) that seeks to enhance the permeability of the built environment (Brisbane City Council, 2011a). WSUD is a planning and engineering design approach that integrates the urban water cycle, including stormwa-ter, groundwater and wastewater management, into urban design to minimise environmental degradation and improve aesthetic and recreational appeal. WSUD is traditionally associated with attempts in Australian cities, from the 1960s, to treat stormwater more holis-tically avoiding rapid stormwater run-off which can cause serious flash flooding (Roy *et al.*, 2008).

Increasingly, urban and regional planners have recognised the need for an integrated management approach to enable cities to adapt and become resilient to the pressure which urbanisation and climate change place on ageing water infrastructure (Donofrio *et al.*, 2009). As a result, as Roy *et al.* (2008) highlighted, Australian States began releasing WSUD guidelines within the mid-late 1990s with Brisbane City Council releasing theirs in 1999. In Brisbane

WSUD has formed part of a total water cycle management plan, first released in 2004 and most recently updated in 2013 (Brisbane City Council, 2013b). *Brisbane's Total Water Cycle Management Plan* is a long-term implementation plan – a tool to guide strategic planning and collaboration with its council's partners, which aligns with the council's long-term community vision (Brisbane Vision 2031). This provides a 20-year implementation plan and framework to 'guide detailed planning around issues such as improving Brisbane's flood resilience' (ibid., p.2).

The *Total Water Cycle Management Plan* is in line with the broader Brisbane Vision 2031 plan (Brisbane City Council 2013a) – the long-term community plan for the city which seeks to ensure that: 'Brisbane is a more *resilient city* – a city that is safe, confident and prepared for natural disasters' (p.29); 'Residents and businesses adapt to Brisbane's changing environment, *are resilient* and find effective solutions to extremes in weather and natural events' (p.27); and that 'Brisbane residents and businesses can *design and plan for resilience* and understand the effects of extreme weather events, including the cycle of drought and flood' (p.28, emphasis added). The plan is in essence an innovative resilience strategy focused on climate change adaptation:

> A changing climate can provide the opportunity for us to be innovative in our solutions. Brisbane is committed to adapting the way we manage public spaces, buildings, waterways, overland flow paths and Brisbane's floodplains to make the city and its community *more resilient to change.* (p.6, emphasis added)

The *Total Water Cycle Management Plan* advances a set of detailed implementation plans, most notably the Water*Smart* strategy (2010) and Flood*Smart* strategy 2012–2031. The Water*Smart* strategy aims to protect and improve waterway health and create well-designed vibrant and liveable spaces that are economically viable, and ensure the long-term sustainable management of Brisbane's water resources as the population grows. The Flood*Smart* strategy is promoted with the slogan '*Together we can build a more resilient city; a city that is safe, confident and ready*' (p.1) and was formulated in large part due to the devastating floods which hit the city in 2011. The strategy has six planned strategic outcomes which seek: a risk-based approach to flood management; an integrated and adaptive approach; smart planning and building; an educated and resilient community; world-class response and recovery; and well-maintained and improved structural assets. As the strategy notes:

> [W]e can be a city that lives well with flooding. This means ensuring that flooding is expected, designed and planned for. *It means adapting our built form to the natural movement of water. It means developing communities that are resilient to weather extremes.* We also need to meet the challenges of the future. Climate change and increasing development will require adaptive approaches to flood risk management. (p.2, emphasis added)

This adaptive and integrated approach is summarised in Figure 6.3, highlighting the key role for urban and regional planners (Flood*Smart*, n.p.).

Within Brisbane's planning approaches that support flood risk management is WSUD. In 2011 Brisbane City Council released a new set of guidance documents which encouraged appropriate use of WSUD features – *Water Sensitive Urban Design: Streetscape Planning and Design Package* (Brisbane City Council, 2011b). The design package was intended for urban planners, civil engineers,

Figure 6.3

The planner's role in flood risk management

Land-use planning and development control

Flood awareness and information

Flood risk management

Flood emergency management

Flood mitigation infrastructure

Flood risk management tools

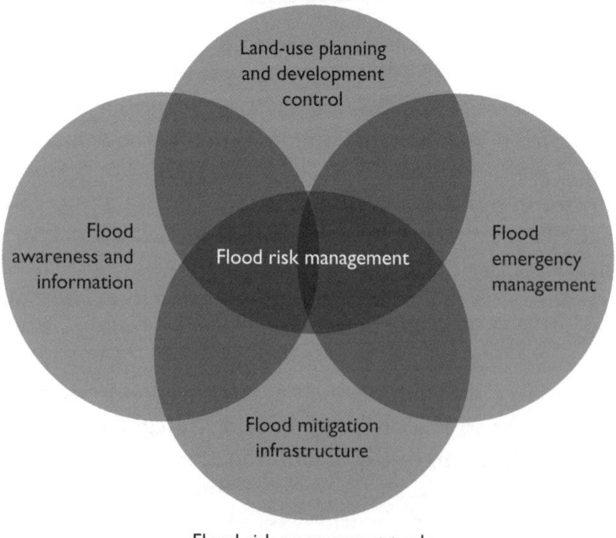

landscape architects and other professionals seeking guidance on stormwater management techniques required in many types of development application. The overarching idea was to create 'water smart streetscapes' using one or a combination of stormwater management devices: bioretention systems, swales, gully baskets and permeable pavement. As the design package notes (p.2) such streetscape interventions can:

> significantly improve the health of Brisbane's catchment and waterway corridors [...] [and] can also help to keep streets green in times of drought, increase visual appeal, increase native habitat and improve drainage, all at minimal cost. For optimal results, stormwater management devices should be considered during the initial concept planning phase of a project. However, they can also be retrofitted into existing urban streets.

In short, WSUD regards urban stormwater run-off as a resource rather than a nuisance or liability, representing a paradigm shift in the way environmental resources and water infrastructure are traditionally dealt with in the planning system.

Climate resilience and transformative planning

The previous sections of this chapter have mainly focused upon climate change adaptation attempts in advanced economies. By contrast this section focuses upon climate resilient development – an approach that typically takes place in less developed nations as a means by which vulnerability can be reduced and resilience enhanced in the face of climate change in ongoing development efforts.

Climate-resilient development

Climate-resilient development, as USAID (2014, p.xvi) notes, 'is about adding considerations of climate variability and climate change to development decision-making in order to ensure that progress toward development goals now includes consideration of climate impacts'. Moreover, climate-resilient development represents a new approach to implementing international development:

> Climate-resilient development means ensuring that people, communities, businesses, and other organizations are able to cope

with current climate variability as well as *adapt to future climate change,* preserving development gains, and minimizing damages. Climate-resilient development is about adding consideration of climate impacts and opportunities to development decision-making in order to improve development outcomes, rather than implementing development activities in a completely new way. Climate risks cannot be eliminated, but negative impacts on people and economies can be reduced or managed. Climate-resilient development helps minimize the costs and consequences of climate impacts so they do not hinder progress toward development goals. (ibid., p.2, emphasis added)

Climate-resilient development seeks to mainstream adaptation and mitigation against climate change and embed better risk management and financing into local planning and development opportunities in a similar way to disaster risk reduction (DRR) approaches and general principles of socio-ecological resilience (see Chapter 2). As Adger *et al.* (2011, p.706) have noted of climate-resilient development:

> There are explicit links made to disaster preparedness and disaster risk reduction; to providing layers of insurance protection, and safety nets where appropriate; and to building 'climate smart' systems. The approach therefore mixes a number of different aspects of resilience thinking, including multiple and cross-scale dynamics; the emphasis on shocks and disturbances to the system; but also aspects of engineering-like resilience.

The climate-resilience development approach seeks to build on existing development practices and facilitate new ways of thinking and working. USAID (2014, p.2) highlights a number of ways in which the climate-resilience development approach differs from traditional development approaches which include future-looking strategic thinking, long-term planning, and embedding flexibility and robustness into developments. These are detailed in Box 6.1.

Advancing a climate-resilient development approach is of course context-dependent but as the Economics Of Climate Adaptation Working Group (containing, for example, ClimateWorks Foundation, Global Environment Facility, European Commission, McKinsey & Company, The Rockefeller Foundation, Standard Chartered Bank and Swiss Re) highlighted (2009, p.13), a number of steps are key to

Box 6.1 *What is different about climate-resilient development?*

Looks forward and plans for the future. Climate change impacts are being felt today, and will continue for centuries to come. Climate change is causing shifts in weather beyond historical experience in many places and the past may no longer be a good predictor for the future. Development practitioners should identify the climate challenges ahead and relate them to current challenges of climate variability.

Identifies climate stressors and utilizes appropriate climate information. Climate stressors should be taken explicitly into account in development planning. Relevant information that aligns with the nature and timescale of your operating environment should be used, ranging from observed trends to modelled projections. For short-term activities, like agricultural extension, information on the next growing season is most relevant. For long-lived infrastructure investments, 50- to 100-year estimations – covering the life of the investment – will be more useful.

Reduces vulnerability to climate stressors. Climate-resilient development must effectively reduce harm caused by climate change. That requires an understanding of what makes someone or something vulnerable, and taking action to reduce those vulnerabilities. Actions that may decrease vulnerabilities include helping people become better equipped to prepare for or adjust to stressors, shifting locations or fortifying high-value areas to reduce exposure to stressors, or changing what people depend upon so they are less sensitive to those stressors.

Promotes flexibility and robustness. Despite great advances in science, climate change impacts are uncertain and will remain so. The continuous changes and occasional surprises of political and economic systems are familiar to development practitioners; the climate system similarly defies precise forecasts.

Embedding flexibility or robustness into development activities involves employing multiple approaches to managing risk, favouring choices that still generate benefits if climate changes to a greater or lesser extent, and managing risk in an adaptive manner.

Continues over time as the needs of countries and communities evolve and climate stressors change. Adaptation is necessarily a continuous process rather than a one-time action because the climate will continue to change, new information about climate stressors will become available and should be integrated into responses, new response options will emerge, and we will learn what works well and what can be improved.

implementing a comprehensive climate-resilient development strategy at the national or local level: creating an inclusive national or local effort; defining current and target penetration of the priority measures identified; addressing existing obstacles to development implementation, such as policy frameworks, institutional capability, and organisation; encouraging sufficient funding from the international community; and recognising and mobilising different roles for each stakeholder. This approach can be exemplified through urban resilience approaches being adopted in Jamaica.

Jamaica's climate-resilient planning approach

In any climate-resilient planning process it is important to frame the planning process and determine appropriate development goals and longer term objectives as well as existing planning laws, regulations, and policies that might facilitate enhanced urban resilience. One notable case of the advancement of a climate-resilience development framework came in 2012 when the Jamaican government sought the support of USAID to develop a new climate change policy to sit alongside the national development plan *Vision 2030: Planning for a Secure & Prosperous Future* (Planning Institute of Jamaica, 2009). Through a series of workshops, gaps were illuminated in Jamaican policy for sufficiently addressing climate change, notably effective governance and funding, but also more regulatory concerns such as the need for proper legislation, effective zoning, and better enforcement of existing building regulations (USAID, 2014, p.14). In identifying a range of climate stressors, Jamaica's climate change approach was properly contextualised and led to a set of adaptation options being advanced.

Subsequently, in the latter half of 2012, Jamaica developed a *Strategic Program for Climate Resilience* (SPCR) as part of the Caribbean Regional Pilot Program for Climate Resilience (PPCR) that aims to assist in climate proofing the country's development. The PPCR provides financing for technical assistance and investment to help highly vulnerable countries integrate climate risk and resilience into their development planning and implementation framework. In so doing it is seeking to move from a 'business as usual' approach to a more proactive and integrative strategy. In Jamaica the SPCR is aligned to *Vision 2030*, and also builds on challenges identified in Jamaica's development strategy. The SPCR is a critical initiative which will assist the country to climate proof its national development though the embedding of climate change adaptation polices across a variety of other policy sectors. For example, in the core area of water and agriculture a range of policy priorities: disaster risk management; flood reduction; poverty reduction; gender considerations; and food security are now integrated within the context of climate change adaptation. Most recently, in 2015, the Jamaican Government announced a $6 million climate change resilience project in the greater Kingston metropolitan area – 'Building Climate Resilience of Urban Systems through Ecosystem-based Adaptation' – as part of a UN Environment Programme focused on Latin America and the Caribbean. As the Jamaica Environment Minister noted of this project (cited in the *Caribbean Journal*, 2015):

> This presents new challenges and opportunities to city planners, environmental planners, the construction sector and to civil society. These are very practical matters – where to build, how to build, and the role that ecosystem services can play – in order to develop and prosper within the new climate reality.

Towards a transformative urban resilience agenda for climate change

Urban areas are on the front line of climate change impacts with many highly exposed and vulnerable to flood risk. Such exposure is often a result of historical path dependencies and locked-in approaches. This chapter has illuminated a range of approaches that have traditionally and more contemporaneously been used by urban and regional authorities, specifically planners, to both mitigate and adapt the built environment (and associated governance mechanisms) through the discourse of urban resilience. This has occurred within the context of increased exposure to climate risk and a heightened sense of uncertainty. As Leichenko (2011, p.164) has noted:

> The notion of resilience is gaining increasing prominence within the literature on cities and climate change. Frequently used terms such as 'climate resilient,' 'climate-proofing,' and the 'resilient city' emphasize the idea that cities, urban systems, and urban constituencies need to be able to quickly bounce back from climate related shocks and stresses. Enhancement of resilience is widely cited as a key goal for both adaptation and mitigation efforts in cities and urban regions.

This chapter has also highlighted that a paradigm shift is occurring, and has been implemented in some urban areas, which is seeing incremental engineered approaches to mitigation being replaced by more natural-focused adaptation schemes implemented by planners, and in so doing creating a built environment and society that is more resilient to climate impact. This is not quite the transformative, adaptive and radical local change highlighted by Pelling (2011) but there are strong signs that in many locations climate change is being differentially framed in terms of practices and governance.

The shift from simply defence and protection for reducing the probability of climate change impacts, notably flooding, to that of prevention and preparedness has now become a key priority of the planning profession and is increasingly being mainstreamed into policy and practice. As White (2008, p.152) noted, 'the current process of emerging natural management [has arisen] as the limitations of the technocratic approach are recognised [and] land is given back for floodplain restoration and more room is made for water'. However, such cultural change is not easy and as Brown (2012) has noted, adaptation to climate change at present seems to be more about incremental change than genuine transformation.

While conservative interpretations of resilience against climate change perhaps dominate, it is important that a more progressive view is embedded within polices and practice of urban and regional planning, embracing adaptability and transformability so as to reduce exposure to both current and future risks. Such an evolutionary resilience perspective, as noted in Chapter 2, rejects equilibrium, certainty and prediction, seeking to draw a much wider array of stakeholders into governance processes as well as develop alternative development trajectories (Davidson, 2010). As White (2013) further highlighted, a move to such a transformative approach would illuminate the dangers of current ways of calculating flood risk (what he refers to as false precision) and remove locked-in decisions. Such adjustment would also facilitate a shift from the dominance of procedural and rational planning orthodoxies to one where uncertainty is embraced and urban and regional planners are increasingly empowered to intervene on a more precautionary basis. However, as we have highlighted in this and other chapters, great care will be needed in governing such new approaches to planning given the real concerns about how climate change adaptation and other forms of urban resilience have implications for social and spatial justice, and actively responsibilise citizens and stakeholders to become risk managers. As Kuhlicke and Steinfuhrer (2013, p.115) recount in relation to flood policy:

> At the same time, *this shift towards a governance of preparedness is quite often associated with new forms of authority and control as well as a changing distribution of responsibilities.* While governments still set flood policy, they at the same time seek to shift responsibility for costs and actions to other segments of society. As a result, those at risk – residents, businesses, farms, infrastructure companies, etc. – are no longer simply exposed to the risk of flooding; rather, *they are gradually transformed into active risk managers as they are encouraged to make decisions and choices with regard to the prevention and mitigation of flood risks.* (emphasis added)

Overall, as UN-Habitat (2011, p.27) has asserted, the response of cities to the challenges of climate change has been fragmented, and significant gaps exist between the rhetoric and the realities of action on the ground. However, through the lens of urban resilience there are signs of progressive and transformative change occurring as:

> the climate change agenda has moved from one of scientific problem framing (climate science and identification of climate impacts) to one more concerned with the implementation of societal responses (mitigation and adaptation), a detailed political, ethical, social and normative analysis has become increasingly important. (McEvoy *et al.*, 2013, p.281)

As with all urban resilience interventions, context is crucial. There is no one-size-fits-all solution; no blueprints for how urban and regional planners should assist cities to adapt to the impacts of climate change. The examples given in this chapter have highlighted the past failure of planning but also illuminated how planners can become a key stakeholder transforming the climate change agenda with a focus upon innovation and change rather than techno-rational and business-as-usual approaches. While there is evidence of advancement in integrated climate change resilience, more challenging is achieving this in combination with sustainable and equitable urban development (see Chapter 10).

Chapter 7

Security-driven Urban Resilience

Urban resilience is traditionally construed in the disaster management literature as being primarily concerned with protection and recovery from natural hazards and/or the effects of climate change. However, as noted in previous chapters, more recently the term is assuming a new guise as it becomes coupled with national security initiatives by governments across the globe. The primary proclaimed objective of these emerging plans is to restrict opportunities for terrorists to penetrate targets and to take measures to mitigate the impacts of successful strikes (Coaffee *et al.*, 2008a; Coaffee and O'Hare, 2008). Although such concerns regarding terrorist threats (as identified by nation states and national governments) are global in scope, and are far from new, such agendas have been pursued more earnestly in the USA and the UK since the 9/11 attacks and the suicide bombings on London's Underground network on 7 July 2005. This is not to say that attempts to thwart urban terrorism did not predate these events, but rather that they have acted as catalysts for increased preventative measures being adopted in the planning and design of places considered to be at greater risk, with increased attention on counter terrorism as a core element of a broader and better funded urban resilience agenda.

In the wake of 9/11, national security policy began to shift to proactive and pre-emptive solutions – what Heng (2006, p.70) referred to as 'active anticipation and reflexive risk management strategies' at a number of sub-national (urban and regional) spatial scales. While recent work suggests that such policy interventions occur in a number of interrelated ways that have 'surged' since 9/11, resultant policy responses have often amounted to little more than extrapolations of ongoing trends reducing the occurrence and perception of crime and terrorism. This, it can be argued, has occurred in four main ways, articulated through the frame of urban resilience (Coaffee and Wood, 2006).

The *first* is through the growth of electronic surveillance within public and semi-public urban spaces, in particular automated software-driven systems (Lyon, 2003). 9/11 proved a catalytic event for the mass introduction of hi-tech surveillance systems – a 'surveillance surge' with the intensification and expansion of existing systems and the adoption of ever more refined technologies now inherently linked to the notion of ensuring everyday urban resilience.

The *second* way is through the increased popularity of physical or symbolic notions of the boundary and territorial closure, for example expansion of the development of residential gated communities and increased protection of entrances and curtilage of airports, civic buildings and major financial districts into which access is restricted. After 9/11 many commentators hypothesised that fears linked to the threat of terrorism would speed up the fragmentation of the city into safe and unsafe zones and have a lasting impact on global cities. Others also documented how the institutional response to terror has led to the 'shrinkage of urban space' as communities seek the sanctuary of purpose-built enclosures (Savitch, 2005).

The *third* way this has occurred is through the increasing sophistication and cost of security and contingency planning undertaken by organisations and different levels of government, intended to decrease their vulnerability and increase preparedness in the event of attack. Most institutions have reviewed and re-evaluated individual risk assessments in order to become more resilient. Full-scale testing and post-evaluation of disaster plans and scenarios are also now increasingly common (Adey and Anderson, 2012).

The *fourth* way is through the linking of urban resilience and security strategies to competition for footloose global capital. Many cities are now overtly linking security to urban regeneration, in terms of both the micro-management of new cultural quarters and gentrification and the macro-management of the urban image through city marketing initiatives, which increasingly play on the importance of the 'safety' of cities as places of business, utilising security and resilience as a vital selling point in their global city offer (Coaffee *et al.*, 2008b). This is also evidenced by the development of city resilience indices by global stakeholders and the professionalisation of resilience assessment for the purpose of capital investment as we discussed in Chapter 5.

These four categories of urban security have become prominent in policy debates, as cities are increasingly scrutinised through the lens of 'resilience'. In practice, this has forced a rethinking of traditional emergency planning and counter-terrorist agendas given the increased magnitude of the threats faced, and the drawing in of a range of non-traditional stakeholders – notably urban and regional planners – into the security policy agenda.

The UK government, like many others, has been developing a range of urban resilience strategies linked to the threat posed to national security by terrorism. Such hostility is not new for the UK, having faced in the past a significant threat from Irish Republican organisations which today is still a concern, though to a significantly reduced extent. Many governments and national security communities have highlighted how new terrorist tactics and targeting strategies have forced a reassessment of threat levels against locations and urban infrastructure. Moreover, while specific targets, such as embassies, military installations and key national infrastructure remain at high risk, a distinctive feature of current threats is that they 'often deliberately strike at ordinary people going about their lives' (Home Office, 2006, p.7). Crowded public places in particular are deemed to be increasingly attractive targets, and must, we are told, be defended. As is outlined in this chapter, however, such initiatives pose significant challenges for urban and regional planners charged with balancing the public interest with security considerations, not least new engagements with police and security services officials in pursuit of this objective.

In unpacking this challenge, and drawing on findings from a range of research projects linked to security-driven urban resilience conducted by the authors, this chapter is structured into three main parts. It first details the pre-9/11 remit for the planner in countering the threat of terrorism, placing the current preoccupation with designed-in security features in historic perspective. It draws on examples from the US, Israel/Palestine and Northern Ireland to exemplify how the ideas underpinning a traditional planning agenda of defensible space or crime prevention through environmental design were 'militarised' in the name of national security. Second, the chapter then turns attention to potential planning-led responses to perceived contemporary threats in the UK, and in Abu Dhabi, providing empirical examples of the mainstreaming of security-driven urban resilience into planning practice. In the third section we reflect upon the significance that this particular peril has for the development of 'resilience' as conventionally understood by the urban and regional planning profession. In highlighting how the role of the professional planner is being reconfigured and being given greater responsibility with regard to contemporary urban security policy, we draw attention to concerns that this raises; concerns that may be shared with other built environment professions such as structural engineers, architects, urban designers and developers. We also highlight that despite a plethora of emerging policy and guidance for urban and regional planners tasked with engaging in the national security agenda, an implementation gap has emerged in effective practice, driven by maladaptive relationships between planners and security specialists. The uneasy linkages between the cultures of planning and policing, which often result in professionals falling back on embedded assumptions and failing to adapt and innovate approaches in accordance with a new normality, is a key characteristic of current security-driven urban resilience approaches. Finally we comment on the impact of the economic recession and how this has made developers and building owners increasingly reluctant to implement the most proportionate security-driven urban resilience measures.

Planning and design for counter terrorism: A historical context

Increasingly, since 9/11, the language of 'resilience' is used to refer to planning policies that embed features into the urban environment that counter the risk of a place or building to terrorist attack, or mitigate the effect of a successful attack:

> [D]omestic security planners have embraced anti-terrorism measures to create a human environment that is difficult to attack, *resilient to the consequences of such incidents,* and protective of its populations and assets. Specifically, anti-terrorism strategies seek to change the fundamental nature of terrorist targets by lessening their real and symbolic value to terrorists while simultaneously reducing their physical vulnerability to terrorist threats. (Grosskopf, 2006, p.1, emphasis added)

Such strategies have important effects upon the built environment, both in terms of what is built and how, but also by what is not built. However, given the uncertain and secretive nature of terrorist risk assessments and concerns of planning professionals regarding engaging with national security policy, many countries have been reluctant to incorporate terrorism prevention within a system of integrated emergency management which includes urban and regional planning communities (Coaffee and O'Hare, 2008).

Moreover, given the intensity of government control over terrorism research and intelligence and the fear that the hazards research label may be used by the power structures to legitimise the nationalistic, ethnocentric and jingoistic aspects of the dominant discourse on terrorism, many in this field are reluctant to lend the umbrella of hazards research to research on terrorism (Mustafa, 2005).

Historical antecedents

Attempts to create urban resilience for, or to defend against, the effects of conflict or terrorism are not new, and are well documented (see for example, Graham, 2004). There are many examples of instances when security and defence agencies have developed initiatives and features with the principal goal of safeguarding particular spaces, such as individual key administrative buildings, frequently with iconographic or symbolic significance (foreign national embassies, memorials, key public buildings and heritage sites), as well as commercial or industrial centres, or transport networks (Sternberg and Lee, 2006).

Current attempts to embed counter terrorism into urban resilience approaches should acknowledge its provenance to notable interventions in the 1960s when planners started to manipulate the built environment to curtail the opportunities for crime and disorder. Advocates of such 'defensive' planning argued that places, particularly residential areas, could be created that would discourage opportunist criminals, and would encourage civic pride, a sense of ownership, and neighbourly surveillance. In the late 1960s and early 1970s architect Oscar Newman undertook a study of large public housing estates in St Louis and New York. Newman developed the concept of 'defensible space', which he viewed as a 'range of mechanisms – real and symbolic barriers [...] [and] improved opportunities for surveillance – that combine to bring the environment under the control of its residents' (Newman, 1972, p.3) and the subsequent publication of *Defensible Space – Crime Prevention through Urban Design* (1972) provoked an intense debate on the relationship between crime and the built environment. Newman argued that defensible space was a means by which residential environments could be redesigned 'so they can again become livable and controlled not by the police, but by a community of people who share a common terrain' (Newman, 1973, p.2). Defensible space offered an alternative to the target-hardening measures that were being introduced to American housing at this time and this concept (and similar ideas such as Crime Prevention through Environmental Design (CPTED) or Secure by Design (SBD) – see Jeffery, 1971 and Conzens *et al.*, 2005) were integrated into UK policy and applied on similar large high-rise housing estates in the late 1970s and 1980s (Coleman, 1985).

Such security initiatives within the urban environment, particularly in 'at risk' places, were again increasingly pursued in the 1990s. Urban form was seen to follow a culture of fear (Davis, 1990, 1998; Ellin, 1997) expressed through, and in some cases even dominating, the built environment; the ubiquitous situation whereby 'virtually every institution – bars, universities, doctors' surgeries, sport, public transportation – takes security very seriously. Burglar alarms, outdoor lights, panic buttons, CCTV cameras and an array of private security personal are testimony to a flourishing market in fear' (Furedi, 2006, p.3). This led to an increasingly sophisticated array of fortification, with surveillance and security management techniques being deployed by security agencies and civilian administrators to protect perceived urban vulnerabilities. This, it could be argued, was an unbalanced response, bearing little relation to the incidence of crime. This apparently disproportionate approach to the introduction of an ever more security conscious citizenry and militarised built environment has had important implications for the everyday experience of the city and, by extension, in the approach taken by urban authorities and the planning profession to countering the risk of terrorism through the protection of economic interests and key national infrastructure.

The militarisation of defensible space

At the same time that the planning profession was initially adopting the principles of defensible space in an attempt to protect communities from opportunist crime, others, particularly military planners, were using similar principles to counter civil disorder and violence. Such interventions, designed to 'target-harden' or fortify areas and buildings, had often quite brutal physical manifestations upon the urban and built environment. For instance, military-style fortifications were employed in Northern Ireland to counteract the Irish Republican Army's (IRA's) campaign against commercial areas, with the security forces constructing 'rings of steel' around commercial centres to create physical barriers specifically designed to limit the permeability of public spaces to paramilitary operations (Brown, 1985; Coaffee, 2000). The features consisted of new traffic restrictions, with barbed wire fences and tall steel barriers limiting entry and egress points to sensitive areas, or to spaces deemed as 'at risk', essentially rendering them besieged citadels. In addition to the fortification of public and shared spaces, segregation was formalised and partially institutionalised as a method of managing and containing civil conflict – a process marked by the creation of vacant 'no-man's' lands which separated conflicting communities, and then by razor wire, armoured vehicles, 'peace' walls and a series of police and army checkpoints (Shirlow and Murtagh, 2006).

Another notable example of the securitisation role of planning which became synonymous with militaristic security planning that significantly impacted upon land use and the day-to-day experience of places is provided by Israel during the 1980s and 1990s. The link between the military and planning in Israel must be viewed not only in a historical context but also in terms of different strategies of intervention at the national, regional and local scales (Soffer and Minghi, 2006) creating a 'securityscape' preoccupied with impending threats, defence strategies and precautionary measures. In this case, as attacks on Israeli settlements threatened public safety, the security forces had an expanded role to play within the planning process.

In more recent times, throughout the disputed territories of Israel/ Palestine, the heightened need for 'national security' has led to ever more brutal and visible territorial defences. For the most part these have been constructed by the Israeli authorities, particularly in response to the risk of suicide bomb attacks originating in the Palestinian territories. Most notably, in 2002 the Israeli Defence Force commenced the construction of a separation 'wall' around substantial sections of the Palestinian West Bank and Gaza strip, linking earlier fences and walls in a formidable barrier in the name of the protection of Israeli areas and Jewish settlements, at an estimated cost of $1.5 billion. 'The Wall' consists of '8-metre-high concrete slabs, electronic fences, barbed wire, radar, cameras, deep trenches, observation posts and patrol roads' (Weizman, 2007, p.12). Access is only through armed checkpoints containing x-ray scanners and its entire length is patrolled by thousands of security guards.

In both of these cases, and in other similar instances, the intervention of the security services and the military has led to stark forms of protection embedded within the built environment, at times so widespread as to effectively normalise heightened security. Such planning-led interventions, though often crude, are generally acknowledged to be, superficially at least, effective in that they prohibit the penetration of targets and the permeability of spaces by potential perpetrators of attacks. Planners and designers in this sense have been an initial guide to the siting of defensive features, but have had little influence over construction or design.

The role of the planner in security-driven urban resilience before 9/11

Despite a host of high-profile terror attacks against economic or iconic targets and subsequent militaristic interventions in many Western cities during the 1990s, it is common for scholars and built environment practitioners to maintain that the inception of counter terrorism in contemporary society can be traced to the events of 9/11. While the events of that day were a major catalyst of this agenda, the role of planners increased after other earlier terrorist attacks, particularly in the United States, caused by vehicle-borne explosive devices penetrating target buildings; the first in a parking area below the iconic World Trade Center in February 1993, which killed six and injured over 1,000 people, and, secondly, the destruction of the Alfred P. Murrah Federal Building in Oklahoma City by a truck bomb in April 1995, killing 168 and injuring over 800. These attacks in the continental United States, along with the simultaneous US Embassy bombings in Dar-es-Salaam and Nairobi in August 1998 (together killing 257 and injuring 5,000 people, mainly African civilians but also many US civilian personnel) and a bomb attack on the Khobar Towers Hotel in Saudi Arabia in 1996 (which killed 19 US service personnel and one Saudi and injured almost 400), led to increased attention being paid to the protection of buildings. Although such attacks were neither entirely unprecedented nor unanticipated, attacks on the streets and public buildings of the continental United States were significant in the mainstreaming of counter-terrorism features within the planning system.

The 1993 World Trade Center attack horrified the US public, which had seemed immune to acts of terrorism that had plagued other parts of the world, soliciting a swift defensive response with both individual buildings and commercial districts increasingly attempting to 'design out terrorism' (Coaffee, 2004). These responses were noted within the wider public with one journalist explicitly referring back to the work of Oscar Newman and noting, 'barricades and bollards have become the newest accessory on this country's psychic frontier [...] You might call it the architecture of paranoia. They [planners] call it defensible space' (Brown, 1995). In response to the Oklahoma bombing, at the time the most devastating act of terrorism in the United States, the US government passed legislation for increased security of federal buildings and for the potential for 'bomb proofing' through greater structural robustness (Executive Order 12977 – 19 October 1995). A great deal of attention was being paid to the fact that the Alfred P. Murrah Federal Building had been so devastated by the explosion (it collapsed like a pack of cards), with experts charged with assessing how buildings could be protected in the future. A review of the impact of the Oklahoma bombing detailed how buildings could be 'hardened' and defended and highlighted how, unlike military facilities, civilian facilities had few standards and guidelines available (Hinman and Hammond, 1997).

In the wake of these incidents, the practical response by statutory agencies was rather reactionary, adopting crude but robust approaches to territorial security, and once again pursuing ideas of defensible space as their key modus operandi, as the American public became increasingly aware of the threat of 'home-grown' terrorism and the vulnerability of the built environment. By extension, the potential role that urban and regional planning professionals could play in 'terror proofing' cities became more apparent. Similar concerns were felt in London at this time as a result of a series of large explosions in the financial core. Here too-crude defensive cordons were erected in attempts to 'beat the bombers' (Coaffee, 2000).

The proactive defence of buildings and structures from explosions per se at this time was not new, however, and it was felt that 'Cold War legacies': 'blast resistant design specialists and the tools they use to understand explosions' was sufficient (Baer, 2005, p.2). Yet, as suggested, most such specialists were deployed to defend not civilian buildings, but military facilities, such as missile silos or bunkers. In response to the threat of terrorist attack against civil buildings, urban planners were now being urged to incorporate resilience for counter terrorism, but with the added challenge of 'budgetary and aesthetic considerations that were never meant to accommodate blast hardening' (Hinman and Hammond, 1997 p.18). These are key issues which, although identified in the 1990s, are only now being recognised and dealt with by the planning profession as they advance security-driven urban resilience strategies.

Such target hardening as a form of defence is not without critique. Architectural critic Martin Pawley (1998) argued that in light of an upsurge in urban terrorism, urban areas could be punctuated by an 'architecture of terror', dominated by the need for increased security, and more generally could become the subject of 'anonymous' design to make them less of an iconic target. Elsewhere it was argued that such secure design may be difficult to regress once established, unless there was a significant decline in the security risk (Coaffee, 2004). By extension, the target hardening or defence of particular places may cause displacement of risk as attention for attack is turned to other places. Others have also been concerned that such defences, including territorial measures, could be an overreaction, as Finch (1996, p.1) argued after the 1996 London Docklands bomb:

> The truth is we do not design buildings to withstand bomb blasts because bomb blasts are the exception to the rule [...] the key point is the defining of the line between risk and recklessness. We do not generally conduct our lives on the basis of the worst thing that could in theory happen.

The mainstreaming of security features into the planning process

In the heightened security climate after the attacks of 9/11, and subsequent Al Qaeda-inspired attacks and campaigns worldwide, many countries have pursued more vigorous urban counter-terrorism strategies, and in so doing have displayed a greater sensitivity to this potential vulnerability. One particular aspect of these initiatives is the physical protection of places perceived to be at risk. As such, this section of the chapter highlights the current context of the threat from terrorism and how attempts to address these threats have been translated into broader legislative and policy agendas of resilience with critical implications for the built environment and for the planning profession. Here we detail the immediate response to the 9/11 attacks before turning attention to the UK and the Abu Dhabi governments' contemporary counter-terrorism policy, again paying specific attention to the implications for urban and regional planners and the planning process.

In a number of countries after the 9/11 attacks, there was substantial pressure for key buildings, including iconic or landmark public and commercial buildings, to be protected from terrorist attack. This led to many robust yet unrefined and obtrusive features almost literally 'thrown' around key sites. Indeed, in some cases security installations needed to be 'seen to be doing something', employing features that are effective, but not necessarily acceptable nor aesthetically pleasing. For instance, it has been charged that the US-wide effort to secure 'key' buildings after 9/11 has, in its rather haphazard and makeshift manifestation, prioritised safety of building occupants over regard for social, economic, aesthetic or transportation considerations (Hollander and Whitfield, 2005). Others have described how the 'guns, guards, gates' posture adopted in the immediate wake of 9/11 was inappropriate, due to the way such measures 'actually intensify and reinforce public perceptions of siege or vulnerability, and thus heighten the sense of imminent danger and anticipation of attack' (Grosskopf, 2006, p.2). In Washington DC, for example, the erection of Jersey barriers and chain-link fences were unpopular with visitors and planners. It was asserted that the defences were more suitable for construction sites: 'the nation's capital has become a fortress city peppered with bollards, bunkers, and barriers' (Benton-Short, 2007, p.426) due both to a lack of funding for 'anything nicer' and a lack of strategic coordination between policy makers.

Others argued that such 'security zones' were unlikely to exhibit any of the characteristics of successful public spaces: 'usability, accessibility, and detailed design'. In fact, many argued, such places may be planned to be less welcoming (Hollander and Whitfield, 2005, p.250). On a related point, there have been concerns regarding the impact that such features may have upon the urban fabric and for the permeability and liveability of places, with, in Washington DC, planning guidance being issued in an attempt to create security that complements or even promotes vistas, open spaces, accessibility and the iconographic significance of the city (National Capital Planning Commission, 2001). This pattern of reactive and retrofitted fortification was repeated in many countries. For example, in London high-profile targets such as the Houses of Parliament and the US Embassy were protected by rings of concrete barriers and mesh fencing (Coaffee, 2004).

Security-driven urban resilience policy in UK policy

To understand the role that urban and regional planners might have in national security agendas we must first understand broader security and counter-terrorism policy (see, for example, Cabinet Office, 2008). The UK's present counter-terrorist strategy is referred to as CONTEST – a long-term strategy for developing 'resilience' against the threat of terrorism. It is divided into four strands: *Prevent*,

Pursue, Protect and *Prepare* (Home Office, 2006). The *Protect* strand specifically aims to secure the public, key national services and UK interests overseas and covers a range of issues such as border security, critical national infrastructure and crowded places, and presents a key role for the planning profession. Others too have charted the shift from 'hard' government targets towards 'soft targets' such as nightclubs, bars and hotels, with the assertion that paying taxes legitimises the targeting of citizens (Dolink, 2007).

On 25 July 2007, shortly after failed car bomb attacks against a London nightclub and Glasgow Airport, and two years after suicide bombers killed 52 people and injured 770 using London's transport network, the then Prime Minister, Gordon Brown, provided a 'statement on security' in which he noted 'the protection and resilience of our major infrastructure and crowded places requires continuous vigilance' (Brown, 2007a). He added that 900 shopping centres, stadiums and venues had already been assessed by counter-terrorism security advisors, with 10,000 other premises given updated security advice. Subsequently, in November 2007, the Parliamentary Under-Secretary of State for Security and Counter-Terrorism (Lord West) presented a review to government regarding how it may best protect 'crowded places, transport infrastructure and critical national infrastructure from terrorist attack' (Smith, 2007).

Although, for reasons of national security, the review was unpublished, numerous statements were made in Parliament and to the press that provided an insight into proposed policy initiatives and their implications for the planning profession. The West review highlighted the need to improve the resilience of, in the words of the Prime Minister, 'strategic national infrastructure (stations, ports and airports) and other crowded places, and to step up physical protection against possible vehicle bomb attacks,' including 250 of the UK's busiest railway stations and airport terminals, ports and more than 100 sensitive installations (Brown, 2007a). He added that the national security state will now work with planners to encourage them to 'design in' protective security measures to new buildings, including safe areas, traffic control measures and the use of blast-resistant materials. In particular, the Prime Minister said that he would make *'improvements to the planning process'* to ensure *'more is done to protect buildings from terrorism from the design stage onwards'* (ibid.). This would, he continued, be conducted with the support of relevant professional bodies (such as the Royal Town Planning Institute and Royal Institute of British Architects) to raise the awareness and skills of planners, architects and police architectural liaison officers in relation to counter-terrorism protective security. In a statement coinciding with the West review, the Prime Minister's spokesman noted the announcements would prepare 'the public for the possibility that they may start to see some changes to the physical layout of buildings where people gather' (Number 10 Press Briefing, 2007).

With regard to this perceived need to reduce the vulnerability of crowded places through the *Protect* strand of CONTEST, a number of general principles were implied with regard to the embedding of protective security into the built fabric of cities: proportionality; collective responsibility; and visibility.

First, it was argued that protective security measures deployed should be proportionate to the risk faced. This desire for proportionality was further outlined in subsequent UK government documentation where it was argued that the risk faced within crowded places should be judged in a standard way in accordance with a 'risk assessment matrix' that would assess the likelihood and potential social, economic and physical impact of terrorist attacks. This would allow local partners to 'prioritise their work to reduce the vulnerability of crowded places to terrorist attack' (Home Office, 2009, p.4). A proportionate approach was deemed necessary in order to minimise disruption to everyday activities and to 'the ability of individuals and businesses to carry out their normal social, economic and democratic activities' (ibid., p.5). More cynically we could argue that this was an attempt to 'pass on' risk (and hence responsibility for urban resilience) from government security services to local stakeholders.

Second, the West review highlighted that cooperation amongst a host of associated stakeholders, most notably private businesses and built environment professionals such as planners, was required in order to make crowded places safer. Here it was explicit that such interventions should be considered *at the start* of a planning process in order that they could be effectively and acceptably integrated into the design of space. Delivering a noticeable reduction in vulnerability was therefore seen not just in terms of the delivery of guidance to local authorities and business by security specialists, but in the actual implementation of measures, through the actions of a range of stakeholders, to increase the safety of those crowded spaces deemed to be at highest risk of attack. This was in line with broader concerns surrounding the overall resilience of cities against a range of hazards that has necessarily broadened out the range of experts and professions whose input should be coordinated (see Chapters 2 and 3).

Third, it was noted that the imposition of additional security features should not, where possible, negatively impact upon everyday economic and democratic activities. This realisation of the importance of the social acceptability of counter terrorism features led to the West review announcing that security features should be as unobtrusive as possible where finding the right balance between 'subtlety' and 'safety' was seen as vital (Coaffee and Bosher, 2008). As argued at this time, the adoption of counter-terrorist principles within designs had often led to visibly unattractive urban design and architecture and the increased control of access to public space. But this need not be so. As one commentator noted: 'we might live in dangerous times, but they don't have to be ugly ones too' (Bayley, 2007). In response to this challenge security features in selective locations have been increasingly camouflaged and covertly embedded within the urban landscape so that to the general public they do not obviously serve a counter-terrorism purpose (Coaffee *et al.*, 2009). Examples of such 'stealthy' features include ornamental or landscaped measures. For example, balustrades erected as part of public realm 'streetscape' improvements in the government security zone in central London in 2008 have also sought to design in security more attractively and inconspicuously (instead of using security bollards).

Figure 7.1

A hostile vehicle mitigation (HVM) barrier at the Emirates Stadium in North London (2007)

Figure 7.2

A spectrum of visible security features

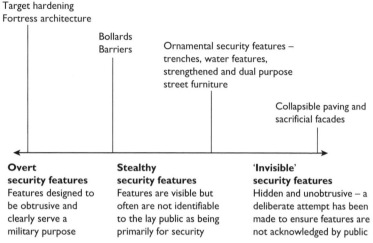

Target hardening
Fortress architecture

Bollards
Barriers

Ornamental security features –
trenches, water features,
strengthened and dual purpose
street furniture

Collapsible paving and
sacrificial facades

Overt security features	**Stealthy** security features	**'Invisible'** security features
Features designed to be obtrusive and clearly serve a military purpose	Features are visible but often are not identifiable to the lay public as being primarily for security	Hidden and unobtrusive – a deliberate attempt has been made to ensure features are not acknowledged by public

Source: adapted from Coaffee *et al.*, 2009.

Further along what has been documented as a spectrum of visible security features (see Figure 7.2) we can also see 'invisible' types of security emerging within architectural practice such as collapsible pavements (so-called tiger traps); although such features come with political challenges in that their very invisibility means they potentially become an uncontested element of political and public policy. This, as one commentator has noted, potentially 'represents the future of the hardening of public buildings and public space – soft on the outside, hard within, the iron hand inside the civic velvet glove' (Boddy, 2007, p.291).

In London, one new development – the new US Embassy – is emblematic of the increased role for planning in security-driven urban resilience and highlights the collective concerns noted above. In February 2010, amidst some controversy, proposed architectural plans were unveiled for the design of a new US Embassy building on a then vacant site in Wandsworth, south-west London. Upon planning permission being granted, building work started in November 2013 and is due to be completed by 2017 at a cost of well over £1 billion. The requirement for a new embassy was deemed vital for 'security purposes', with the existing embassy site seen as vulnerable, and difficult and costly to protect from terrorist attack, given its constrained location. The current embassy site in Grosvenor Square, central London, has, since the events of 9/11 become a defended citadel surrounded by residential and commercial premises, and has seen much public protest regarding the high fences, concrete barriers, crash-rated steel blockers and armed guards that currently encircle the site to protect it from vehicle bombing (Coaffee, 2004).

In more recent times the existing embassy – dubbed 'the fortress in the square' – is said to have offended the 'aesthetic sensibilities' of local residents, some of whom have moved away rather than live near a perceived terrorist target (Coaffee *et al.*, 2009). The 2010 design for the new embassy and the rationale for relocation from the current site incorporated in a singular design a number of the characteristics of contemporary security-driven resilient protective design as embodied in the *Protect* strand of the UK counter-terrorism strategy (CONTEST). Moreover, it can be argued that in an international context, many states, notably the US and UK, are 'visually exaggerating interests of national security through the architectures of overseas embassies' with the aim of transmitting a message of physical defence from attack (ibid., p.500). Even in the most liberal of cities, embassies are being subjected to acute target hardening with resultant impacts upon the everyday city. As such, the aim of ensuring an impregnable sealed site has become a key modus operandi for designers of many embassies worldwide.

In more recent times, the fortress emblem design of many embassies, which was common in the Cold War period and, in many cases, intensified in the immediate post 9/11 era, has begun to pay increased attention to the aesthetics of architectural design, and the wider impact such structures can have upon surrounding areas and communities. With this key principle in mind, the current plans for the new US Embassy in south-west London sought to incorporate a number of innovative and largely 'stealthy' counter-terrorism design features. Many of these features are reminiscent of medieval times, notably the blueprint for a stronghold castle: a protected castle keep surrounded by moats or ditches which could be crossed using ramparts. The lead architect from Pennsylvania firm KieranTimberlake noted that his designs had been stimulated by European castle architecture and that, in addition to the use of a blast-proof glass facade, he had also sought to use landscape features imaginatively as security devices. This was to minimise the use of fences and walls to avoid giving a 'fortress feel' to the site. Ponds and multi-level gardens were also suggested as security features, in part to provide a 30-metre protective 'blast zone' around the site. Referring to his largely glass-based design, the lead architect further noted in *The*

Figure 7.3

The initial design for the new US Embassy at Nine Elms, London

Source: © KieranTimberlake/studio amd.

Guardian newspaper that 'we hope the message everyone will see is that it is open and welcoming' and that 'it is a beacon of democracy – light filled and light emitting' (Booth, 2010, p.13).

In short, the design (see Figure 7.3) highlighted a number of key features of contemporary counter-terrorism philosophy: the need to integrate effective protective security into the design of at-risk sites; the increased importance of built environment professionals such as planners, architects and urban designers in security planning; and the need to consider the visible impact of security measures, and where appropriate, make these as unobtrusive as possible.

More generally, and in line with these core principles of proportionality, collective responsibility and visibility, the intention since 2007 in the UK has been to develop a national framework for the rolling out of protective security within crowded places. This is in order to deliver a sustained and noticeable decrease in urban vulnerability over the long term. The development of such a framework has had a number of constituent elements linked to the urban and regional planning process, including:

• Drawing on existing expertise in local areas such as crime and disorder reduction partnership and local resilience forums where the police, local government and other key stakeholders (such as planners) come together and work collectively to reduce vulnerability.

- Developing a national network of well-trained counter-terrorism specialists and security design advisors who can provide guidance and advice to local planners with regard to threat levels faced and the proportionate use of protective security interventions.

- The creation of performance management indicators at local level to assist local government to focus on the requirement of reducing the vulnerability of crowded spaces against terrorist attack. The use of such performance management tools indicates that a local authority and its partners, in liaison with the local police and specialist counter-terrorism security advisors, will have a statutory duty to ensure that the protection of crowded places is 'robust' (DCLG, 2007a).

- Improving the skills base of urban and regional planners through workshops run by the National Counter Terrorism Security Office (called Project Argus Professional), and through delivering enhanced training schemes for local police involved in urban planning and design guidance – called architectural liaison officers (see NaCTSO, 2010).

- The production of bespoke planning guidance (non-regulatory) to upskill the epistemic planning community with regard to the embedding of security features into the built environment. In March 2010, the same month as the designs for a new US Embassy in London were unveiled, the UK government, as part of its *Working Together to Protect Crowded Places* programme of work, released a set of technical and procedural guidance documents for built environmental and security professionals concerned with reducing vulnerabilities in urban areas: *The Planning System and Counter Terrorism* and *Protecting Crowded Places: Design and Technical Issues* (Home Office, 2010a and 2010b; see also revised version re-released in 2014). This was followed a year later by a specialist design guide from the Centre for the Protection of National Infrastructure: *Integrated Security: A Public Realm Design Guide for Hostile Vehicle Mitigation* (Centre for the Protection of National Infrastructure, 2011).

- The potential to enhance the business case for the implementation of security measures through so-called dual use design (Coaffee and Bosher, 2008). In delivering an enhanced level of security, there are of course questions of cost to address and in terms of economic efficiency there is now a tremendous opportunity, especially for new-build projects, to simultaneously embed energy efficient and security features into the built environment which can 'contribute to the larger goals of an economy less vulnerable to energy supply and infrastructure disruptions and to generate long-term energy cost savings that will in turn lower the net cost of essential security improvements' (Harris *et al.*, 2002, p.6).

Planning for safety and security in Abu Dhabi

The UK has perhaps gone furthest in advancing a role for urban and regional planning in security-driven urban resilience. The UK approach is now undergoing policy transference as other countries seek to adopt similar approaches, albeit within their own particular planning context.

As part of their 2030 vision, and drawing extensively on the experiences in the UK, in 2013 the Abu Dhabi Urban Planning Council produced the *Abu Dhabi Safety and Security Planning Manual* (SSPM) to 'ensure the creation of safe and secure communities that enhance the quality of life and reflect the Emirate's unique identity' (Abu Dhabi Urban Planning Council, 2013, p.9). Specifically, the SSPM presented 'planning and design guidance that will embed counterterrorism protective security in our built environment, *reducing vulnerabilities and increasing the resilience of our communities*' (ibid., p.21, emphasis added).

The SSPM allows planners, in conjunction with a range of other government stakeholders, to guide the development of safe and secure communities. Here *community safety* comprises strategies and measures that seek to reduce the risk of crimes occurring and their potential harmful effects on individuals and society, including fear of crime, by intervening to influence their multiple causes, while *protective security* is an organised system of protective measures implemented to achieve and maintain security. The SSPM combines the three disciplines of personnel, information and physical security in order to create 'defence in depth', where multiple layers work together to deter, delay, detect and deny an attack (ibid., p.20). The manual is an attempt to develop an integrated development process where planners can work with other stakeholders to advance urban resilience and do so in a way that allows the principles of safe and secure planning to be embedded into the development process at an early stage. As the SSPM (ibid., p.13) notes:

Good planning and design of the built environment are central to community safety and protective security, yet crime and security issues rarely receive sufficient attention early in the development process. The purpose of the Manual is to ensure that safety and security are embedded in development proposals and this is best achieved using an Integrated Development Process.

Eight planning principles are presented in the SSPM that underpin the approach to safety and security planning (see Table 7.1). These

Table 7.1 *The eight key principles of the SSPM*

Principle	Focus	Description
Principle 1	Access and connectivity	Balancing safety and security with movement of vehicles and pedestrians and ensuring street design complies with the Urban Street Design manual
Principle 2	Structure and spatial layout	Ensuring that the configuration of the built environment does not contain vulnerable areas and is structured in a way that manages risk appropriately
Principle 3	Ownership	Safety and security can be enhanced if occupants and users have a sense of ownership and responsibility over places
Principle 4	Surveillance	Appropriate levels of natural and electronic surveillance can enhance safety and security but this must be balanced with the need for shading and privacy
Principle 5	Activity	Ensuring that places have an appropriate mix of activity and use patterns that reduce crime and are welcoming to legitimate users
Principle 6	Physical security	Physical security should be used in an appropriate and proportionate way, using risk assessment and where possible integrated sensitively into the urban fabric
Principle 7	Public image	Places should be well maintained and managed and seek to promote a positive public image and a sense of identity
Principle 8	Adaptability	Places should be adaptable to change in order to enhance safety and security and change of use should be considered in planning and design

are seen as universal considerations, regardless of the development, but need to be applied differently according to local context (ibid.).

These eight planning principles have been developed into specific policy statements, which have sought to engage planners to embed principles of safety and security at all stages within an integrated and holistic development process. This represents a proactive attempt to change planning culture and to make safety and security a core consideration alongside other planning stipulations, to schedule safety and security early in the development process, and to introduce best practice principles for both new and existing development. This involves, in particular, engagement in a process of risk assessment to judge the likelihood and impact of crime or terrorist risk, and ensure that community safety and protective security arrangements in new and existing developments, 'must be fit-for-purpose, appropriate and proportionate to the risks' (p.22). Notably, planners, working with developers, are encouraged to make decisions on 'risk treatment' required based upon whether intervention would be tolerable or intolerable to the effective operation of their buildings, and advised that 'risks should be treated as early as possible and where measures can be most appropriate and effective' (Abu Dhabi Urban Planning Council, 2013, p.254). This process also involves planners working together with a range of non-planning stakeholders that have traditionally had little input into the planning process. Planning for safety and security is also very much seen as a pragmatic balancing act, recognising that 'few organisations will have the resources and mandate to mitigate every plausible scenario' (p.77). As further noted:

> It is rarely possible or cost effective to implement every security countermeasure for every conceivable scenario. However integrating security throughout the planning and design process enables the project team to strike a responsible balance between the level of risk, available resources and appropriate mitigation measures. (p.74)

The final policy direction advanced in the SSPM differentiates the Abu Dhabi model of security-driven urban resilience from that operating in the UK and other parts of the world, in that the SSPM has an *owner pays* stipulation where 'costs associated with community safety and protective security fall where responsibility for safety and security lies: with the owner' (p.22). To aid this the manual is supplemented by an online decision support tool that may be used during the pre-planning stage of a project to gain an appreciation of how much influence safety and security will have on development proposals. Moreover, unlike other planning systems, the SSPM is strongly enforced through regulations. For example, by Urban Design Policy VII – U23 Crime Prevention, which states that developers should 'complete a set of guidelines for crime prevention through building and landscape design and henceforth manage development to facilitate the safety of environments and maintain Abu Dhabi's excellent record on crime' (ibid., p.20). Powers under the Emirate of Abu Dhabi's Environment, Health and Safety Management System also allows municipalities to monitor and enforce good practice.

The SSPM also seeks to work with local context and thus does not prescribe any particular solutions, acknowledging that 'safety and security risks differ from one place to another and that the solutions that work in one place might not work in another' (p.20) and that 'there is a need to take into account the local situation and for all those involved in developing, managing and maintaining the built environment, to work collaboratively and holistically to address safety and security risks' (ibid.). It is intended that this process implements security-driven urban resilience principles that are bespoke to Abu Dhabi Emirate. Here the Urban Planning Council has amended international best practice in safety and security interventions to take account of culture and religion (the importance of privacy means that surveillance, overlooking and screening need to be handled carefully so that residents do not feel uncomfortable), the hot dry climate (for example, buildings are aligned and narrow paths created for increased shading which restricts sightlines of surveillance), the fast pace of development (which means that safety and security principles can be applied as part of a master plan, rather than being restricted to individual plots) (p.31) and vernacular built form.

As previously noted, the SSPM is part of the broader Vision 2030 programme that is ambitious and involves significant development. The Abu Dhabi 2030 Urban Structure Framework Plan (2011) is a programme of urban evolution that seeks to optimise the city's development, laying the foundations for a socially cohesive and economically sustainable community that preserves the Emirate's unique cultural heritage. Accordingly it reflects a 'next generation planning' mindset. As part of this 2030 Vision a wide-ranging government-funded implementation programme is being rolled out through the SSPM charged with identifying any safety and security improvements needed to existing buildings or new developments. Such appropriate securitisation of the built environment is seen as essential in sustaining and promoting future economic growth and ensuring that Abu Dhabi 'remains safe, secure and welcoming as it continues to grow and attract a range of diverse activities, people and opportunities' (Abu Dhabi Urban Planning Council, 2013, p.19). This priority is in line with what the government of Abu Dhabi sees as its primary goals: a safe and secure society and a dynamic, open economy (Abu Dhabi Government, 2008, p.6).

Planning security-driven urban resilience measures: From circumvention to co-option?

Prior to 9/11 and in its immediate wake, security interventions were rather crude, dominated by the need for physical robustness and, in some instances, designed to be a potentially intimidating and *visible* deterrent. However, there is now increasing pressure to promote 'good design' and 'landscape elements' in defensive features. The effects of the promoted policies and initiatives upon the built environment are potentially considerable and as Table 7.2 illustrates, a range of generic stakeholder perceptions, often with competing rationales, must be negotiated.

A more thoughtful planning process has the potential to create physical and social improvements so that the crime of terrorism does not continue to destroy places but rather is dealt with comprehensively and proportionately. Yet, despite the promoted status of urban and regional planning professionals in such activities, their precise role in national protective security and that of the statutory and professional context within which they operate is not, in many cases, clear. More fundamentally, there are emerging concerns regarding the efficacy of planning professionals in engaging in these agendas (Coaffee and O'Hare, 2008). Attention is now turned to briefly discussing these emerging themes and concerns.

As suggested, it is not completely clear as to how the emerging security agenda, as it has been outlined thus far, is to percolate into planning practice. There are a number of options available, though some are more likely to be adopted than others. In most contexts it is *unlikely* that designing in counter-terrorism features will be enforced by stringent regulatory controls (although this is the case in Abu Dhabi). It is much more likely that features will be pursued using a variety of incentives for building developers or users, or

Table 7.2   *Emergent (and indicative) stakeholder perceptions of designing counter-terrorism features*

Built environment professional/stakeholder	Dominant emerging perception
Planner	Potential mediator amongst other vested interests
Architect	Protect ability for innovative design
Urban designer	Innovative design and public usability
Landscape architect	Embed landscape elements into counter-terrorism strategies
Structural engineer	Ensure physical robustness
Surveyor	Cost suppression
Developer	Usability and cost
Police	Physical security and crime/terror prevention
Emergency planner	Mitigation of risks from a wide range of hazards and threats
Public space manager e.g. town centre manager, or building user	Vibrant, safe and 'operational' spaces
Insurer	Decreased risk and attack mitigation of impact

through the development of training courses and decision support frameworks that help a variety of built environment professionals (not just planners) adopt such approaches to urban resilience and embed them into the their design of buildings and places in ways that assist broader sustainable development criteria.

Indeed, there is the possibility that pressure may come from the users of buildings and public places, mirroring the uptake of designing out crime schemes for which the victims' rights movement of the 1980s acted as a catalyst, raising the spectre that there is a threat of increasing liability on the part of private land owners (see, for example, Conzens *et al.*, 2001). Ironically, however, it is also proposed that without regulations, and possibly without the threat of sanctions against those who do not take account of this, predominantly, state and security forces-driven agenda, planners or developers will ignore these pressures. By extension, attempts to regulate in this field may be treated as an unnecessary and costly burden. While the agenda coming from governments tend to favour an approach which sees the adoption of security-driven urban resilience as 'best practice' and something to be encouraged in a proportionate way within the planning profession, there is no doubt that when comparing the systems in operation in the UK to those in Abu Dhabi, a strong regulatory system is undoubtedly helpful in facilitating the adoption of this agenda.

More fundamentally for the planning profession, serious concerns have emerged as to whether engagement with attempts to embed safety and security features into the built environment represents the legitimisation of more general, and highly contested, generic foreign and domestic policies. Additionally, it could be questioned whether this represents an associated (further) loss of autonomy for planners and other professionals. Does the engagement of planners in this agenda normalise ever more pervasive and omnipresent security? Does it represent a further 'responsibilising' of the planning profession (see Chapter 2)? It has been argued that the 'right to the city' has been under siege prior to 9/11 – 'the false use of the threat of terrorism is only an accentuation of already existing trends' and that as a result policies dealing with urban security and urban resilience have become increasingly anticipatory and premised on a 'planning for the worst' (Coaffee, 2009, p.299; see also Marcuse, 2006).

Others charge that technological developments and design imperatives create security that is 'almost' invisible to the eye, or 'light touch' (Briggs, 2005) bringing aesthetic and access benefits, but also serious challenges: 'Who makes decisions and how they are monitored?' 'Where does power lie?', 'How will technologies be used in public and private spaces?', 'What is the balance between civil liberties and security with regard to the "war on terror"?' and 'What role will planners find themselves playing?' Others still have asserted that the lack of public input in the process and the rhetoric expressed in support of 'hypersecurity' plans raises a concern as to whether 'the prioritization of security over access to public space may be linked to a broader social–political agenda that seeks to restrict public space in general' (Benton-Short, 2007, p.445).

In a broader sense, concerns have also arisen regarding the attention that is being provided to the particular threat of terrorism, both against the context of the range of more likely and more catastrophic threats (for example widespread flooding) that face the contemporary city, but also, more practically, due to the already heavy workloads of planners. Questions must therefore be asked regarding how public perceptions may skew the real nature of risks, potentially distracting decision makers from genuine priorities and generating disproportionate responses. It is, therefore, possible that engagement with the counter-terrorism agenda may represent not just a potential co-option of the profession – a responsibilisation into the security agenda – but also a capitulation to the goals of terrorism itself (Coaffee and O'Hare, 2008).

As we have highlighted, planning and planning-related design and construction measures to enhance security are increasingly promoted as integral aspects of overall urban resilience. The aforementioned historic cases of counter terrorism in Israel and Northern Ireland highlight instances where security in public areas assumed a militaristic stance, with the planning process and professional planners playing a minor or even negligible role. Even in instances where built environment professionals had an input, this was dominated by the need to physically secure areas, with the process dominated by the military and security services. In many respects the professional planner was circumvented in the name of national security. With time, the role of professional planners has increased, to the situation today where they, and other built environment professionals, are considered to be essential partners in the development of national strategies for security, urban resilience and disaster relief and recovery tasks. Yet critical concerns and questions have arisen regarding the efficacy and appropriateness of the profession's engagement with such agendas.

In recent years the introduction of counter-terrorist concerns into broader urban resilience agendas has illuminated a number of key features of importance when planners and other built environment professionals consider mitigation of urban vulnerabilities of all kinds. Without doubt, the threat of terrorism has increased attention to and funding for urban resilience. Key features of the evolving security-driven urban resilience praxis for planners to consider therefore include:

- The importance of a proactive and front-loaded approach – design and management issues should, if possible, be dealt with at the drawing board stage of any development. This will improve effectiveness and decrease potential cost as retrofitting features is usually more expensive and is often less aesthetically appealing.

- The key role of training and skills development to raise awareness of options that are available to all those involved in the decision-making process, or that hold a stake in developments.
- The improved integration of and development of potential synergies between different policy streams, for example crime, environmental sustainability, climate change mitigation and counter terrorism, to better make the financial case for security investment.
- Appropriateness in terms of balancing risk mitigation with aesthetically pleasing and acceptable design. Acceptability here is related to the obtrusiveness and cost of proposed interventions as well as revenue concerns about management and maintenance.
- The importance of a well-organised disaster risk system to manage the urban environment and to affect design modification as appropriate according to social, political and economic criteria.
- Urban resilience through security and emergency preparedness is increasingly becoming affiliated with branding practices and utilised by governance regimes to promote and brand particular locales as safe, secure and resilient to attack, and emerging as a factor in the attraction of inward investment as security, marketing, economic development and regeneration have become necessarily intertwined (Coaffee and Rogers, 2008).

Although in this chapter we have focused upon the hardware of urban resiliency as related to countering terrorism, there should also be a growing awareness of the importance of the collective governance of risk mitigation (see Chapters 2 and 3). Resiliency solutions should involve a wide variety of stakeholders from the public, private and community sectors as demonstrated by the focus in many areas upon community and social resilience.

Given the range of threats against urban areas that have been identified, the broad scope of potential hazards, and the sheer devastation and unpredictability of their impacts, embedding urban resilience and mitigating risk is undoubtedly a huge challenge. On this note, like others we would argue that urban resilience must 'not be too prescriptive' (Bosher *et al.*, 2007; Coaffee *et al.*, 2008a). It should, rather, enable urban and regional planners and other built environment professionals to collectively make informed decisions regarding the proactive integration of security and resilience activities during the design, planning, construction, operation and maintenance of existing and future development projects.

Chapter 8

Coping with Large-scale Disasters

Recent natural disasters such as Hurricane Katrina (August 2005) and Hurricane Sandy (October 2012) in the US, the Queensland floods (December 2010) and the (Tohoku) Great East Japan earthquake (March 2011) as well as major terrorist incidents such as 9/11 and 7/7 have put increased emphasis on how quickly equilibrium is achieved following a large-scale shock. The highly integrated and global nature of social, natural and technical systems has meant that disaster risk reduction or disaster resilience has grown in prominence as a field of study and as a policy-framing device for planning. Within this area of planning for large-scale shocks, particular emphasis has been placed upon so-called 'Black Swan' events – low-probability but high-impact events. Such events defy the normal compensatory operations of risk management and insurance systems, and have dramatic, far-reaching and long-lasting effects which urban and regional planners are increasingly tasked with responding to. As Taleb (2007) argued in *The Black Swan: The Impact of the Highly Improbable,* such a focus upon these type of catastrophic events can be disproportionate in terms of effort and cost; they can also create a myopia amongst policy makers, affecting strategy development aimed at mitigating more frequent but less immediately impactful risks or slow-burn events which may have dramatic consequences when undetected (see Chapter 9).

There is a large and emergent literature on management and planning responses to cope with disaster management (Berke *et al.,* 1993; Olshansky, *et al.,* 2006), generally framed around technical, operational, social and economic (TOSE) requirements (Bruneau *et al.,* 2003) and preparedness, response, recovery and mitigation of systems to achieve equilibrium (i.e. to bounce back) (Olshansky and Chang, 2009). National policies and strategies for embedding resilience have tended to emphasise the coordination and response to 'shock' events, framed in terms of civil contingencies from this 'equilibrium' perspective and have tended to locate the community as the first line of defence to shock events and often as the principal tool for bouncing back (Edwards, 2009). However, large-scale disasters trigger very different reactions according to context; communities are often destroyed and their involvement in the rebuilding process is irreconcilable with more technical solutions designed to mitigate future loss from natural hazards.

As we highlighted in Chapter 2, Gunderson and Holling (2002) introduced the notion of panarchy in recognition of the effect of path dependency and feedback loops over time and across systems, especially relevant to socio-technical systems such as planning. Panarchy acknowledges that system cycles may not be fixed or sequential but may be nested and interact across time and space highlighting how a sudden shock event can trigger disruption across multiple network assemblages (see for example Olshansky, 2011). Such panarchic events signal a need for multi-agency and multi-scalar responses: in such instances the initial shock poses a threat to integrated systems increasing susceptibility to 'cascade failure' within and between a range of infrastructural systems. The resilience of such complex networks to cascade failure, particularly in urban settings where networks are spatially proximate, has become increasingly important given the interconnectedness and interdependences between multi-scale and multifunctional networks ranging from the Internet and electrical transmission grids to social and economic networks. Although often designed to cope with anticipated challenges through compensatory systems, spare resources or *redundancy* (see Chapter 2), such networks are susceptible to unexpected threats. The paradox of such systems makes the properties of resilience both an advantage and disadvantage and as we noted in Chapter 4: 'as complexity of that compensatory system grows, it becomes a source of fragility itself – approaching a tipping point where even a small disturbance, if it occurs in the right place, can bring the system to its knees' (Zolli and Healy, 2013, p.28). Holling (2001) further argued that a 'tipping point' is reached when nested systems are 'over connected'. In such circumstances systems are least resilient as the over connectedness and overabundance of resource is 'an accident waiting to happen' (Holling, 2001, p.394) with 'the possibility of black swans [...] engineered in' (Zolli and Healy, 2013, p.28).

In this chapter we primarily consider the 2011 Great East Japan earthquake (東日本大震災), or *triple disaster* of earthquake–tsunami–nuclear meltdown, as a panarchic Black Swan event and consider efforts at pre- and post-disaster resilience planning strategies. The 2011 earthquake is also referred to as the Fukushima earthquake because of its devastating impact on the Fukushima Daiichi nuclear power plant on the coast of Fukushima prefecture in north-east Japan. In this chapter we will refer to the 2011 events as the 'Tohoku earthquake' as the majority of the 15,891 people killed, and the many tens of thousands that were displaced, lived within Tohoku – a region to the north of Tokyo on the main island of Honshu consisting of six prefectures: Fukushima and also Akita, Aomori, Iwate, Miyagi and Yamagata. This *triple disaster* resulted in cascading technical failures of the Fukushima nuclear plant, radiation contamination and power failure across the region, creating disruption within social, economic, ecological and environmental networks and logistics systems which continues to contribute to ongoing perceptions of risk (Frommer, 2011).

The remainder of this chapter is ordered in four main sections that take a chronological (pre-, during and post-incident) approach to the Tohoku earthquake and subsequent cascading events following the massive tremor that hit Japan on Friday 11 March 2011. We draw specifically upon field visits to Japan and detailed dialogue with planners responsible for the disaster management and post-disaster reconstruction efforts to address how principles of resilience are being increasingly being adopted in urban and regional planning practice as the governance of risk in Japan becomes more precautionary.

In the first section of this chapter we set out the planning and resilience context for Japan, noting the largely technical, managerial and centralised approach to disaster management that has been adopted over many decades and across numerous spatial scales there. Second, we focus upon the immediate impact of the Tohoku earthquake and associated events, before the third section illuminates post-reconstruction plans and planning processes operationalised in the wake of it. From this analysis we draw out a set of planning lessons in the final section that can be used to enhance future resilience of disaster-prone areas and cities worldwide and illuminate attempts to enhance the whole resilience cycle, from anticipation and preparation for shocks through to recovery from them.

Anticipating shock: The planning and resilience context for Japan

As highlighted in Chapter 3, while there is a dissonance in many countries between urban and regional planning and disaster management, this is not the case in Japan. Japan is an extremely disaster-prone country subject to natural hazards of volcanoes, earthquakes and tsunamis: it contains 7% (108) of the world's active volcanoes and in the decade to 2010 experienced almost 20% (212) of total worldwide earthquakes measuring magnitude 6.0 or more (Japan Cabinet Office, 2011 p.1). Risk and planning mitigation to avoid disaster are therefore heavily ingrained in Japanese planning across spatial scales. Japan's contemporary planning and disaster management system is underpinned by practices embedded in late nineteenth-century legislation which continues to provide the jurisdiction and coordination of disaster planning management at neighbourhood, city, region and national level. This period of Japan's history, known as the Meiji Restoration, represented a concerted effort toward modernisation and industrialisation and an opening up to Western values and influences. The development of the planning system and land management regulation borrowed heavily from the West, especially the USA, UK and Germany. The threat of natural disasters and the need for Japan to compete globally meant that disaster management was writ large within the modern planning system enshrined in the Erosion Control Act of 1897 (砂防) which regulated the development of land adjacent to natural hazards such as land slippage following earthquake, flood and volcanic eruption. While this act marks the start of Japan's modern era of disaster planning, the cornerstone of Japan's contemporary resilience and disaster management planning is the 1961 Disaster Countermeasures Basic Act. This was enacted two years after the largest typhoon (Ise-wan) in modern Japan's history killed more than 5,000 people and injured almost 40,000 (Japan Water Forum, 2005, p.52). Ise-wan caused unprecedented flooding of the main island of Honshu with extensive inundation of industrialised land and built up settlements and the 1961 Act therefore underpinned large-scale flood defence investment across Japan's coastline.

While Ise-wan exposed vulnerability of Japan's industrialised seaboard, the Hanshin-Awaji earthquake of 1995 (more commonly known as the Kobe earthquake) exposed the fragility of Japan's older urban centres and infrastructure (especially low-income housing and neighbourhoods). Prior to the Tohoku earthquake, Kobe represented the largest real estate loss of any natural shock event in Japan, destroying essential infrastructure such as waste management, transport and communications to a value of ¥6 trillion (almost 3% of gross national product) (GNP). The speed of development after the Second World War had resulted in maladaptive construction methods that were driven by economic necessity rather than safety or disaster mitigation. This led to a concentration of poorly constructed wooden apartment blocks in older inner and downtown areas of industrialised cities such as Kobe. In these areas the sub-division of plots had resulted from increasing segregation and deprivation within Japanese cities and the functioning of these poorer areas for temporary and casual workers living in dilapidated and over-crowded conditions, employed in so-called 'three K' employment: Kitanai, Kiken, Kitsui (dirty, dangerous and demeaning work). The physical and social conditions of Kobe created the circumstances for a powerful set of civil society groups, such as trade unions and residents' associations, to come together and demand neighbourhood improvements, and resulted in a flourishing of *Machizukuri* (literally *town manufacture*, translated as *community development*) councils. These longstanding neighbourhood associations – stretching back to the 1960s in Kobe – mean that the city is unique in Japan in having a high degree of autonomy in some policy areas. Healey (2010, p.85) notes that at the beginning of the twenty-first century the city had more than 100 of these resident-based community groups or *Machizukuri* registered with Kobe city authority.

But despite the flourishing of community development in Kobe, the highly centralised allocation of resources and decision making did little to alter the living conditions or the highly segregated nature of Kobe's housing and neighbourhood conditions. While real estate redevelopment and the housing bubble of the 1980s had transformed large parts of Tokyo's housing stock, poor housing conditions and structural inadequacy of housing in some parts of Japan continued into the 1990s. According to 1993 census data, less than half of dwellings in areas that would be significantly affected by the 1995 Kobe earthquake (i.e., Kobe, Nara, Wakayama) had flushing toilets, whereas almost 95% of dwellings in Tokyo had such amenities at that time (Japan Statistics Bureau, 1999, p.127). The majority of the 6,500 people that perished in the Kobe earthquake lived in the 70,000 poorly constructed dwellings that were destroyed as a result of the quake. More than 90% of deaths occurred in the first quarter of an hour as a result of being crushed or suffocating to death beneath collapsed buildings (Kobe Earthquake Memorial Museum).

While some degree of autonomy of planning existed within Kobe's *Machizukuri* it was inadequately positioned to prevent the significant loss of life and housing in its poorest neighbourhoods. It did, however, have a large influence in steering resilience planning practice and the improvement of mitigation and risk reduction associated with building collapse in urban areas across Japan. Lessons learned from the Kobe earthquake, the setting up of a Hyogo disaster prevention centre in Kobe and working with the residents' groups affected led to the adoption of a cyclical approach to disaster management (*Prevention/Mitigation*, *Preparedness*, *Response* and *Rehabilitation/Reconstruction*) between 1995 and 1999 as well as five Acts of Parliament and two legislative amendments to deal with mitigation measures. These included the Earthquake Disaster Countermeasures Act (1995), Promotion of Earthquake-Proof and Retrofitting Buildings Act (1995), the Promotion of Disaster Resilience Improvement in Densely Inhabited Areas Act (1997) and the Support for Livelihood Recovery of Disaster Victims Act (1998). These interventions significantly strengthened mitigation and prevention through:

- investment in the development of improved construction methods;
- the redevelopment of transport and waste management infrastructure in metropolitan areas;
- improved neighbourhood design;
- greater emphasis on pocket parks to assist in mitigation of fire and flood; and
- increased commitment to the development of community planning (*Machizukuri*) to enhance social resilience.

Between 1945 and 2011 almost 100 additional Acts of Parliament or amendments to existing legislation in Japan aimed at either regulating land use or introducing and implementing special measures to deal with disasters and sudden shock events (Japan Cabinet Office, 2011). During the post-war period, major shock events such as the Kobe earthquake and the Ise-wan typhoon have proved pivotal in strengthening measures to prevent flooding and building collapse and developing resilience planning. The introduction of the 1997 Densely Inhabited Areas Act was perhaps the first time *resilience* had been translated within disaster planning legislation in Japan (the word *Seibi* within the Japanese name of the Act (整備) literally means 'maintenance' but is translated from the Japanese as resilience). But the Kobe earthquake also highlighted weaknesses in the resilience of communication systems and coordination of response. While policy was adopting resilience language there remained a failure of political leadership in adopting resilience principles in practice and in recognising quickly enough how the national implications of the Kobe disaster impacted beyond its local and regional manifestation.

The most significant change post-Kobe was therefore the introduction of a Minister of State for Disaster Management. This ministerial post was created to strengthen the political arm of practical mitigation, response and disaster planning relief efforts and, within the Cabinet and a Cabinet Secretariat, overall control of security and risk management. Directors of the various aspects of planning and disaster management for natural hazards such as earthquakes and volcanoes, as well as anthropogenic shocks (exemplified by the sarin attack on the Tokyo metro in 1995) thus had a direct reporting line to the Director General for Disaster Management within the Cabinet Office. The introduction of much greater political accountability in the Cabinet Office would supposedly strengthen the responsiveness and coordination of future disaster relief.

In developing its resilience planning system over more than a century, Japan has in many ways become an exemplar of 'precautionary governance'. Pre-emptive risk management activities are undertaken to map urban vulnerabilities, plan for high-impact 'shock' events and develop and enhance practical and technical expertise to aid both mitigation and recovery from disruptive challenges (De Goede and Randalls, 2009). Japan has established evacuation procedures and measures for people requiring assistance during disasters for all local authorities, with large-scale disaster reduction drills carried out in every region and prefecture annually on what has become known as Disaster Reduction Day (1 September). Despite the preparation for large earthquakes (especially preparations for Tokyo-centred quakes) the magnitude and cascading nature of the 2011 Tohoku earthquake led to a reassessment of the technical and managerial measures that formed the cornerstone of the traditional Japanese disaster management approach. As we will also see in the following sections, the Tohoku earthquake and associated effects were not only physically and psychologically devastating but also served to illuminate a set of serious 'slow-burn' challenges that Japan will need to confront over the next decades. The Tohoku earthquake has also led to a reassessment of the hierarchical nature of disaster management policy and reinvigorated a call for greater community resilience to be advanced.

The triple disaster of March 2011

The Tohoku earthquake hit at approximately 14.46 Japan Standard Time on Friday 11 March 2011. It was the largest earthquake in recorded history to hit the country and was the fourth most powerful worldwide since modern records began in the early twentieth century (Fukushima Action Research, 2013). The epicentre was located in the Pacific Ocean approximately 70 kilometres east of Sendai in the north east region of Tohoku. The earthquake triggered tsunamis of almost unprecedented height that inundated large parts of the coastline of north-east Japan and quickly enveloped strategic sites such as Sendai airport. Within minutes the earthquake triggered a chain of events that would lead to the triple disaster. According to Japan's National Police Agency, as at May 2015 15,891 people were killed as a result of the earthquake and 2,579 persons remained missing more than four years after the event (Japan Times, 2015). The vast majority of deaths (15,824) occurred in the three prefectures of Iwate (4,673), Miyagi (9,539) and Fukushima (1,612).

Following the Kobe earthquake of 1995 a system had been established to automatically distribute impact data on earthquakes and other natural disasters. As a function of the Integrated Disaster Management Information System, earthquake events are reported within ten minutes of a tremor measuring 4.0 or above and similar measures are in place for tsunamis and volcanoes. Satellite imagery and GIS systems are also distributed to survey damaged areas and made publicly available. Almost immediately following the Japan Meteorological Agency's (JMA) detection of the earthquake an estimated impact and warning of tsunami was issued. However, measures in place to provide structural resilience and disaster response following the Kobe earthquake were exposed as insufficient. The authorities had not anticipated such a large earthquake hitting the Japanese eastern seaboard and had not planned for the volume of water and degree of inundation that resulted from a tsunami that was unprecedented within Japan's contemporary history. The tsunami predictions were a lot lower than the reality subsequently experienced and contributed to the chaos and confusion that followed as a mixture of poor communication and mishandled evacuation procedures resulted in large-scale fatalities from drowning. This included 250 disaster relief volunteers that perished in the first few minutes after the tsunami hit the coastline (Hasegawa, 2012).

Information and communication systems had been strengthened up to February 2011 with a system of satellite mobile telephone communication systems backed up with terrestrial systems for local authorities. The vulnerability of Japan's coastal areas meant these were linked, via wireless communication systems, to public broadcast loudspeaker systems within neighbourhoods. Social media

was also utilised with Twitter proving useful for 'tracking the public mood of populations affected by natural disasters as well as an
early warning system' (Doan *et al.*, 2011, p.58) in the immediate
aftermath of the Tohoku earthquake. The first tweet originated in
Tokyo less than 90 seconds after the earthquake occurred (ibid.,
p.62). However, there were widespread communication and power
systems failures and many communities had to largely rely on local
knowledge and word of mouth to get information and react to the
unfolding of events. The local radio communications systems across
the Tohoku region were severely affected and subsequent research
on evacuees established that loss of power and the damage to public announcement systems and pylons resulted in little more than a
tenth of those fleeing responding to radio alerts by the local authority (Hasegawa, 2012).

The sudden shock of the earthquake also exposed underlying
vulnerabilities of cascading and interlinked systems (*panarchy*). An
example of this is how the triple disaster exposed the path dependencies and inadequacies of Japan's electrical transmission systems.
In this regard Japan is probably unique in the developed world
in having two electricity systems that are essentially independent
of one another and hence lacking vital interoperability resilience.
The Tokyo region and the area to the north and east of Tokyo has
emerged as a system that has developed on 50Hz AC generators
while the west of Japan, centred on the Osaka–Kinki region and
westwards has emerged as a 60Hz region. The 'frequency frontier'
is marked by the intersection of the Fujigawa and Itoigawa rivers in
Shizuoka and Niigata Prefectures respectively. The two 'electricity
regions' have developed separately using generators supplied by different suppliers. In the case of Osaka and the west these were originally supplied by USA whereas the generators supplied to Tokyo
in the Meiji Restoration era (late nineteenth century) originated
from a company that became AEG in Germany. This disharmony
of national frequency and the separate development of the electricity grid in Japan has never been resolved. The unfolding situation
following the earthquake was therefore compounded by the failure
of the national electricity system to work in a way that supported
the affected region by redistributing power from the west of Japan
(which was largely unaffected by the earthquake), to the east and
north of Japan which experienced blackouts and major disruptions
to power supply as a result of the failure of the Daiichi plant. This
meant that when the earthquake and tsunami resulted in power
shortages in the Tohoku and Tokyo regions after 11 March almost a

third of power was lost in east Japan and power could not be shared from the western half of the country.

In the chaos that resulted from power cuts and a failure of communications systems more than two-fifths of people affected relied on their own judgement, or that of friends and relatives, to make their way to safety (Hazegawa, 2012). Some residents died as a result of investing too much confidence in the hazard maps produced by local authorities to guide the evacuation process. These were based on estimates of the areas that would be inundated under much lower magnitude tremors than the 9.0 Tohoku quake and proved wholly inaccurate given the unprecedented scale of the earthquake and tsunami. In effect the maps created a sense of certainty in the minds of residents while directing people to evacuation points that would subsequently become inundated.

Alongside these failures in the response to the tsunami, a parallel set of pre-disaster planning failures were occurring in relation to the nuclear disaster at the Fukushima plant. Despite the fact that the reactors went into an emergency shutdown (Scram) procedure almost as soon as the earthquake hit the region, coordinated evacuation did not take place until more than 48 hours after the event took place. The National Diet Investigation Commission (The National Diet of Japan, 2012) reported that less than 20% of affected residents were aware of the accident on the first day while less than 10% were informed that they should evacuate. This state of affairs has been partly explained by the 'Myth of Absolute Safety' created by the Japanese government regulators and the operators in claiming that a severe accident in Japanese nuclear power stations would never occur. The investigation into the nuclear accident, for example, identified the failure of management of the plant and that this was a 'failure made in Japan'. Moreover, the Minister for Economy, Trade and Industry responsible for overseeing the nuclear industry in Japan acknowledged that 'there was an unreasonable overconfidence in the technology of Japan's nuclear power generation' and that the nuclear industry's 'thinking about safety had a poor foundation' (Onishi, 2011). This culture contributed to the failure of national government to react quickly and communicate radiation levels. In the absence of up-to-date information from central government or TEPCO (Tokyo Electric Power Company – the owners of the nuclear plant) municipal governments made decisions to evacuate their residents. In some cases this resulted in the evacuation of residents to areas downwind of the plume such as Fukushima City and Okuma City where exposure to radiation was higher.

The culture of absolute safety permeated advanced planning on evacuation procedures and basic training. Hasegawa (2012) reported on evidence that evacuation drills and exercises had been conducted mainly in a radius between one and three kilometres from the nuclear plant and that the scenarios envisaged were of a small-scale tsunami with no significant radiation leakage. Interviews with evacuees from villages close to the stricken plant established that only 1 in 50 evacuees from the vicinity ever participated in evacuation drills while the majority were unaware of procedures. On the day after the explosion at the No.1 Reactor Building, lunch was cooked and served outside school buildings in an area that was used as an evacuation centre for tsunami-affected residents close to the plant. It is clear that evacuees were not informed of the severity of the accident or that they would not be able to return to their homes within the subsequently declared exclusion zone. As a result many had abandoned their homes without any essential supplies such as extra clothes, money, food or legal documents (Hasegawa, 2012).

These failures in consistent communication were matched by a failure of geophysical defences. Coastal forest defence systems built in many areas of Japan, especially in the tsunami-prone Tohoku region, could not be relied upon to mitigate Black Swan events such as the Tohoku disaster and in many cases forests planted as a means of coastal defence exacerbated events. Forested areas around Kesennuma City in Miyagi Prefecture were felled by the inundation of the fast-flowing tsunami. This resulted in a deluge of timber being dragged across the landscape and acting as large battering ram that exacerbated damage to buildings and vital infrastructure (Fritz *et al.*, 2012). Two-thirds of the 230 kilometres of protective coastal forests in the region were heavily damaged by the tsunami that reached 15 metres in height in Rikuzentakata City and 'destroyed a 200-metre-wide forest before heading inland and laying waste to large sections of the city' (Cyranoski, 2012, p.142). The power of the tsunami resulted in cars, industrial equipment and shipping being swept inland and destroying everything in its path. Figure 8.1 gives an indication of the power of the tsunami and shows how a 200-foot-long, 330-tonne fishing boat was swept almost 1km from its docked position at Kesennuma port into a residential neighbourhood.

The inadequate coastal defence mechanisms and evacuation attempts in the midst of such powerful and destructive forces highlighted a range of maladaptive responses linked to the unexpected scope and scale of the disaster as it unfolded and cascaded (Ando, 2011). The earthquake hazard assessments, for example, turned out

Figure 8.1

No. 18 Kyotokumaru, Kesennuma City, Miyagi Prefecture, Japan, March 2013

to be incorrect while many residents did not receive accurate tsunami warnings. In addition to this, previous embedded knowledge of tsunamis in older residents contributed to a failure to act quickly and evacuate. Some older residents had previously experienced a delay of 10 to 15 minutes between the tremor of the earthquake and inundation from tsunamis. In the case of Tohoku however, it took up to 40 minutes for the tsunami to hit the coast after the initial shock. Some of those that had evacuated on the basis of previous experience of tsunamis returned to their homes and drowned:

> Fifty percent of local residents above 55 years old experienced the 1960 Chile tsunami, which was significantly smaller than that of 11 March. This sense of 'knowing' that 'the tsunami will be small' based on their previous experience put their lives at very high risk. (Ando, 2011, p.412)

As a result, the elderly and people with disabilities became the biggest victims of the tsunami. Hasegawa estimates that more than 60% of those that died were over 60 years old (Hasegawa, 2012).

Another maladaptive feature of the disaster was a heightened sense of complacency founded on a false assumption of safety and the presence of the existing sea-wall defences. The sea walls existing at the time of the disaster (see Figure 8.2) reached up to six metres in height in some parts of the region and gave the impression for many residents that they would protect neighbourhoods close to the sea. This sense of complacency reflected a failure to understand the mechanics and threat of tsunami, as Ando (2011, p.412) noted: '[residents] believed that with the presence of a breakwater, only slight flooding would occur and moving to the second floor at home was sufficient'. Finally, the inadequate initial response to the Tohoku earthquake and unfolding events in Fukushima can also be explained by the technocratic, managerial and hierarchical nature of disaster response management. The Prime Minister at the time, Naoto Kan, did not visit the devastated region until the beginning of April 2011, three weeks after the earthquake, somewhat symbolising the distanced, uncoordinated and technocratic reaction of the state. Criticism was subsequently levelled at the national government for reacting slowly and for not setting up a disaster relief centre within the region but conducting operations from the Cabinet Office in Tokyo.

Post-disaster reconstruction and resilience planning

The 2011 disaster exacerbated existing problems of shrinkage as a result of population ageing, low fertility rates and net outward migration that peripheral and rural regions in Japan such as Tohoku had faced over the previous two decades (Matanale and Rausch, 2011). The macro-economic causes of Japan's shrinkage – economic stagnation, deflation and concomitant fiscal difficulties in its public finances experienced since the early 1990s – were exacerbated by further immediate population loss as a result of the disaster. The population of the northern rural city of Rikuzentakata, for example, fell by almost a fifth in the year after the earthquake. Meanwhile, cities along the eastern seaboard of the Tohoku region, such as Sendai, Kesennuma and Ishinomaki, stood at a major turning point as they attempted to reconcile their planning response to rebuild after the earthquake in the midst of a projected loss of more than a quarter of the regional population between 2010 and 2040 (Sendai City Council, 2014).

Ubaura (2015) refers to a paradigm shift in urban and regional planning following the Tohoku earthquake, given the unprecedented set of pre-existing conditions of slow-burn shrinkage together with the triple disaster. After 1945, urban and regional planning in Japan took place under conditions of expansion and growth but in the wake of the disaster an 'equilibrium' approach to resilience planning in Tohoku appears infeasible and unachievable given the combination of events. The region therefore faces a challenge in reconciling short-term rebuilding with long-term repositioning of the region. For example, the Ministry of Land, Infrastructure, Transport and Tourism (MLIT) aims to foster growth of an internationally viable manufacturing corridor by improving transport corridors between the poorly connected east and west coast of northern Japan. However, there is a need to reposition the region and reinvent communities by revitalising the economy with innovative projects (e.g., renewable energy supply) rather than concentrating solely on the traditional notion of reconstruction via 'mega' construction projects that are embedded in assumptions of connectivity to the Tokyo economy and conurbation.

Residential relocation, land-use planning and resilience

The immediate task has therefore been for localities to get lives back on track and induce a sense of normalcy; this has not been a straightforward process. Given the change in the regional and national planning paradigm (Ubauru, 2015), and despite high exposure to large-scale disasters and associated risks, the absence of an overarching law for local redevelopment planning in Japan has not helped to improve coordination or speed of recovery (see Murakami and Murakami Wood, 2014, p.243). MLIT's creation of a Reconstruction Agency in 2012 resulted in a set of coordinated enquiries into the reconstruction needs of localities and the declaration of Disaster Area Relocation Zones that guide the development process and central funding. A parallel set of arrangements were initiated by the Fisheries Agency within the Ministry of Agriculture, Forestry and Fisheries (MAFF) to protect the fishing industry and coastal ports. However, MAFF and MLIT came up with two different approaches that involved, on the one hand, relocation to higher ground or, on the other, disaster prevention by extending and heightening levees or sea walls to prevent future inundation from tsunamis. The conflict between these approaches played out in post-disaster reconstruction efforts in a number of Japanese cities as we will describe.

Local authorities in cities such as Sendai, Kesennuma and Ishinomaki had disaster mitigation and planning regulations designed for relatively frequent tsunami occurrences, i.e. tsunamis that happen every decade or several times over the century. Such protection measures were of limited value in the event of 'Black Swan' events such as Tohoku earthquake where the tsunami reached run-up heights (the height above sea level) of almost 40 metres in some parts of the region and travelled up to ten kilometres inland. Protections against these very large-scale tsunamis that occur once every thousand years need to be tackled using a mix of technical–structural and social–community-based solutions. However, the planned approach in the immediate aftermath of the tsunami has been to extend sea walls for more than 200 miles along the Tohoku coastline and in places increase the height to up to almost ten metres. Figure 8.2 shows the height of the sea walls in Kesennuma (an area badly affected by the tsunami) that were in place at the time of the tsunami and Figure 8.3 shows the construction of a new wall along a stretch of the same coastline showing the height above the existing line of the sea wall. The previous sea defence is less than half the height of the newly planned wall and had been decorated and painted by local school children.

These technical solutions have divided communities and been seen by some as not serving the needs of residents, business and the

Figure 8.2

Existing sea wall defence at Kesenumma, March 2013

Figure 8.3

Implementation of extension and heightening of the sea defences in
Tohoku prefecture

environment. Many citizens were not happy that 1,214 hectares
and about 2,000 homes would be declared unsafe for habitation as
part of Sendai city's zoning plan and some have threatened to sue
(Cyranoski, 2012). Research by Shinshu University and the Japan
Society of Urban and Regional Planners into the experiences of residents resettled away from their original home having been displaced
by the tsunami found a high level of dissatisfaction with the quick-
fix approach that cities have been adopting which appears to be the
emerging response as the reconstruction efforts gather pace (Uehara
et al., 2015, p.119). A prescient reason for the construction of sea
walls and the emerging relocation strategies of local authorities
relates to memory and loss of tacit knowledge associated with such
shock events. Sendai and the broader region were devastated by tsunamis in 1896 and 1933 and while survivors moved up to the hills,
later generations returned. As noted by Fumio Yamada, the head of
Sendai's reconstruction division, 'if you just warn people, if you don't
have it in law, people will come back' (Cyranoski, 2012, p.142).

Central government therefore works on the basis that planning needs to build in long-term memory to prevent return or

complacency in the utilisation of land. As a result local authorities are caught in a double bind of planning for a future population in the context of shrinkage while working within the framework of the Disaster Area Relocation Zones designated by the Reconstruction Agency and underwritten by the 2012 Basic Act on Reconstruction (Tomita, 2014, p.243). The highly centralised and top-down approach to reconstruction managed by MLIT and MAFF continues to shape outcomes locally. However, in order to access necessary funds for reconstruction local authorities must declare inundation zones and plan mitigation measures such as sea walls to protect existing communities. Local authorities such as Sendai therefore need to enforce the construction of inundation zones and sea walls in order to access central reconstruction funds. This has had the effect of dividing older and younger communities (Tricks, 2012). But it has also pushed a 'planning for the worst case' through new laws introduced by the Reconstruction Agency in Japan on 'tsunami resilient' cities that require local authorities to develop forecasts and simulations of worst-case tsunamis (i.e. once every 300–400 years). Where a tsunami is projected to rise to four metres, newly designated relocation zones and inundation sections are declared and residential housing is not permitted. Five mitigation and land readjustment strategies have emerged as local authorities work within the parameters of the Reconstruction Agency requirements for designation of inundation zones and Disaster Area Relocation Zones as shown in Figure 8.4:

1. Relocation of residents and households to higher ground within the local authority area.
2. Aggregation of existing housing units within the existing neighbourhood and the construction or heightening of sea walls in areas affected by the tsunami.
3. Raising land adjacent to low-lying areas and the strengthening of sea defences.
4. A combination of the relocation of households and land raising.
5. Repair of essential infrastructure allowing people to remain in the area.

Figure 8.4 captures the emerging planning approach of local authorities to meet the planning requirements of the Reconstruction Agency's policy on declaration of Disaster Area Relocation Zones (see Murakami and Murakami Wood, 2014; Ubaura, 2015). Schematically, Figure 8.5 also shows the emerging plan (in profile) of tsunami-resilient cities that Japan (in this case Sendai) aims to build.

Figure 8.4

Reconstruction patterns and planning approaches in Tohoku region following the earthquake

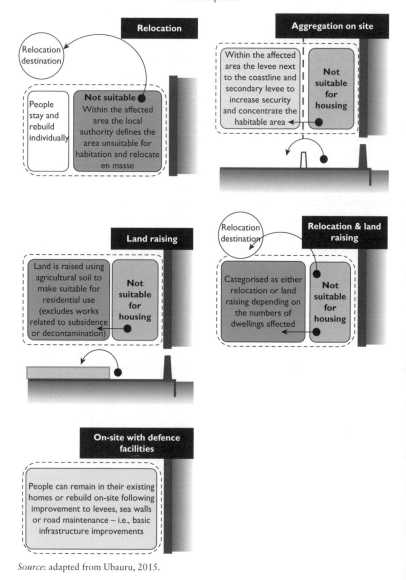

Source: adapted from Ubauru, 2015.

Figure 8.5

Plan for a tsunami-resistant/resilient city

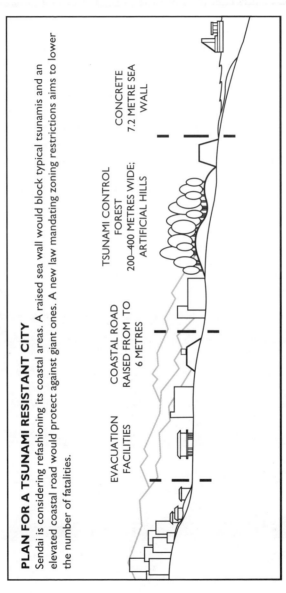

PLAN FOR A TSUNAMI RESISTANT CITY

Sendai is considering refashioning its coastal areas. A raised sea wall would block typical tsunamis and an elevated coastal road would protect against giant ones. A new law mandating zoning restrictions aims to lower the number of fatalities.

EVACUATION FACILITIES

COASTAL ROAD RAISED FROM TO 6 METRES

TSUNAMI CONTROL FOREST 200–400 METRES WIDE; ARTIFICIAL HILLS

CONCRETE 7.2 METRE SEA WALL

Source: adapted from Cyranoski, 2012.

Figure 8.6 dramatically illustrates how the implementation of various planning and land adjustment mechanisms is being developed in practice. It shows the port area of Ishinomaki City north of Sendai which has been designated as a Type 1 relocation zone requiring the clearing of the site. Satellite images taken nine months prior to the tsunami (25 June 2010) show a densely populated residential neighbourhood but it is noticeable that just over one week after the tsunami (19 March 2011) the area was almost totally cleared having been completely devastated by the impact of the flood. Residential properties located here are vulnerable to tsunamis in excess of four metres. One year after the tsunami, demolition and clearance was well under way and by April 2014 temporary facilities to support the clearance operation had been dismantled together with some of the port infrastructure that had remained largely intact despite the impact of the tsunami and earthquake. In this situation forestation was both an aid and hindrance. Despite

Figure 8.6

Ishinomaki City Port 'Disaster Area Relocation Zone'

25 June 2010   **19 March 2011**

8 February 2012   **1 April 2014**

Source: Map data ©2015 Google, ZENRIN Imagery ©2015, Cnes/Spot Image, DigitalGlobe accessed 27 May 2014.

the fact that forest defence system failed to protect communities and caused significant damage across parts of the region, adjacent industrial and residential areas in elevated positions to the west and north of the most severely impacted areas were largely unaffected and were also protected by a forested boundary. Therefore, this area is subject to forestation as the government remains committed to it as a strategy because of its potential to counteract the effects of high-frequency, lower impact events:

> [T]he Japanese government has decided to invest ¥59 billion in replanting trees in Tohoku. Proponents argue that the trees also serve other purposes, such as providing a wind break that stops sand from blowing inland. And there is evidence that the forests have slowed tsunami waves resulting from some smaller quakes. Even last year there were some examples of success. In Hachinohe, which was hit by waves higher than 6 metres, the trees stood firm and blocked more than 20 boats from being swept inland and causing further destruction. (Cyranoski, 2012, p.142)

Any remaining housing in the MLIT-declared Disaster Area Relocation Zones are subject to land readjustment measures and clearance. Figure 8.7 highlights an example of a modern and supposedly tsunami-resilient house built on 'stilts' to withstand low-level inundation. It is evident that the tsunami inundated the ground and first floor of the elevated building while sweeping away all surrounding and adjacent properties in the neighbourhood. As the house is situated within the newly declared tsunami inundation zone as part of the Disaster Area Relocation policy in Ishinomaki City, the owners would have had to relocate to an area on raised land or a readjusted urban area while receiving compensation from the local authority via the national Reconstruction Agency.

The common response to disaster and post-planning recovery has been that residents either acquire land themselves to build their home, move into temporary sheltered housing or public housing more permanently or reconstruct their home elsewhere under a comprehensive relocation plan. In many cases the design of new tsunami-proof areas could not be established until the number of homes that are to be constructed was decided. This has created a long delay and stand-off between relocation and mitigation investment and a trade-off between short-term and long-term planning outcomes. In the absence of strong compulsory purchase procedures,

Figure 8.7

Disaster resilience housing within the 'tsunami inundation' zone near Ishinomaki
City, Miyagi Prefecture and government signs declaring the area a tsunami
inundation area or Disaster Relocation Zone

private speculators were also buying land and pre-empting attempts
by central and local government to acquire land thereby undermining a coordinated response to relocation. The reuse of sites
left vacant by relocation plans have become problematic and also
contribute to shrinkage. Areas designated Disaster Area Relocation
Zones in particular have become blighted because government has
different responsibilities depending on whether the land is residential or industrial. After the Tohoku earthquake many land parcels

have become devalued and there is growing recognition that current planning methodologies need to be revised:

> Land readjustment may have been appropriate during the age of growth and expansion; however, it is doubtful whether the LRP [Land Readjustment Policy] is appropriate for shrinking, peripheral communities, where increasing land values after re-plotting cannot be assured. However, there are currently no other viable re-plotting methods. *Current urban planning methods need to be immediately reviewed and updated.* (Miyake, 2014, p.248, emphasis added)

In the following section we reflect on what changes in the culture and practice of planning are implied from the unfolding events and draw out more general implications of resilience planning for large-scale disasters.

Learning from Tohoku: Recovery, redundancy and rebuilding communities

Disaster planning and an equilibrium model of resilience is hard-wired into the planning system in Japan which has proved extremely effective in preventing innumerable loss of life in the midst of large-scale disasters. The panarchic events of the Tohoku triple disaster, however, signalled a number of systemic failures and left central and local government unprepared for the unfolding of events resulting in several thousand deaths, many of which could have been avoided had a more flexible and less centralised process of planning been adopted. As we have noted above, technical forecasting measures designed to predict and assess earthquake hazards across Japan turned out to be incorrect which resulted in many affected coastal towns receiving inaccurate tsunami warnings. Meanwhile, previous knowledge of tsunamis and a failure to understand the mechanics and threat of tsunami resulted in unnecessary deaths as communication systems failed. Some residents assumed safety because of an overreliance on highly technical solutions such as sea walls which induced a sense of complacency amongst some communities. In the absence of systematic community-based practices and evacuation drills, the systemic response was therefore highly dependent on a set of centralised technocratic, managerial and hierarchical processes. Early academic scrutiny of the urban and regional planning implications arising from the 2011 triple disaster in east Japan has speculated that these systemic failures, the resultant deaths, and continued threat from nuclear radiation could have a profound influence on altering the Japanese planning system.

To be resilient against panarchic events such as the Tohoku triple disaster requires a variety of planning and disaster management responses and interventions. A key aspect of moving towards a more evolutionary approach to urban resilience requires greater emphasis on community-based planning (Japan's *Machizukuri* system). To some extent the triple disaster has stimulated grass-roots activism and participation amongst young people especially in response to the nuclear dimension that has challenged the technocratic disaster response embedded in the planning system (Tricks, 2012). Increasingly the national government is being challenged to accommodate change and to allow communities to have more input into the longer term planning, while recognising this has been stifled in the past by an older, more conservative culture in areas that suffered from shrinkage prior to the Tohoku earthquake. Some have also begun to argue that the unfolding events following March 2011 could rebalance social relations and planning practices in Japan (Murakami and Murakami Wood, 2014, p.237).

But Japan's planning system remains obdurate as the country struggles with fiscal retrenchment and progress on planning and rebuilding the areas affected by the Tohoku earthquake has inevitably stalled, with a growing frustration amongst many communities that progress on reconstruction has been lagging (Suzuki, 2015). Highly technical, top-down reconstruction solutions aimed at equilibrium (adaptation) of existing sets of socio-spatial relations come into direct conflict with proposed schemes focused upon redefining (embedding adaptability into) the role of villages and coastal communities devastated by the flooding. More broadly, there is tension between adaptation and adaptability – between resilience approaches that aim for 'bounce back' versus approaches that challenge assumptions about energy production, consumption, land use and demographic change and aim to evolve the role of the region.

Quick technical fixes such as the building of sea walls and the declaration of disaster zones give the illusion of recovery but actually stall the remodelling of spatial–social relations by preventing 'open consideration of the social, economic and environmental sustainability of these fishing villages' (Tomita, 2014, p.244). Such top-down solutions also raise questions about the proportionality of response in dealing with future events and who benefits from reconstruction efforts. Constructing sea walls that protect communities from events that happen every thousand years may induce complacency in communities, making them think they are totally safe from natural hazards. At the same time construction of large-scale infrastructure projects such as sea walls along the Tohoku coast benefits large construction industry highlighting the nexus between the liberal government and big business which was strengthened by the disaster (Murakami and Murakami Wood, 2014, p.240).

The Tohoku quake revealed the integrated dependencies of systems and how failure in one system triggered panarchic failure. The lack of progress in developing an adequate resilience plan partly reflects a lack of a coordinated spatial and strategic recovery plan, but it also reflects path dependencies in the underlying set of cultural, social and economic relationships. In Chapter 2, for example, we noted how the risk industry and insurance underpins an equilibrist approach to resilience planning policy. Quick-fix technical interventions have been pursued following Tohoku as these were practices that allowed local authorities to access funding as part of the Basic Act on Reconstruction (2012). State-sponsored solutions tend to be less progressive and lead to a 'business as usual' approach with planning policy underpinning the preservation of underlying assumptions in social and economic behaviours. The requirement to replace like-for-like infrastructure as part of reconstruction and renewal efforts under Japanese legislation following a disaster puts enormous onus on local authorities to deliver outcomes that favour an equilibrium approach to resilience: bouncing back to a steady state of what existed prior to the disaster. Moreover, such cyclical maladaptation is designed into the regulatory systems of the planning process through such legal requirements. As Tomita (2014, p.244) starkly illustrated:

> The reconstruction of ruined low-lying areas generates another concern about the concentration of large-scale facilities. Japanese law, from 1951, states that damaged or ruined public facilities have to be rebuilt as before. All port facilities, therefore, will be restored as they were prior to the tsunami, despite some fishing villages now being extinct or effectively amalgamated with other villages when they moved to new, shared hillside locations.

These cultural traits and embedded tendencies towards equilibrium may explain the 'deadlock in bottom-up community development approaches' (Murakami and Murakami Wood, 2014, p.239) resulting in some arguing for the reshaping of governance processes in shrinking regions to bolster social capital (Dimmer, 2012, 2014). But the triple disaster also revealed a set of underlying relationships to nuclear energy that influence governance relationships. For example, a tendency towards insularity and 'reluctance to question authority' may explain why the momentum appears to have stalled despite increased emphasis on community planning after the Kobe 1995 earthquake. Equilibrium approaches to resilience, emblematic of a disaster-based tradition for planning, reflect cultural traits that maintain rigidity and certainty but may not be susceptible to flexibility and adaptation that could incorporate new sets of social and economic relationships. A traditional Japanese proverb, deru kugi wa utareru (出る釘は打たれる), translates as 'the nail that sticks up will be hammered down' and may be a cultural barrier to evolutionary adaptability, diversity and change within governance and civil society. While the value of planning is recognised, its values and cultural traits may make transition to an evolutionary model of resilience more demanding and reflect a lack of novelty and diversity in the planning process. This lack of redundancy and diversity to affect change in planning cultures provides another interlocking set of barriers to transition. The failure to diversify energy production away from nuclear (infrastructure), the lack of interoperability between the two electricity systems, the system of planning that determines what was destroyed must be replaced (equilibrium) and an ageing population within population-shrinking regions in Japan (lack of diversity) points towards a moribund set of contextual influences on the planning system. Meanwhile, Japan continues to experience deflation and shrinkage, a tendency towards a political constituency that is conservative and embedded in a set of political networks, and corporate path dependencies appear to prevail in the medium term. This includes a cultural mindset that had consequences for how Japan responded to the triple disaster:

> What must be admitted – very painfully – is that this was a disaster 'Made in Japan'. Its fundamental causes are to be found in the ingrained conventions of Japanese culture: our reflexive obedience; our reluctance to question authority; our devotion to 'sticking with the program'; our groupism; and our insularity. (The National Diet of Japan, 2012, p.9)

Urban resilience has been viewed by some in the West as an opportunity to innovate and adapt when confronted by a shock event. However, for Japan to evolve a new set of planning trajectories for the Tohoku region will require innovation in the production of energy, and the relationship between citizens and production of energy in shrinking regions to diversify and create more resilient energy futures for them. The triple disaster revealed underlying path dependencies on energy and the fragility of nuclear safety in the midst of such shocks. Altering the 'energy' trajectory of shrinking regions such as Tohoku is crucial to developing alternative pathways of development and interrupting the memory of the shock. Large infrastructure projects in Japan such as energy and transport are decided at a federal or national level. There is minimal input from community groups or consultation with those most affected by the siting of these infrastructures; an inextricable set of relationships that need to alter post-Tohoku and Fukushima.

It is noticeable that the National Diet of Japan identifies the problem of the triple disaster as endogenously located: the explanations of the cause of the shock are blamed on a management culture. This is important as it ringfences the problem and ensures that the technologies of nuclear, for example, are not brought into question. Therefore, despite the initial decision of the Japanese government to mothball nuclear and widespread political backlash against nuclear decisions to restart nuclear facilities (despite a court injunction against the reopening of the Takahama plant north of Kyoto in April 2015), the decision, in April 2014, to allow some residents to return to the Fukushima plant exclusion zone reflected a strong impulse in central government to maintain equilibrium and the nuclear energy policy nexus. Globally the number of nuclear plants increased from 547 to 558 in the 12 months after the disaster (Holloway, 2012) and there are strong political and economic impulses that serve to maintain domestic production. Not least of these is Japan's reliance on importing fossil fuels from countries such as China (which weakens its role in the region) and its determination to sell its nuclear technologies to emerging nations consuming nuclear energy such as Vietnam and Indonesia in order to bolster its influence in the region.

These underlying fundamental relationships play a significant role in maintaining the status quo and resisting key changes to urban and regional planning mechanisms that could alter sociospatial relationships. These have proved difficult to resist because of in-built path dependencies and an approach to planning which has deep-rooted equilibrium impulses as a result of longstanding policies on disaster management. The shadow of Fukushima therefore remains over the region, making the problems that the region faces almost 'beyond planning'.

From a strategic and longer-term perspective on planning what Japan tells us is that the traditions and values of disaster preparedness and planning are ingrained into civic society, cultural practices and building and construction. Such persistent urban resilience can be symbolised by Tokyo's Sky Tree, opened in May 2012 and at the time of construction the world's second tallest structure at 634 metres. It stands at the heart of a seismic zone – a daring feat of engineering vividly symbolising the Japanese approach to disaster management embedded within systems of urban and regional planning. The Tohoku earthquake struck during its construction and the tower withstood damage from the fourth most powerful earthquake in recorded history thanks to its earthquake-resistant innovative structure comprising a central concrete pillar connected to external steel elements through a system of shock dampers (Euronews, 2015).

But while Sky Tree and the announcement of the Tokyo Olympic Games to be held in the summer of 2020 represent symbolic moments of resilience for Japan, the future resilience of communities affected by the triple disaster seems less assured. Several lessons can, however, be drawn from the triple disaster relevant to wider issues of planning and resilience. The earthquake and tsunami demonstrated the *invisibility* of risks while revealing underlying fractures which continue to compound restructuring and planning efforts. These risks were in the embedded assumptions about the safety of nuclear and an exposed energy supply network that was not interoperable. Planning for energy requires diversity and interoperability to enable micro-generation and transference of energy across scales; the earthquake revealed these rigidities and lack of redundancy within planning policy for energy diversity in Japan. The sudden shock also demonstrated how the set of assumptions and practices to deal with a disaster could not incorporate a real-time situation on the ground into hazard plans. Responses to shock events need to build in some redundant capacity to adapt to circumstances as they unfold or evolve. The transition to evolutionary resilience appears to be much harder in Japan because of the traditions of disaster reduction and a highly homogenous society. This has created the conditions for an equilibrist framing of resilience efforts within planning. In more diverse and less disaster-prone countries the transition to evolutionary resilience is likely to be more progressive. These are issues that we return to in Chapter 10.

Chapter 9

Preparing for 'Slow-burn' Shock Events

While much work has been undertaken to assess the degree of resiliency following disasters and sudden shocks, the concept of resilience remains under-specified for 'slow-burn' events and non-specific threats (Pendall *et al.*, 2010). Martin and Sunley (2015) argue that slow-burn events are not relevant to the theoretical and analytical development of resilience studies within regional economics, arguing that it is the *sudden* shock event that reveals the resilience of the system and its ability to adapt. However, for urban and regional planning systems, they ask: 'resilience of what, to what, by what means, and with what outcome?' (p.12). Their assertion raises important questions for how the urban and regional planning community responds to long-run events that occur across temporal and spatial scales, for understanding urban futures through foresight techniques, and for the study of urban resilience more generally. The problem attenuating for spatial systems is therefore in the precise spatial and temporal *location* of the long-run or slow-burn event: *when did the event begin* and *what territory is affected?* Events such as the recent 'credit crunch' and global economic recession, and the impact of austerity measures that have resulted from the credit crisis as well as long-term events such as population loss, urban shrinkage, low housing demand and neighbourhood abandonment illuminate the problem of measuring resilience of *what*, by *what means* and with *what outcome* across time and space.

In this chapter we illustrate the relevance of an evolutionary and anticipatory approach to resilience through the role of agency and the importance of understanding the cumulative decision making that contributes to slow-burn stresses within urban and regional planning systems that are illuminated by shock events as well as serving to exacerbate their impacts. We relate this to ideas of 'hysteresis', as used by economists, to illuminate the permanent impact of shock events on the natural thresholds of systems. Such accounts

219

argue that the memory of the disturbance lingers in the systems after the shock has subsided (often termed 'remanence'), through, for example, the altered behaviour of decision makers (Romer, 2001; Cross et al, 2010; see also Chapter 2). Such shock-induced behavioural change can notably have the effect of changing the trajectory of an economic system. As Martin (2012, p.8) notes, 'there is, then, a close relationship between the idea of "ecological" resilience – specifically in the case where a shock is such that it displaces a system beyond its "elasticity threshold" – and the notions of hysteresis and remanence.' However, both ecological resilience and hysteresis, although attractive propositions, are essentially equilibrist readings of how systems change in response to shock, and fail to sufficiently account for the impact of the complexity added by social, political and agent-based behaviours and for the cumulative impact of more persistent underlying slow-burn stresses.

In this context, our focus in this chapter is on regional housing which provides an illustrative example of the capacity of regional systems to adapt: a lens through which to consider the evolutionary versus equilibrium (Chapter 2) and adaptive versus maladaptive (Chapter 4), features of slow-burn events that operate across temporal and spatial scales. This chapter in particular highlights that slow-burn events *are* highly relevant for urban resilience practice and that the purpose of an evolutionary *process*-driven account of resilience is the ability to avoid 'tipping points' and to adopt appropriate anticipatory policies. Our analysis here draws from a range of research carried out by the authors for local and regional authorities in England from the late 1990s looking at the internal consistency of sub-regional approaches to national guidance on strategic housing market assessments and issues of regenerating low-demand housing. The later research contributed to the shaping of the decisions on investment in Housing Market Renewal – a national programme of interventions in housing markets in the north and Midlands of England that ran between 2003 and 2010 – as well as evaluation of the implementation of the programme locally and regionally.

In the remainder of this chapter we first consider the 'sudden shock' event of the 2008 global economic crisis from an evolutionary economics viewpoint. Here we highlight how traditional equilibrist resilient approaches to such events fail to provide adequate causal antecedents, and illuminate how we can better analyse slow-burn events through viewing them as complex, interconnected socio-spatial systems operating at multiple scales and timeframes and with many feedback loops – what we described as a *panarchy* in

Chapter 2. Second, we then apply this panarchy reading to an analysis of historic and contemporary housing markets at the regional scale, exemplified by a detailed consideration of the problem of low-demand housing in Liverpool, England. Third, in analysing housing markets we focus upon the specific role of *agency* within evolutionary resilience interpretations of slow-burn events whereby the obdurate and often locked-in behaviours of agents within the epistemic planning community serve to steer the market in path-dependent ways illuminating the difficulties of changing traditional ways of working. Here we highlight how specific agents and their behaviour in a relatively closed policy (epistemic) community influenced the form and effect of strategic regional housing policy through the selection of certain prescribed measures of assessment. Fourth, we conclude the chapter by arguing that, in hindsight, UK regional housing strategy lacked appropriate 'resilience' mechanisms to anticipate change as it occurred locally, and alternative pathways of action (i.e. redundancy and diversity in the policy-making process) as mechanisms to enable policy to react. This reading illuminates the need for a more evolutionary perspective on regional scale resilience that incorporates flexibility, redundancy and diversity; one that utilises resilience not just as the ability of a region to accommodate shock events, but extends it to the long-term ability of regions to develop new pathways to growth and adaptation. This we argue is best achieved through more loosely coupled networks and structures that are not locked into previous pathways of action.

Slow-burn events and self-restoring equilibrium dynamics

A significant turn in the development of the resilience narrative within urban and regional planning coincided with a period of economic recession following the 2008 global credit crisis. The credit crisis is illustrative of the problem of classifying system shocks and whether an equilibrium or evolutionary response is appropriate. The aftermath of the financial crisis is still being played out (as at October 2015) and it is clearly not desirable to return to the pre-shock state. While the credit crunch was a systemic shock (defined arguably by the fall of Lehman Brothers on 15 September 2008) it cannot be classified in the same way that a system shock such as a flood or earthquake (or for that matter a terrorist attack) is defined given that slow-burn stresses occur as a result of the accumulation of prior modifications to a range of interlinked systems. Long-run or 'slow-burn' events such as deindustrialisation and urban shrinkage (Pendall *et al.*, 2010) are an assemblage of different events and involve longer term processes of structural change within systems. The sudden shock of the credit crunch resulted in almost immediate widespread recession with longer term implications for social, political and cultural systems. More specifically it heralded a period of stalled investment and a reduction in employment in construction and the planning profession.

The foreclosure of debts in sub-prime markets in the US cascaded across systems and had multiple impacts across spatial scales. The endemic hysteresis within the shock makes the credit crunch both a system shock and slow-burn event – its origins lay in the deregulation of banks, extension of credit to very low-income groups with poor credit ratings, models of urban development dependent on property-led regeneration and global equity and, inevitably, the rise of the buy-to-let industry as a mechanism to distribute investment risk and maximise off-plan housing sales and profits. However, while we consider the interaction of slow-burn events and shocks as central to developing resilience practice in urban and regional planning and illuminating different spatial impacts, Martin and Sunley (2015, p.16) have argued that the explanatory potential of resilience for regional economics and planning is not in the analysis of slow-burn events but in how adaptive regional systems are to sudden shock events:

> [T]he idea of resilience should be distinguished from that of long-run adaptive growth, and is best confined to the study of shocks, including any 'reactive adaptation' that such shocks may initiate. Otherwise, there is the risk that the concept of resilience takes on a plethora of meanings and interpretations and loses its analytical purchase.

This appears a reasonable position to take given that capitalism and regional economies are driven by 'creative destruction' wrought by capitalism's pursuit of change to maximise surplus value (Schumpeter, 1976). However, understanding slow-burn events across urban and regional systems illustrates adaptive capacity and the ability of regional systems to adapt to, or absorb, economic change. This is pivotal to our conceptualisation of how resilience is an evolutionary process and how places 'bounce forward'. The concept of 'self-restoring equilibrium dynamics' (Martin and Sunley, 2015, p.4) embedded within mainstream economics has arguably influenced the adoption of a normative engineering equilibrium-based model of resilience thinking within regional urban economics and regional planning. This equilibrium approach has meant that economic resilience is viewed as the process of embedding disaster mitigation philosophies into the everyday practice of governance and ensuring the ability of regional economies to continue to maintain capacity and play their role in global economic networks. The self-restoring equilibrium dynamics implicit within engineering approaches to resilience is transferable to the analysis of system performance maintenance across global logistical supply chains; perturbation in a regional economy may trigger malfunction across entire global systems resulting from the failure of utilities, transport, or energy in the event and its impact on business continuity (Rose, 2007, p.385). This highlights the importance of understanding the absorptive capacity of regional economic systems and how such systems maintain function when shocked (ibid., p.384).

In socio-technical (Smith *et al.*, 2005) systems such as urban and regional planning it is, however, never clear what the system boundaries are. Christina Beatty, Steve Fothergill and Paul Lawless's research on mining closure and regional labour markets (Beatty and Fothergill, 1996, 1998; and Beatty, Fothergill and Lawless, 1997) demonstrated that large plant or mining closures, as shock events occurring at a single point in time, are preceded and followed by methods of *absorption, displacement* and *reclassifying* of the unemployed across scales. Households, companies, local authorities and national government all play a part in these adaptive strategies. This occurs in such a way that the precise impact of the scale, location and duration of the shock is hidden. For urban and regional planning, the shock does not present a dichotomy between pre- and post-shock states as it is difficult to pinpoint a clear delineation of responses that occur after a shock at a single point in time. Slow-burn events may be concealed for long periods of time, indicating the ability of parts of the system to absorb shocks, accommodate change and continue while system resources are reorganised; the ability to 'reorganize while undergoing change so as to still retain essentially the same function, structure, identity and feedbacks' (Walker *et al.*, 2004, p.2) may be a function of a resilient system. However, it may also hide dysfunctional practices and systemic failure (maladaptation) that goes undetected for long periods. At some point the system may be unable to absorb the shock and a new equilibrium, which may be less favourable than the pre-shock state, may emerge. This is characteristic of housing markets in which fixed assets and sunk costs lag behind the *creative destruction* of economics and the free market's messy ways of attempting to deliver progress.

We noted in Chapter 2 the increasingly contested nature of resilience thinking and practices and the nature of constantly changing non-equilibrium systems that has led a number of researchers to argue for a more *evolutionary* approach to be adopted. Critiques of equilibrium models of socio-ecological systems (SES) and the adaptive cycle led to modification of the approach by Gunderson and Holling (2002) to account for the unpredictable nature of change and interactions between systems. Unpredictability is especially relevant to socio-technical systems such as urban and regional planning, where the adaptive cycle is affected by rigidities and path dependency of planning decisions interacting with micro- and macro-level factors. Together these influence housing and economic behaviour over spatial and temporal scales.

Gunderson and Holling (2002) introduced the notion of *panarchy* in recognition of the effect of path dependency and feedback loops over time and across systems. Processes of urban change do not occur in a fixed, sequential pattern; systems interact and may be nested. Panarchy is a heuristic device – an artificial construct which attempts to account for limitations in an equilibrist single cycle approach to understanding urban complexity (Holling, 2001, p.394) and has become a key conceptual framework accounting for urban and regional economic resilience and adaptation (Simmie and Martin, 2010).

At each stage in the cycle and within each nested system, there is the opportunity for experimentation and reorganisation that is influenced by both 'bottom-up' and 'top-down' processes. The failure to experiment and create the conditions for reorganisation and dynamism within this set of asynchronous and dynamic processes may be due to a region being locked in positively (due to cumulative advantage/agglomeration) or held back through a lack of *physical*, *institutional* or *productive* capital or what Simmie and Martin (2010, p.16) refer to as 'institutional hysteresis and unchanging cultures'. This institutional hysteresis creates feedback loops that result in negative symbolic capital or *remanence*: 'the effect of the shock is permanent, not transitory – there is "memory" of the shock ("remanence")' (Martin and Sunley, 2015, p.5), resulting in feedback loops that both influence and effect interlocking systems.

Advances in evolutionary economics and urban planning have modified aspects of the panarchy model to develop the explanatory potential of resilience beyond bounce-back approaches (Folke *et al.*, 2010, p.25). Evolutionary resilience demands anticipatory systems to manage continuous change, and to avoid major system perturbation and advance the adaptability of governance responses in enhancing the resilience of regional systems. As we have seen in Chapter 2, Davoudi (2012, p.304) highlighted how 'evolutionary resilience promotes the understanding of places not as units of analysis or neutral containers, but as complex, interconnected sociospatial systems with extensive and unpredictable feedback processes which operate at multiple scales and timeframes'.

Panarchy and regional housing markets

For urban and regional systems in the UK one of the most challenging system failures of the past 25 years has been the problems engendered by low demand and abandonment of housing and neighbourhoods in parts of the north and midlands of England. The emergence of 'low demand' as a housing policy concern was first signalled by the detection of various processes that challenged conventional housing management wisdom. Housing policy in the UK up to the late 1980s arose out of the council house building programme of the post-war era and was highly municipal in nature. Consequently the strategic housing role of local authorities did not extend much beyond the management of council housing until the development of strategic partnerships between local authorities and social landlords emerged from the early 1990s as a result of the 'privatisation' of council housing following the Right to Buy (RTB), changes in the subsidy of new affordable housing and large-scale stock transfer. Many local authorities affected by low demand became aware of the growing problem across the social housing sector and estates subject to RTB from the mid-1990s onwards. But by the late 1990s it became apparent that housing problems in post-industrial northern cities could not be tackled on an ad hoc single-tenure basis, but required a strategic approach (Murie *et al.*, 1998). The problems were quite different from the micro-management concerns of dealing with 'difficult to let' social housing stock (Power, 1997; Power and Mumford, 1999). That low-demand conditions appeared pervasive throughout areas of private sector housing as well as social housing estates (DETR, 2000a) indicated that a more strategic and market-focused approach to understanding the problem was necessary (DETR, 2000b). A wide-ranging research programme and evidence base on low-demand and empty homes was assembled between 1998 and 2003 (Murie *et al.*, 1998; Lee *et al.*, 2001; Nevin *et al.*, 2001), indicating a wide-scale problem of changing demand for different parts of the market and abandonment of some areas of inner cities arising from a mixture of macro- and micro-level factors. It was not until the late 1990s, therefore, that the problem became systematically evidenced in academic and policy reports. This was followed by central government policies supporting urban regeneration and changes in planning policy to stimulate so-called urban renaissance. As part of a broader package of measures to deliver sustainable communities, UK government invested in a £2 billion programme of housing market renewal and strengthened guidance on foresight and monitoring of housing markets across scales (local, sub-regional, regional etc.) to deliver this agenda. In the next section we explore some of the key aspects of what emerged as a panarchic model of housing demand in Liverpool in north-west England and in the subsequent section reflect on the role of agency in developing evolutionary urban resilience responses to such slow-burn shock events characterised by such low and changing demand for housing.

Changing demand in Liverpool

To illustrate these issues we consider the case of the city of Liverpool in north-west England. Between 1950 and 2000 the population of Liverpool shrank by almost half and in some inner city neighbourhoods more than 30% of the housing stock was empty (Lee and Nevin, 2003) (Figure 9.1). From 1945 onwards, incremental changes in welfare policy, the expansion of state-subsidised housing, assumptions about the Keynesian welfare state and full employment were followed by 1970s restructuring after the oil crisis and IMF intervention and subsequently by changes in urban management and the rise of urban entrepreneurialism in the 1980s and 1990s. As a result of these incremental changes in macro and micro context for Liverpool, its population reduced from 875,000 to 475,000 between 1945 and 2000 (Lee and Nevin, 2003). What became apparent was that while housing and planning officials 'on the ground' in Liverpool were aware of the problems of low demand and abandonment in their 'patch' from the early 1990s, the political will and resources to address the problem were absent.

Figure 9.1

Boarded up shops and housing in Granby, Liverpool L8, April 1999

The abandonment of some large swathes of housing can be explained by a series of cascading events (panarchy). Processes of decentralisation of population arose because of planning assumptions taken from the perspective of Keynesian economic and welfare policies, underpinned by assumptions of full (male) employment and high birth rates that over-estimated population projections and household formation rates. The creation of New Towns within the sub-region (Merseyside) (i.e. Runcorn, Skelmersdale and the Wirral) and new housing opportunities encouraged the migration out of the city. By the early 2000s a steep gradient related to income and housing location existed – for example out of a sample of 22,000 public sector workers in the city, almost 40% of administrative and clerical staff and almost 65% of professional and highly qualified medical staff lived outside the city (Nevin *et al.*, 2001).

The economic housing trajectory of Liverpool arose partly from geographical and morphological path dependency and the importance of the River Mersey in the development of the city's economy. Traditionally, low-income housing was located in either terraced streets or in new estates such as St. Andrews Garden, inspired by modernist European architecture in the 1920s and 1930s – and seen as a revolutionary approach to working-class housing based on the horseshoe design of the Hufeisensiedlung (Horseshoe Estate by German architects Bruno Taut and Martin Wagner). Neighbourhoods were developed close to the docks and the city centre. As automation, containerisation and deindustrialisation swept through the city in the 1960s and 1970s, the jobs in these traditional locations disappeared, resulting in household, market and state-led responses. For example, different strategies to cope with the deskilling of the workforce and high unemployment were adopted by households so that their behaviour concealed the underlying structural problems in housing supply and consumption. This did not necessarily result in migration out of the city but often involved the use of occupational pensions and redundancy payments to invest in housing. At the same time there was a failure of the city to diversify its economic base, which would have repercussions for changing demand for housing in future waves of economic development (Harding *et al.*, 2004).

This is to simplify a set of processes in a highly chronological fashion and throughout this period cultural changes, underpinned by social welfare restructuring, interacted with local changes in the economy and housing supply. The expansion of higher education created a generation that was able for the first time to access a university education with state-subsidised student grants. Students were also able to access more affordable and regulated housing in the private rented sector with the provision of Fair Rents rather than 'market' rents and 'secure' rather than shorthold tenancies. The grant and subsidy system for this new generation in higher education increased both social and residential mobility and expanded opportunities to leave the city. The failure to diversify the economy or modernise parts of the housing stock and neighbourhoods meant many did not have a reason or desire to return and this contributed to a skills shortage. While the city expanded its university provision which provided some inward migration and graduates remaining in the sub-region, the expansion of higher education resulted in further concealment of underlying structural problems in the wider housing market. This occurred through processes of 'studentification' as part of the traditional housing stock built close to the city core and designed to house low-income workers was given over to student housing (Groves *et al.*, 2003).

But the process of displacing working-class housing was incremental and fragmented, with the 'studentification' process initially market-led. This was mainly through the actions of private sector landlords who took advantage of abandoned inner city private sector properties at auction or advertised in the local press and commodified ex-council housing that had entered the market following the RTB. This process of commodification partly revitalised some stock (in the autumn of 1999 an advertisement in the *Liverpool Echo* for five properties on the same street had an asking price of £7,500 for the lot) that had been subject to processes of residualisation (Forrest and Murie, 1988; Lee and Murie, 1999). Subsequently the process of 'studentification' was steered by the universities themselves through delivery of bespoke student housing by local universities and the private sector, which ironically further weakened fragile markets by reducing demand for such 'studentified' inner city properties.

Initially, the actions of private sector landlords in housing students concealed underlying problems. However, a parallel set of acquisitions of previously private sector stock was made by a number of housing associations or Registered Social Landlords (RSLs) operating across the city. For example, in Granby (an area of 18,000 households) more than a dozen RSLs were responsible for 60% of the housing stock (Lee and Nevin, 2003). Public policy governance arrangements were consequently highly fragmented and there was a general failure to integrate social housing with other tenures into an overall strategy. Consequently, RSLs operating in the inner city had adopted different investment strategies with some acquiring more properties and some disinvesting.

But this also resulted in a highly volatile mix of competition for a declining number of rental property clients as there was an increasing oversupply of housing at the lower, entry-level, end of the market. High rates of unemployment and structural problems with the economy endured by the city from the 1970s onwards resulted in political instability from the early 1980s. Fractures in the local Labour Party were embodied in the influence of the 'militant tendency', reflecting a fundamental schism between local politics and national economic policy under Thatcherism. The Deputy Leader of the city council, Derek Hatton, pursued, as putative leader of the council, a 'deficit budget' policy using loans from abroad to invest in additional social housing provision (so-called 'Hatton' housing). This compounded the problem of oversupply of low-income housing and created further instability in the market, especially given the need for housing diversification, the movement towards demand or 'aspiration'-led housing polices from the mid-1970s and changes in urban governance from the 1980s (Harvey, 1989). The housing market, characterised by a volatile mix of population loss, declining demand from low-income households and oversupply was further destabilised by changes in housing subsidy and a move away from bricks and mortar subsidy to portable housing benefits in 1982. This had the impact of allowing rapid changes in occupancy of inner city areas and increased the volatility of churn and turnover in neighbourhoods.

The overall impact of each of these factors was to create and sustain a vicious cycle of decline, cumulatively disadvantaging existing residents and locking them into processes of social exclusion. High levels of social polarisation and economic segregation in inner city areas at the time gave rise to social conflict and in inner city Liverpool in 1981 and 1985 (and in other cities and towns across the UK during this period) resulted in a series of major social conflicts and riots. For many years the riots in Toxteth (and Brixton in London and Handsworth in Birmingham) became synonymous with inner city decline and all that was 'wrong' with British cities. The memory of the shock (riots) endured to create a *remanence* (Martin and Sunley, 2015) that had its own feedback into future waves of housing demand. Thus, despite the fact that the main causes were often external to those events this *remanence* located the action far from its causes (see Chapter 2 where we referred to the central criticism of resilience being in its endogenous location of causation). In carrying out our research in the late 1990s and 2000s we found that the deeds of ownership of a large proportion (in excess of 20%) of empty housing in inner city Liverpool were held by solicitors and recorded on the Council Tax register as 'executors of will' – where the last remaining occupant was deceased and the property was held intestate, the payee was recorded as such. Vacant housing resulting

Figure 9.2

Panarchy in regional housing markets: Low demand within cascading
regional and national housing systems

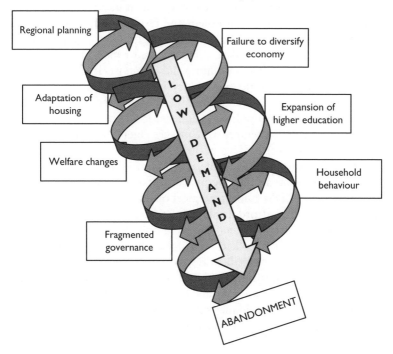

from the death of a sole surviving household member signalled
the end of a set of processes of abandonment that had its roots in
a myriad set of interlocking processes and systems. Figure 9.2 is
illustrative of a set of processes that interacted over time and space
resulting in the low demand and abandonment in housing markets
in England that surfaced in the 1990s.

Evolutionary resilience in slow-burn events and the role of agents

Local authorities needed to move beyond a 'housing condition' or
traditional 'housing management' approach to tackle these problems. In the early 2000s it was recognised that a wider perspective
on structural processes, including how land-use planning interacts

with regional economies and labour markets in giving rise to low demand conditions, was required (Murie *et al.*, 1998; DETR, 2000a, 2000b). The response of urban and regional planning policy to problems of low demand and abandonment became increasingly direct in its framing of the problem and response during the period 1997 to 2010. A range of evidence was assembled that increasingly recognised the uneven and rescaled nature of markets and that a 'natural' state of resilient equilibria did not exist. In these circumstances the role of agents and policy instruments to intervene in market conditions was seen as highly necessary and emblematic of a Third Way in British politics (Giddens, 1997), writ large in planning practice where attempts were made to blend neoliberalism and social welfare concerns. This period culminated in highly detailed guidance relating to the completion of regional spatial strategies (RSS) and associated planning instruments such as regional housing strategies (RHS) and strategic housing market assessments (SHMAs) as well as affordable housing targets for regions produced by the now defunct National Housing and Planning Advice Unit (NHPAU). While not explicitly stating so, these arrangements were aimed at creating more resilient regional housing markets following a period of highly dysfunctional and volatile market conditions. In the following section we consider some of the evidence assembled as part of centralised guidance on tackling low demand and understanding regional housing trajectories.

Implementing regional housing strategy to deal with slow-burn shocks

As noted above, planning policy during this time was highly directive in nature and the data, analysis and interpretation of housing circumstances and trajectories for sub-regions drew on a range of evidence such as statutory local authority returns as well as census, employment and HM Land Registry data. As the assessments took place during a period when house prices reached their peak there was a heavy emphasis on the analysis of house prices and affordability. This was reflected in extensive description of house price trends at local authority and sub-district level and development of proxy affordability measures comparing house prices to average earnings.

Because of the fixation on house price affordability, analysis of some aspects of market conditions was often omitted or not dealt with in great depth. Stock condition, fitness and obsolescence played a major role in the dynamics of low demand and housing market trajectories (Ferrari and Lee, 2010). However, in much of the evidence these factors were not considered in any detail and housing needs were interpreted as housing 'aspirations' and 'growth' leading to greater emphasis on the term housing 'opportunities'. This reflected the fact that the evidence was assembled during a period when the policy drivers affecting supply and competitiveness were aligning and housing was being articulated most clearly through the 'lens' of economic performance. In the absence of integrated analysis of housing needs (nationally, numerous separate housing needs studies had been undertaken using different methodologies by different survey contractors), housing requirements tended to be extrapolated from economic trends that had prevailed in the period leading up to the SHMA (i.e. the period of economic growth prior to the credit crunch). When a linkage was made between the economy and the wider housing market this was seen as unequivocally positive and the impact 'linear'. For example, forecast trend data showing improvement in economic prosperity was translated on to housing demand and summarised in one SHMA as resulting in: '*an acceleration of existing trends in the pattern of housing demand, a continuing shift to owner occupation [...] demand for more space, [and] ability to pursue aspirations*'. Meanwhile the forecast strength in the overall economy was extrapolated as evidence of a potentially significant increase in the income distribution with major implications for the housing market. On closer inspection, the projected rise in incomes represented an average increase of less than 1.9% per annum – significantly below the rate of house price inflation at the time of the assessment. Underlying these examples was a problem of making incorrect claims about small group behaviour based on an analysis of large group data (ecological fallacy) and the failure across regions to differentiate the impact of the economy on *people* and *places* i.e. across different households and neighbourhoods.

The initial premise of SHMA research and intelligence affected the way in which housing, regeneration and broader planning policy was configured regionally and locally. In the case of migration, for example, its importance for the economy was asserted without challenge and led to the conclusion, in more than one SHMA, that economic performance could only be maintained by increasing supply and encouraging migration in order to expand the economically active population. However, the case study region contained a large unskilled population that was significantly above the national average. Raising skills levels and economic activity rates could have simultaneously reduced inward migration while putting downward pressure on demand for new build to attract migrants. Factoring in the potential impact of employment and training policies could have therefore influenced decisions on future levels and types of house building.

The overall effect of the under-specification of detail resulted in a narrative emphasising the need to drive for greater private sector housing supply in order to put downward pressure on house prices and for housing growth irrespective of current conditions of existing stock or the economic circumstances of existing residents. One sub-regional assessment concluded that there was *no current demand for social housing* and that private sector housing should be encouraged to attract inward migration to bolster economic performance. This narrative of growth reflected some deep-seated vested interests in particular policy options and outcomes at the regional level. The SHMAs were undertaken by four different private sector consultancies specialising in property and economic development that included a global real estate advisor; all, to varying degrees, had an interest in growth and the legitimation of a particular development path. Underpinning this was the fact that central government guidance on SHMAs was also developed by a private sector property consultancy (ODPM, 2004; DCLG, 2007b).

These strategic housing market assessments reflected and underpinned a trajectory of housing growth in inner cities that was changing the nature of supply and the pattern of ownership in the UK market. While housing supply had been in general decline in the post-war era, falling from a peak of 352,540 dwellings completed in 1968 to a post-war low of 157,150 in 1995 there was a resurgence of housing outputs against this long-term downward trend in the 2000s with a post-1995 peak of 175,560 completions in 2007 (DCLG, 2011a). A significant proportion of the resurgent housing supply delivered during this cycle was apartment dwellings in northern towns and cities. For example, starting from a very low base of city centre apartments, 12,000 were built in Liverpool city centre between 2002 and 2007 with similar patterns in other cities in England (Unsworth, 2007, p.7). Many of these developments were funded via arms-length private investors raising equity through the buy-to-let market and bought 'off-plan'. The number of buy-to-let mortgages to private individuals in the UK increased by more than 3,500% from less than 30,000 in 1996 to more than one million in 2007 (CML, 2008). Overall, gross mortgage lending trebled from £119 billion to £364 billion in the UK between 2000 and 2007 (Parkinson *et al.*, 2009, p.16) with £67 billion invested through the buy-to-let route over a ten-year period to 2006 (House of Commons, 2006b, p.100). As a consequence private sector 'equity leveraged' buy-to-let investment displaced private financing of social housing investment which totalled less than £38 billion over a longer, 17 year, period (i.e. between 1988 and 2005 from the introduction of the 1988 Housing Act which allowed housing associations to finance new build through raising private equity for the first time).

At the height of the housing boom the Council of Mortgage Lenders (CML) found evidence of a strong trend towards 'middle-aged' investors in their mid-to-early 50s with high levels of private equity supporting the point of investment (CML, 2005). As a result of these trends in buy-to-let investment the number of one or two bedroom dwellings as a proportion of total completions increased dramatically from 34% in 1996 to almost 60% in 2009 (DCLG, 2011b). At the same time the waiting list for three and four bedroom properties in the social rented sector increased by more than 40% and 80% respectively between 2002 and 2010 (HSSA, 2011). The market, however, continued to deliver a high proportion of smaller dwellings despite evidence being presented at a parliamentary select committee on affordable housing arguing that, while there were an increasing number of smaller households, this did not necessarily mean that the requirement across the board was for smaller houses or flats:

> We are in danger of developing too many monolithic one and two bedroom apartments on the assumption that households will be smaller. Households will still have friends and where they have been divorced and have families, they will want their kids to stay over. (House of Commons, 2006b, pp.25–26)

These trends were underpinned by a set of analyses and prescriptive guidance that saw the necessity of altering house price gradients and creating the conditions for a revolution in supply of city centre apartments to deliver urban renaissance policies. Evidence assembled in SHMAs was largely based on a paradigmatic view of house prices, urban competitiveness and the need to supply high-density housing within brownfield sites in order to influence competitiveness and social inclusion agendas that prevailed prior to the 2008 credit crunch. The credit crisis, like low demand, was a slow-burn

event. Its seeds were sown in the expansion of off-plan sales and
by-to-let mortgages in the mid-1990s. Why, therefore, was regional
housing so inflexible and deficient in its ability to anticipate these
slow-burn events? In the next section we consider the role of agents
in developing a shared vision and how this provided the conditions
for these outcomes.

Agency and the regional 'epistemic community' in evolutionary resilience

Martin (2012) and Bristow and Healy (2014) refer to complex
adaptive systems theory as most relevant for understanding the
resilience of regional systems. Here, adaptive resilience has been
defined as the 'ability of a system to undergo anticipatory or reactionary reorganization of form and/or function so as to minimize
impact of a destabilizing shock' (Martin, 2012, p.5). As we have
shown in this chapter, a wide range of stakeholders within regional
systems provided the adaptive capacity to alter the trajectory of
regional planning for housing. We have also illustrated how a set of
interlocking *panarchic* processes resulting in low demand and abandonment was addressed by a set of shared views and official documents designed to address these problems. The approach was an
assembly of normative positions – a rigidity trap – on low demand
and urban renaissance which drew on prevailing paradigmatic positions on house prices, affordability (in the south of England) and
low demand (in the north) developed by an epistemic community
within planning that operated at local, regional and national level.

An 'epistemic community' embodies a 'shared set of normative,
principled and causal beliefs derived from analysis and shared
notions of validity' and which leads to a 'common policy enterprise'
(Haas, 1992, p.3): data analysis and the presentation of empirical evidence, policy prescriptions and narratives within core planning documents represent the connected network underpinning the
adaptive capacity within the regional housing system. The 'evolutionary adaptive capacity' of regional housing was represented by
all those involved in the SHMA process including regional housing and planning professionals, members of regional assemblies and
private sector consultancies. These *agents* within the *epistemic community* interpreted and responded to trends and sanctioned investments and policies that affected the exploitation of urban–regional
resources. The embodiment of the 'causal beliefs' of the epistemic
housing community were laid down in a number of key documents

and practices which set the tenor and direction of planning and housing policy at all scales (national, regional and local):

- Visionary documents such as the Urban Task Force's 'Towards an Urban Renaissance' (Urban Task Force, 1999) and Planning Policy Statements (PPS) reflected a shared set of normative and principled beliefs.
- The Regional Spatial Strategy (RSS), Regional Housing Strategy (RHS) and associated strategic housing market assessments (SHMAs) provided the evidence base underpinning those normative or shared causal beliefs.
- Procurement and letting of contracts to private consultancies and development of a narrative around 'growth' and 'supply' demonstrated evidence of shared notions of validity in pursuing competitiveness and affordability policies.
- The Barker Review of Planning and Housing (Barker, 2004) set out a common policy enterprise of growth and housing development as a core component of competitiveness and affordability. This was also underscored by the appointment of Kate Barker, a Treasury economist, to review and overhaul planning in England (Barker, 2004) placing a presumption in favour of development at the heart of the system.

Subsequent revision of national planning policy urged local authorities and regional partnerships to 'take into account the needs of the regional economy and have regard to economic growth forecasts' (DCLG, 2006, p.12) when allocating housing. Economics and the competitiveness discourse for regional housing was strengthened when Communities and Local Government (DCLG) rebranded itself in 2007 as an *economics* department asserting that '*economics is at the heart of all activities of the Department*' (DCLG, 2007c, p.4). These shifts in government policy and the rebranding of the department responsible for housing represented examples of a *common policy enterprise* (Haas, 1992, p.3) within the epistemic community. During the period 1997–2007 housing was elevated as a key variable in delivering economic competitiveness and contributed to unprecedented levels of city living. Regional planning and housing agents were locked into a 'supply–growth–house price' paradigm that resulted in the development of a narrative that viewed housing as a principal driver to unlock economic potential.

There was a collective pressure for the development of new housing and a greater release of land to increase *choice* and deliver *flexibility* as part of this narrative that was underpinned by a uni-variate and descriptive analysis of house prices and short-term economic performance. Research processes and intelligence emphasised data and monitoring but lacked a more discursive approach that offered outcomes or scenarios to that 'supply–growth–house price' paradigm. As demonstrated above, a number of factors aligned to create a contradictory set of pressures for the delivery of housing at a regional level, and the normative policy framework of expanding home ownership and increasing supply of smaller units to meet household demand was supported by the expansion of financial instruments and supply of credit. The delivery of a higher proportion of smaller dwelling units was justified as a means of addressing house prices and securing economic competitiveness. But the failure to triangulate data or provide alternative narratives resulted in a displacement of housing needs with 'expressed demand' for housing typified by the buy-to-let phenomenon which was supported by a set of causal beliefs within the epistemic narrative. Unevenness in demand and supply reflected unevenness of housing-based equity and resulted in a distortion of the housing cycle affecting future waves of development and resilience of urban–regional systems.

These causal beliefs and practices were symptomatic of a deductive equilibrist view of regional and national housing planning requirements as opposed to an inductive evolutionary approach attempting to reconcile multiple trajectories and interoperability between systems. Evolutionary resilience as it applies to complex adaptive systems such as regional planning and housing requires agents to understand the evolutionary nature of housing consumption and its interaction with other social and economic policies across temporal and spatial scales. The implicit expectation in the pre-credit crunch period of regional planning in England was that planning and housing agents responsible at the regional level would respond to social and economic needs and that the needs of households was key to economic resilience. Regional and city-regional actors would, it was hoped, provide a dampening mechanism within an adaptive regional planning system – checking the excesses of macro-economic policies and creating a narrative that fitted local context. What is evident is that the mechanism by which regional agents understood and reacted to events (SHMAs) drew on very limited evidence and interpretation and was underpinned by regional spatial strategies (RSS) founded on macro assumptions within a Treasury model of housing supply and house prices (Barker, 2004). There were no regional variations or assumptions about differences in housing markets or consumption within the model. The regional epistemic community (RSS, SHMAs and associated adaptive capacity) did not provide a dampening mechanism against macro-economic and housing policy.

When it arrived, the credit crunch demonstrated elements of being both a sudden shock and a slow-burn event – it showed how brittle macro housing policy was to shock and revealed underlying weaknesses in regional planning systems. This continues to have implications for regional housing trajectories (slow-burn event) and led to the reorganisation and abolition of regional planning for housing in England. This moved planning for regional economic and housing change to a rather unfettered path with limited diversity (redundancy) in intelligence gathering and assembly of evidence to assess the risks and trajectory of panarchic events that we described in the first sections of this chapter. The suddenness of the credit crunch shock also revealed these underlying structural problems of resilience and the absence of redundancy (diversity) in the regional epistemic planning community in England. As we discussed in Chapter 2, redundancy is recognised as a key property and means of improving the resilience of systems defined as through the addition of substitutable elements or alternate pathways (Bruneau *et al.*, 2003). It can therefore be expressed as the degree to which systems are insured against loss of function (Gitay *et al.*, 1996). Haas had previously warned that technical uncertainty and global complexity raise questions over the ability of policy actors to ever fully appreciate the anarchic nature of the systems that they manage (Hass, 1992, p.2). Translating the concept of redundancy to social–technical systems such as regional planning suggests that a more variegated and distributed set of actors should be harnessed in order to deliver outcomes that meet urban and regional needs.

Gunderson and Holling's adaptive cycle suggests that resilience is greatest when connections are loose. 'Looseness' would suggest that policy makers should play a much more laissez-faire role in order to distribute connectivity and increase adaptive capacity. But an unfettering of markets does not take account of their unevenness: this chapter has demonstrated that left unchecked, regional housing markets do not possess a 'natural' self-restoring equilibrium. Low demand is illustrative of the cascading nature of panarchic systems interacting over time when there is too much looseness in regional planning systems, when they are left unchecked or when there is a failure to recognise the longer term implication of interactions between systems. Agents' interventions can also be damaging if their set of values are based on a limited set of criteria and are equilibrist in nature. There is a need for some intervention to rebalance and continual monitoring for slow-burn issues underlying dysfunctional aspects of markets. Self-restoring 'natural' equilibria approaches, however, result in a withdrawal of regional agents and accord with the policy of abandoning regional governance arrangements and the emphasis on *real economies* and localism in the UK (LGA, 2007). This reflects an ideology of self-reliance and *responsibilising* central to equilibrist resilience frameworks and thinking (Pendall *et al.*, 2010) and raises important questions about the strategies pursued for delivering evolutionary resilience in complex adaptive systems such as regional planning and the alternative pathways available to evolve during or following 'shock' events.

Understanding slow-burn events and their implications for developing urban and regional resilience

Housing plays an important role in regional economic systems. Firstly, it provides the basis on which different housing and neighbourhood environments require adaptive and diverse housing types and markets. Secondly, it illustrates processes of transition to an urban renaissance characterised by housing and property-led investment and a post-political environment in which housing investments are largely uncontested. Thirdly, housing provides a litmus test for long-run trends in the national and regional economy and the sunk costs that reflect different economic eras. Finally, slow-burn regional trends captured in changes in housing demand, consumption and production reflect the ability of housing markets indirectly, and households more specifically, to absorb change. These processes initially conceal, but eventually reveal, underlying scalar effects related to long-run changes in the economy and therefore also provide a litmus test for the adaptive capacity of regional systems to adapt to slow-burn events.

The problem that emerges for socio-technical systems (i.e. regional planning) in dealing with long-run or slow-burn events is an unequal capacity to absorb shocks across space. Places (housing markets, regions, city regions) are uneven in their resources and ability to withstand shocks. Such unevenness reflects positive or negative feedbacks, 'lock-in' or path dependency i.e. previous eras

of development and the legacy of investment in the built environment (Robertson *et al.*, 2010). In Chapter 2 we highlighted that
more flexible linkages between agents can enhance system responsiveness to foster greater system resilience and remove systemic
rigidities (Pike *et al.*, 2010). However, building a more anticipatory
and flexible governance into urban and regional planning is often
stymied by path dependencies in public policies which are characterised by the way in which 'initial moves in one direction elicit further moves in that same direction; in other words the order in which
things happen affects how they happen; the trajectory of change up
to a certain point constrains the trajectory after that point ... path
dependency is a process that constrains future choice sets' (Kay,
2005, p.553). The resilience of a system can often be weakest when
overconnected or moribund and unable to adapt if there are insufficient connections or ties. While path dependency is a feature of all
systems, socio-technical systems such as urban and regional planning are distinguished from other systems in that agents have the
ability to alter the trajectory of place so that path *dependency* need
not be path *determinacy*. Consequently, agents can be the 'shock' as
a result of strategic (non-)decision making and the construction of
evidence to support policy narratives.

Slow-burn events and the changing nature of anticipatory methodologies for resilience planning across urban and regional systems
are an essential element of embracing resilience practices in planning. Maladaptive features within the functioning of regional systems have raised questions of the relevance of the equilibrium model
for such systems and (as more specifically addressed in this chapter)
for regional housing systems. Regional housing market outcomes
and strategic planning for housing provide a lens through which we
can understand the role of planning stakeholders as agents in monitoring changes in land use, how agents understand the interaction
of different demographic and economic factors across scales, and
how this feeds into policy.

In such policy narratives the principle of a 'self-restoring' resilience mechanism was seen as central to building long-term regional
resilience and anticipating sudden events that may result from slow-
burn processes. However, the effect of various shocks, including
economic decline, are often not instantaneous or simultaneous in
their impact. As illustrated in this chapter, housing abandonment
and the credit crisis were a result of a *panarchy*: the cascading,
hysteresis and systemic interaction of events. The adaptive features
of the system over time reinforce the relevance of 'slow burn' as

a framing device for resilience horizontally and vertically across spatial/temporal scales and systems.

The adaptive capacity of agents

The role of path dependence and the hysteresis nature of housing outcomes across scales illustrate the importance of resilience as a device for understanding the role of agency within complex adaptive systems such as urban and regional economies and regional planning. Urban and regional resilience involves the adaptive capacity of agents to different kinds sudden and slow-burn shock events; it includes preparedness and response and how the mechanism by which the shared beliefs of the epistemic community are arrived at. As we noted in Chapter 2, for social-ecological systems (SES) a number of critiques have emerged from various authors including the *responsibilising* nature of resilience and how it is being applied in a way that 'locates the action' in an endogenous way and fails to accommodate the role of agency and power, and locates the solutions of urban resilience with those affected rather than with causative external factors or agents.

In analysing low-demand housing and the policy response that emerged during the build-up of the conditions for the credit crisis we have demonstrated how policy actors within the epistemic planning community were insufficiently anticipatory in their response to both of these slow-burn events. In England, the introduction of regional spatial strategies (RSS) and strategic housing market assessments (SHMAs) was a means of coordinating the complexity of economic and housing interactions for the purpose of planning at the regional scale and coordinating these connections, 'linkages and dependencies'. The expectation was that SHMAs and increased regional 'interference' would lead to greater alignment of local social and economic needs to housing outcomes. However, none of the strategic analyses were anticipatory of, or prepared for, the credit crunch and so did not have a diversifying strategy (a Plan B) to cope with sudden shock events. In a period of less than a decade, strategic housing market policy at a regional level had grappled with the slow-burn effect of low demand, developed strategic measures that appeared to take an increasingly aggressive private sector approach to regional housing policy and in the aftermath of the crisis began to emphasise inclusion and affordable housing.

Responses to sudden and slow-burn events interact with and shape each other. The role of agents in adapting to events and the

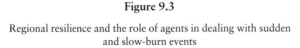

Figure 9.3

Regional resilience and the role of agents in dealing with sudden and slow-burn events

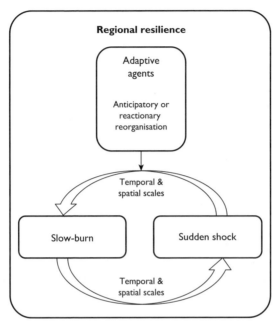

roles of path dependency and path optimisation mean that these types of event are simply two sides of the same coin (see Figure 9.3). Interventions by the epistemic housing and planning community continue to have evolutionary consequences in the future (remanence). In this respect, while agents are not wholly responsible for outcomes at regional level, they contribute through narratives that are either unchallenged or are developed within a narrowly drawn paradigmatic view.

We can only conclude that prior approaches (like SES resilience) are limited and that we need to move into more transformative pathways. To (re-)establish an evolutionary approach to regional resilience (for example in England, where our case study for this chapter has been located) requires reinstituting strategic regional planning with an emphasis on the constituency and methods of governance and foresight. The critical role for urban and regional systems policy makers is the ability to assess the degree of redundancy necessary within regional socio-ecological systems in order to mitigate future shocks. How agents construct narratives and respond or adapt to the unfolding of events is therefore of most significance for resilience in regional planning systems. Our analysis, and those of others (see for example Pike, Dawley and Tomaney, 2010) suggest that in order to avoid path dependency and lock-in, 'loosely coupled networks and loosely coherent institutional structures' (Boschma, 2015, p.733) are most resilient to both shock events and more persistent 'slow-burn' stresses; and that understanding historical trends and decision-making processes 'is key to understand how regions develop new growth paths, and in which industrial, network and institutional dimensions of resilience come together' (ibid.). Regional planning strategies and approaches therefore require increased redundancy or *novelty* and *diversity* in approach. This equates to greater variation and triangulation in analysis to counter macro-level views and narratives of economic and housing market behaviours.

Slow-burn events are the cornerstone of spatial planning across scales. It is the role of planning to ask the right questions and to frame housing market behaviours across scales to facilitate an evolutionary response to resilience and to transition away from an equilibrist and static view of resilience. Policy makers and the epistemic planning community involved in foresight at the regional scale need to embed broad interpretivist analyses of the interaction between systems to test alternative plausible outcomes. The alternative, as we have illustrated, is a moribund core set of causal beliefs that are left unchallenged by voices outside that epistemic community.

Chapter 10

Anticipating the Future: Planning the Resilient City of Tomorrow

In its dialogue paper on *Raising Standards in Urban Resilience*, presented at the Seventh World Urban Forum in Medellín in 2014, UN-Habitat identifies resilience as a cross-cutting theme that can holistically tackle social, economic and environmental inequalities (UN-Habitat, 2014). In the midst of growing uncertainty and complexity, urban and regional planners are increasingly tasked with enhancing resilience and protecting lives, property and infrastructure and to do so they must coordinate their activities horizontally and vertically across local government, with the private sector and other civil society stakeholders. Increasingly urban and regional planning is seen as a remedy to an ever-increasing array of socio-economic problems, policy priorities and risks facing contemporary society for which anticipatory or pre-emptive resilient responses are required. In relation to city building, resilience can be viewed as:

> simultaneously, a theory about how systems can behave across scales, a practice or proactive approach to planning systems that applies across social spaces, and an analytical tool that enables researchers to examine how and why some systems are able to respond to disruption. (Vale, 2014, p.1)

Within the context of planning, urban resilience should therefore be viewed as a continuous process or journey, helping to define the problems at hand and continually seeking to develop planning processes to mitigate emergent issues through adaptation, innovation and cooperation.

Although we would argue that urban resilience is most effectively deployed and embedded at the local level, its discourse resonates at the global scale and is increasingly shaped through ongoing

245

programmes of action. This global resilience project is being coordinated through, for example, the UN and World Bank as well as an increasing array of transnational organisations that seek to advance urban resilience while maintaining and reinforcing a neoliberal urban economic system (see Chapter 5). The overall goal in translating such international resilience narratives to local planning contexts is 'to build resilience to shocks by adapting the environment or social practices (Coaffee 2008) to mitigate against the effects of that shock and to ensure system function (notably in relation to integration into the global economy) is maintained' (Welsh, 2014, p.21).

As we have highlighted throughout the course of this book, to enhance urban resilience necessitates adaptability and innovation and, above all, requires planners to think and act in new ways. Planners cannot function in isolation and must be part of a more integrated urban management nexus where collective ideas about resilience are developed alongside a range of other stakeholders (Coaffee *et al.*, 2008a). The quest for enhanced urban resilience also requires an integration of physical, socio-political and economic aspects as well as the development of new tools and assessment frameworks to evaluate the impact and efficacy of past, current and future resilience requirements at a number of interlocking spatial scales. As we have noted, new relationships are being forged by urban and regional planners with other built environment professionals and with other professions not traditionally seen as part of the planning nexus such as emergency managers, the police and climate scientists (see, for example, Crawford and French, 2008).

While the rhetoric of urban resilience has abounded and its merits have been highlighted in urban and regional planning circles, the reality on the ground is that there is still an 'implementation gap' in delivery (Coaffee and Clarke, 2015). The multiple, inconsistent and incoherent ways in which the urban resilience discourse is deployed in planning practice has limited the transmission of urban resilience ideas across the many disciplinary and organisational boundaries required to trigger transformative change (Coaffee and Bosher, 2008; Fünfgeld and McEvoy, 2012). Instead, common responses to the urban resilience agenda amongst urban and regional planners have tended to be incremental, ad hoc, reactive, and with a focus on maintaining stability rather than fundamentally changing established modes of action. However, resilience has been shown to have extended the reach and repertoires of both sustainability and risk management as core planning ideas with a focus on preparedness and adaptive capacity to manage uncertainty, rather than simply a focus on 'defence' and returning to a balanced position or 'steady state'. A core way in which urban resilience discourse has achieved this is through providing a new and integrated lens through which to view the problem in hand and provide new planning solutions. This is illustrated in Figure 10.1 which highlights the often isolated policy discourses of sustainability and risk management being drawn together under the banner of resilience, and in so doing shifting the inherently conservative nature of policy making towards more progressive and flexible solutions.

The practice of urban resilience is currently in a transitionary phase between equilibrist and evolutionary approaches and requires the mainstreaming of future-looking techniques and strategies that focus upon adaptability in the everyday practices of urban and regional planners to complete this paradigm shift. In this chapter we address the question of how we can most effectively combine multiple *resilience* perspectives in an effective whole-systems *resiliency* strategy; and ask how urban resilience can be embedded as a set of principles for envisioning future local place-making activities and increasingly precautionary governance behaviours. This will involve, for example, increased emphasis on anticipating major challenges with a long-term view, new modes of risk assessment, the

Figure 10.1

Alternative scenarios for balancing sustainability and risk management

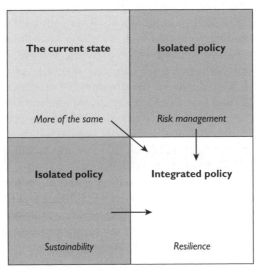

development of individual and institutional coping strategies, and, importantly, providing the appropriate training and advice to planners and other built environment professionals.

This chapter is divided into three main sections. First we draw out the core themes which have emerged throughout the book as a way of highlighting the continual prominence of the urban resilience discourse for planning practice in addressing issues of risk, crisis and uncertainty. The second section of this chapter focuses upon how we might mainstream urban resilience into the central discourses and practices of urban and regional planning. Here we will argue that the search for enhanced urban resilience is key to our future urban imagination/vision and to our cities of tomorrow. In this sense resilience represents a break from previous eras of planning history where stability was sought through deductive and positivist methods that attempted to model the future from the past and fit planning requirements to those predictions. Resilience, we argue, represents a new planning era where uncertainty and volatility predominate and where new and increasingly flexible repertoires of action are required. The third section reflects on how urban and regional planning practice might transition towards more evolutionary resilience. We ask how the implementation gap in urban resilience practice can be closed, and pinpoint a series of constraints or maladaptations that currently hinder the uptake of resilience in planning. As a counterpoint we also illuminate how some planning communities are beginning to embrace the progressive potential of urban resilience through further education and training. We finally set out a set of key principles and learning points through which resilient thinking can be mainstreamed and sustained within planning practice. By way of a postscript we reflect upon three core and integrated post-2015 dialogues which have deployed the discourse of resilience, explicitly and implicitly, and that will have significant implications for urban and regional planning in the years ahead: first, the Sendai Framework for Disaster Risk Reduction 2015–2030 which was adopted by UN Member States in March 2015 at the World Conference on Disaster Risk Reduction held in Sendai, Japan; second, the UN Sustainable Development Goals released in September 2015, and third, the Conference of Parties (COP) that signed up to the UN Framework Convention on Climate Change held at the Paris Climate Conference in December 2015, also known as COP21, with the aim of achieving a legally binding and universal agreement on climate change adaptation.

Planning for risk, crisis and uncertainty

A multifaceted and multi-scalar urban resilience discourse has emerged over the last decade-and-a-half which has reflected political priorities and international frameworks, and which has been subject to an ever-increasing critique from 'critical resilience' scholars. In this section we bring together this ever-expanding body of work with our empirical findings to highlight a range of core issues for planners to consider when practising urban resilience. Here we focus upon issues of clarity and the precise meaning of the term resilience and how this affects control of planning policy agendas; professionalisation, the growth of the resilience industry and the importance of context; maladaptive design and implementation; transitions and cultures of planning; and finally the concept of reflexivity in relation to planning's role in evolutionary resilience.

Clarity and control

As resilience discourse has become increasingly embedded within the repertoires of planning practice many have questioned its utility as a progressive and transformative agenda. As we initially unpacked in Chapter 2 and 3, and further illuminated through our empirical studies presented in Chapters 6–9, resilience has the potential to significantly shape future planning agendas through linking hitherto disparate agendas and stakeholders, and suggesting new frameworks of analysis and evaluation. However, critical attention is required to ensure that issues of definitional clarity and concerns over governmentalising control are addressed. For example, Porter and Davoudi (2012) have argued that planning needs to adopt a critical lens when addressing the new buzzword of resilience that appears to be replacing sustainability as the 'go to' term in planning rhetoric: 'planning has a long history of absorbing new concepts and translating them into its theories and practices. Resilience is no exception' (p.329). The concern here is that the fuzziness and malleability of the term, and its multiple and inconsistent uses in planning practice, could impede effective resilience implementation and dilute the progressive nature of its claims.

Notwithstanding clarity over definitional issues, urban resilience has also been subject to significant critique from a growing band of critical scholars keen to illuminate the dangers of uncritically accepting the resilience agenda at face value. In particular, critics have argued that rather than empowering local communities – which are most receptive and adaptable to locally experienced impacts of crisis – the devolution of responsibility for resilience practices is connected to the broader project of neoliberal governance. For these scholars, the use and scaling of resilience policy has clear geographical, political and ethical attributes: respectively, it is a centrifugal flow of power from governmental centres (and the state itself), with perceived conservative motivations and pernicious effects upon various publics. As we showed in Chapter 2, such critical commentary has focused upon how resilience has been weakened by associations with neoliberalism and post-politics within an apparent period of permanent crisis, articulated through the processes of anticipation, localisation and responsibilisation:

> [R]esilience discourses, as mobilised through the institutions of government, seem to have a number of implications. They foreground a concern with technologies of preparedness and planning, disperse uncertainty and responsibility for being prepared and respons-able throughout the system, and are institutionalised in apparatus of government and governance to fashion adaptive subjects that act autonomously to secure the system against exogenous and endogenous shocks. (Welsh, 2014, p.21)

Moreover, many examples highlighted in this book have shown how planners have been identified as a key set of actors in enhancing urban resilience and in effect *responsibilised* or co-opted as a result of knowledge sharing between state and professional groups in order to foster increased resilience. This for some represents 'a potentially more permeating form of institutionalisation' (Malcolm, 2013, p.311) of the urban resilience agenda.

Our empirical evidence has highlighted many practices that would support such a reading of government control at a distance. In Chapter 7 we highlighted how, in the UK, planners were increasingly given greater responsibility for counter terrorism (badged as resilience) amidst attempts by the national state to advance a security policy that called for a collective and multi-stakeholder response. We also noted how a lack of a regulatory 'stick' meant that the advancement of this agenda into concrete form was seldom implemented. By contrast, in Abu Dhabi, a strong top-down autocratic planning system has been established whereby security concerns need to be met (and paid for by the developer) as a condition of planning permission.

In Chapter 6 we again highlighted how urban and regional planners are being expected to engage with climate change adaptation as an everyday activity. As greater emphasis is placed on planners in developing resilience responses to urban complexity and as planners become more embedded in resilience discourse, then there is a greater risk of exposure to litigation when things go wrong. While not as obviously responsibilising as security-driven urban resilience, the story of recovery after Hurricane Katrina, explored in Chapter 6, threw up a potentially dangerous legal precedent – notably that the US Corps of Engineers were being sued for not properly maintaining the Mississippi River–Gulf Outlet canal. On 19 November 2009, the court found the Army Corps responsible for the flooding with the judge noting that the 'Corps had an opportunity to take a myriad of actions to alleviate this deterioration or rehabilitate this deterioration and failed to do so' (CNN, 2009). He also accused the Army Corps of decades of negligence and of 'insouciance, myopia and short-sightedness'. While this decision was successfully appealed in 2012 such decisions are not unprecedented. In a further example, Italian scientists were jailed in 2013 after they failed to predict the 2009 L'Aquila earthquake and for failing to properly assess and communicate the risks to residents. Although such charges were again successfully appealed the fear is that such prosecutions will mean that few scientists will want to take responsibility for predictive statements or for risk assessments that turn out to be inaccurate. This fear of litigation has become part of the narrative of urban resilience in many areas and is being used as an 'incentive' for planners and other built environment professionals to ensure that proper risk analysis is carried out and acted upon where required.

In terms of 'control' of the urban resilience agenda there are clearly tensions of scale. On the one hand, the building of urban resilience is arguably most effective when it involves a collaborative network of civic institutions, agencies and citizens working in partnership with a commonly agreed strategy (Coaffee *et al.*, 2008b). On the other hand, however, there is still a tendency of governing and steering from a distance on behalf of national governments that set the strategic direction of travel for urban resilience objectives (often depoliticising it) and largely supply the funding for the implementation of resiliency measures. On balance many countries still favour a traditional, vertical command and control structure rather than the horizontally integrated approach favoured in so-called evolutionary urban resilience. Not only does this state of affairs lead to a tension between the aspiration and wishes of localities and prescriptive top-down viewpoints, but on the ground it can play out as tensions between rapid restorations and longer term sustainable and equitable change in planning processes – as we demonstrated with respect to Hurricane Katrina and the triple disaster in Japan in Chapters 6 and 8.

Professionalisation and the importance of context

As we have highlighted, notably in Chapter 5, there is a tendency for initial urban resilience agendas to be codifying and prescribed. We would argue that, in particular, assessment frameworks for city resilience are becoming increasingly professionalised. The techno-rational nature of resilience assessment is illuminated by the Rockefeller 100 Resilient Cities' Chief Resilience Officer concept, and at an everyday level by the training and skill set development required by planners, or other local officials, to undertake the urban resilience assessment process that is recommended in a number of highly influential contributions in this growing area. In Chapter 5 we highlighted examples of scorecards for cities, collection of evidence and depth of monitoring over time that imply considerable commitment, skill and resources for completion and engagement with such assessments. These assessments are aimed at embedding particular criteria into existing urban governance structures but also influencing the nature of governance emerging in highly bifurcated cities, especially in developing nations. The bar is being set so high that many cities may not have the capacity or expertise to deliver and so are encouraged to buy in requisite expertise; further fuelling the rapid growth of the urban resilience industry. As UNISDR points out in the context of developing a resilience assessment: 'some skills, knowledge or experience may be purchased from specialist consultancies, or supplied on a one-time basis by aid agencies' (UNISDR, 2014b, p.11). Notably, there are emerging attempts by a consortium of international organisations and networks to advance an agreed and, arguably, one-size-fits-all approach for assessing urban resilience, tied to enhancing development and growth (see Chapter 5).

While these emerging frameworks might allow useful lesson sharing between cities and perform an important advocacy function for local communities and local policy makers seeking knowledge exchange, there is considerable difficulty in making comparisons between cities as many of the measures are subjective and are dependent on the judgement of the assessor: 'while the scorecard aims to be systematic, individual scores are often unavoidably subjective' (ibid., p.3). Such urban resilience assessment mainstreaming is therefore not unproblematic. What is apparent is that the explosion of interest in measuring urban resilience has occurred at a time of significant withdrawal of the state. Therefore, while there is an interest in targeting those areas that are most vulnerable and least resilient in order to maximise the value of limited public investment, austerity and public sector cuts have made planning increasingly vulnerable and the value of planning questioned. Local authorities need to come up with innovative ways of handling these cuts, but downsizing of budgets and personnel erode the 'institutional memory' and adaptive capacity of cities to create and embed resilience practices in planning. The growth in interest in measuring resilience of cities therefore chimes with urban entrepreneurialism (or disaster capitalism) and the need to identify and nullify risks for global capital. This is perhaps a more cynical view of why resilience has emerged as a key facet of new planning discourses.

What an increasingly prescribed and professionalised urban resilience assessment process also highlights is the importance of paying attention to local context, traditions and tacit knowledge. As Bourdieu (1977) famously noted, while the substance of knowledge shapes decision making, the context of knowledge production crucially frames the possibilities of human action. The conditions underpinning knowledge production are thus crucial and fundamental within this production are relations of (differential) power which shape what certain social groups come to understand as the scope of their response options, influence and actions. Thus the real danger of streamlining measures of resilience into one index, or a set of key performance indicators, is that 'subtleties and contexts can be lost' (Weichselgartner and Kelman, 2014, p.9). Moreover, we, like others, have highlighted how the role of local tacit knowledge and memory in creating, imagining and enacting resilience processes can feed into urban and regional planning processes (see also, Beilin and Wilkinson, 2015). For example, as we highlighted in Chapter 8, local experience was a key feature of community resilience that was sadly ignored in many cases during the 2011 triple disaster in Japan. More positively we also highlighted in Chapter 6 how such localised knowledge resources are being deployed to help shape climate-resilient development in many developing nations. Moving away from one-size-fits-all models and utilising local cultural history requires 'more sophisticated policies and decision-making tools that are capable of reconciling supranational and national objectives with local situations' (Caputo *et al.*, 2015, p.14).

Throughout this book we have emphasised the importance of the context in which resilience planning processes takes place and that this can be more salient than the national and increasingly international guidance that is being produced by governments and international NGOs and bodies such as the UN. The tension that exists within the resilience discourse in planning between top-down and positivist epistemologies and values and more interpretivist and organic approaches highlights the risk of creating a prescriptive and normative framing for cities as they attempt to centralise and codify resilience practice in a way that divorces *context* from *mechanisms* and resilience *outcomes*. These are, of course, not mutually exclusive registers of action, for example the mainstreaming of urban resilience within masterplans alongside a commitment to participatory approaches, or with community benefit in mind. Planners need to be alive to the trajectory towards professionalised top-down frameworks and the empirical chapters illustrate the need for planners to develop locally contextualised responses.

On this note it is encouraging that there is increasing evidence of urban resilience approaches that engage with a wider array of stakeholders and communities to seek social acceptance for planned interventions. For example we highlighted in Chapter 6 how residents are increasingly being given a voice in post-Katrina reconstruction planning and equally, in this instance, how engineering approaches are working with, rather than against, nature in designing coastal flood defences. A further example can be given by BIG Architecture's *Dryline* which aims to convert Manhattan's hard shoreline into a continuous network of landscaped parks to buffer storm surges, challenging the assumption that flood infrastructure has to be detrimental to urban character, and highlighting the co-benefits of considering issues of urban design and enhanced urban resilience in unison. As one of the designers responsible for the *Dryline* plans highlighted, conjuring up previous episodes of legendary New York planning history:

> We like to think of it as the love-child of Robert Moses and Jane Jacobs [...] Our project must have Moses' scale of ambition, but be able to work at the fine-grain scale of the neighbourhoods. It shouldn't be about the city turning its back on the water, but embracing it and encouraging access. (cited in Wainwright, 2015)

Maladaptive design and implementation

Through a study of historical examples noted in Chapter 4, we highlighted a number of constantly recycled maladaptive features within planning processes that illuminate the importance of learning from the past. Learning lessons from prior experiences may resemble an approach to resilience that is equilibrist in nature. However, in order to deliver the adaptive and flexible forward-planning strategies for resilience it is necessity for cities and regions to have a shared narrative that can embrace and understand the past in developing responses to maladaptive design. We showed how the seeds of New York's destruction during Hurricane Sandy were sown through a range of maladaptive planning procedures and practices from decades past. Such practices locked in vulnerability as a result of underlying values of planning practice that reflected inappropriate hazard mitigation measures. In this instance existing flood walls and defences were overwhelmed, flooding streets, tunnels, subway lines and, most notably, the city's main energy plants at Battery Park, which led to widespread electricity blackouts. The flood walls protecting the city's power plants were insufficient to deal with this 1-in-100-year storm event. Others have highlighted the inaccuracy of New York's quantitative flood maps (Peterson, 2014) or the problem of unsuitable development locations, driven by flawed risk management processes that assumed a low probability for shock events occurring (Wagner *et al.*, 2014). We saw similar historical patterns of institutionalised planning failure illustrated by the impacts of Hurricane Katrina and the Tohoku earthquake and tsunami (Chapters 6 and 8) where highly technical engineering approaches, which ultimately failed, were seen to give a sense of assurance to local populations and where hazard maps were based on low-probability scenarios.

A recurring theme has been how such maladaptive planning processes were set in train many years before their failure of deficiencies became apparent – often referred to as path dependency or lock-in – whereby institutional outlooks, relationships and configurations in place are obdurate, and prior plans are fixed and alternative scenarios inhibited. This is what classic resilience theory identifies as a 'rigidity trap' where management by command and control can lead to institutions lacking diversity and becoming highly connected, self-reinforcing and inflexible to change (Gunderson and Holling, 2002). Despite the inherent flexibility imbued by new approaches to urban resilience, to date there have been few attempts to link macro-level structural changes in society (e.g. national or regional economic restructuring) with micro-level resilience strategies (change in communities), once again drawing attention to the continual tension and distinction between equilibrium and more evolutionary approaches. In Chapter 9 we further argued for the importance of underlying slow-burn events as illustrative of the need for evolutionary approaches to urban resilience that are flexible, demonstrate reflexivity in understanding path dependencies, past events and interventions and employ foresight to gauge how the future may unfold in order to anticipate how interventions may be adaptive. Our analysis of low demand (slow-burn) and the credit crisis of 2008 (both a 'slow-burn' and sudden shock event) demonstrated how the epistemic planning community was insufficiently anticipatory in its response to both of these events. The role of path dependence within housing markets over time and space illustrated the importance of resilience as a device for understanding the role of agency within complex adaptive systems such as urban and regional economies and regional planning. As Martin and Sunley (2014, p.110) noted, 'a complex systems viewpoint on regional or city resilience [...] avoids exaggerating the endogenous determinants of a local economy's resilience and neglecting the importance of its "external" connectedness, linkages and dependencies'. Urban resilience therefore needs to deal with the complexity of prior decisions on current and future outcomes (hysteresis) within interoperable systems over time and space. How localities and local planning communities cope with such path dependency and are successful at breaking into new streams of action is a core variable explaining why some areas more than others are resilient.

Transitions and cultures

The nature and future of planning systems, including all the policies and procedures through which planners coordinate land use with wider development objectives, inherently reflect political, economic and social circumstances. As urban society engages with pressures of risk, crisis, uncertainty *and* change, the character and detail of the planning system, in theory, should respond. The way in which it responds will have major implications for the outcomes that it achieves. Increasingly, the quest for enhanced urban resilience is a powerful driving force shaping the transition of international planning systems. Such transition has been driven by a persistent undercurrent of the need for fundamental change and in response to increased urban risk, accelerated by a range of catastrophic disruptions, rapid urbanisation and complex and interconnected urban challenges.

While increased commitments to urban resilience have begun to shape planning objectives in cities around the world, and can be expected to do so over the next decades, planning policy is also under huge pressure to deliver a host of other objectives in an era of fiscal retrenchment. Similarly, there are stark choices to be made about the character of the planning system that would most effectively deliver urban resilience. For example, the planning system that most efficiently delivers large-scale infrastructure solutions is likely to be different from the system that most effectively delivers diverse and decentralised local approaches. Planning systems do not drive values and priorities, but they do bring together key mechanisms for implementing them. In this context, planning systems are constantly key arenas of political and institutional debate.

In Chapter 8 we showed how the exposure to natural hazards has hard-wired resilience approaches to planning that emphasise recovery from sudden shock events. The panarchic and cascading nature of complex urban systems means that sudden shocks can reveal the underlying fragility of systems and that they are simply different sides of the same coin of slow-burn shock events. Specifically, the triple disaster of the Tohoku earthquake demonstrated a number of wider relevant issues for planning and resilience. These included the invisibility of underlying structural problems in the region revealed by the sudden shock of the earthquake and which continue to compound restructuring and planning efforts. Also illuminated were the institutional rigidities and lack of redundancy within planning policy resulting in an inability to respond effectively to events as they unfold; while the traditions and 'values' of planning can be very obdurate. In short, planning traditions that borrow from, or are reliant upon, a tradition of disaster and risk reduction, or lack diversity within civic society, have greater difficulty in transitioning to evolutionary resilience pathways.

Japan's triple disaster demonstrates something more fundamental, not just about the *value* of planning within the resilience turn but also the *values* of planning. The values of stakeholders and the orientation of planning cultures will increasingly drive the momentum and transition towards a planning culture that can embrace interpretivist methods of practice and blend these with traditional positivist methods in planning of predict and provide. The future is not fully determined but the path dependency of decisions that are based on past modes of consumption and practice have a tendency to lock in planning practice to a set of values that repeat the past. Some planning cultures are more susceptible to a shift in practice to embrace the evolutionary resilience principles that we highlight below. The social integrationist approach of the Netherlands, for example, is more capable of closing the implementation gap in evolutionary resilience practice compared to the UK which emphasises land management and has recently moved to a highly localised but increasingly liberalised set of values (Nadin, 2010). New planning methods and ways of thinking about the role of planning are also significant in shaping new planning values and in the process challenge traditional linear assumptions embedded within planning. Evolutionary and transformative notions of resilience that are defined by change and flux 'challenges the adequacy of planners' conventional "toolkits" such as extrapolation of past trends in forecasting and for reducing uncertainties' (Davoudi, 2012, p.303).

In Chapter 3 we gave examples of how planning can meet this challenge in which approaches to urban resilience are proactive, adopt a long-term view and plan for multiple adaptation pathways to enhance diversity and redundancy. New methods and techniques in foresight are required of the urban and regional planning community to better understand an uncertain future and which should 'not be accomplished through the use of forecasts, but rather through the utilization of a structured approach to uncertainty. Urban design and planning can develop plans based on trends, projections, and forecasts, which do not usually leave space for the unforeseen' (Caputo *et al.*, 2015, p.13). Flexible approaches to Adaptive Delta Management, highlighted in Chapter 6, demonstrate the pursuit of a scenario-based approach to advance a range of adaptive pathways in order to cope with uncertainty and indeterminacy. We need to advance planning methodologies that consider 'statistical uncertainties, scenario uncertainties, or sometimes ignorance' (Jabareen, 2013, cited by Caputo *et al.*, 2015, p.13) as well as predictions or anticipation of future risks as a prerequisite to 'uncertainty oriented planning' (ibid.) and the delivery of resilient cities.

Reflexivity

Reflexivity is a key concept in the social sciences and the increased emphasis on planning for risk and uncertainty requires reflexive planning professionals and planning departments that 'constantly monitor their behaviour and experiences, and make adjustments in the light of new information' (Burgess, 1999, p.149). Beck (1992a) drew on the concept of reflexivity in his risk society thesis to highlight the ability of individuals and institutions to produce, through a consideration of the past and present, knowledge about the future which will affect current practices. He argued that through reflexivity, society can adapt and come to terms with new risks. Extending Beck's idea of reflexivity into urban resilience practice, White (2008, p.154) argued that 'the reflexive city is therefore aware of cause and effect and has a constant remit for critical reflection, while being proactive in developing positive feedback loops to ensure its future wellbeing'. We are living in an age of more visible risk, where individuals and governments have ever more knowledge about the possibility of a seemingly growing number of undesirable events occurring, such as flu pandemics, economic crashes, terrorism or flooding. As we have highlighted, it is imperative to learn from the past and to plan and design out maladaptation in the built environment and associated governance processes. The shift we have outlined from technical and equilibrium approaches towards more evolutionary approaches represents this reflexive process of change encompassing a more proactive, adaptive, multi-stakeholder, longer term and socially acceptable way of building urban resilience *for all*.

Viewing the world in this way is also a question of epistemological position. As we have argued throughout, the vast majority of the work done to date under the banner of urban resilience is framed through deductive and top-down approaches which are difficult to operationalise within the complex adaptive systems that make up cities. Such deductive approaches weaken the potential of the resilience approach in practice though a failure to fully take account of social, economic and political realities and important questions of power and agency. Through our own empirical research we have sought to illustrate that inductive reasoning (a bottom-up approach) is a more effective and nuanced approach to delivering urban resilience *in situ*. Our approach has placed great value on co-production and engaging planning and planning-related practitioners and policy makers from the outset of the research process, helping to identify and frame the challenges of urban resilience and connect to the real world of practice. Our approach to the study of urban resilience is thus grounded in pragmatism, particularly at the local level, where 'propositions could only be judged by the result produced when put into practice' (Zanetti and Carr, 2000, p.433). But such change is often premised upon implicit and explicit ideas of key managers and administrators acting pragmatically to balance a host of competing and often contradictory priorities to deliver 'what works' in complex policy arenas, and upon providing a menu of alternatives, selected according to local contingency and in line with a deliberative democracy. Urban resilience is therefore both a concept that allows us to understand complexity and unpredictability – both of practices of planning as well as the effects of planning intervention – but also an objective of policy underpinned by pragmatic philosophy (Raco and Street, 2012; Majoor, 2015).

Urban resilience as a new planning paradigm

Throughout this book we have highlighted the way in which resilience is being interpreted through planning responses while at the same time noting the problem of transferability of a concept conceived outside the realm of planning. The problem that attenuates for the resilience turn in planning is the enduring legacy of equilibrium approaches that have their roots in engineering and ecological models and the tendency to equate resilience with emergencies and preparedness for sudden shock events. This is as much a product of the calculated rationality of the risk industry and models of insurance cover for guarding against risk (replacing what is lost or returning to a state of normality) as it of is the problems endemic in resilience approaches in terms of responsibilising and the issues of scale.

Urban resilience fundamentally challenges conventional ways in which planners have conceptualised the world and practised the art of planning. Naturally, planning is always orientating itself towards the future; it is 'an explicit exercise in imagining the future' (Healey, 1996, p.218), constantly reconciling current circumstances with past investments in search of the city of tomorrow. However, with rising levels of urban risk and vulnerability, urban resilience represents a paradigm shift in thinking – what Lowenthal (1992) referred to as a 'rupture of continuity' – away from modernist foresight that sought equilibrium, stability and sustainability towards a post-modern form of planning where the focus was on the 'recognition of interdeterminacy, incommensurability, variance, diversity, complexity and intentionality, etc. that question the very nature of planning' (Allmendinger, 2002, p.28, cited in Connell, 2009, p.86). Here, in the resilience paradigm, a concern with uncertainty and volatility dominate discussions of an uncertain future and fundamentally problematise current planning approaches and the tools used to envision and forecast the future.

A core purpose of planning has always been to control an uncertain future by preparing plans that in essence bring the future closer to the present and provide stability for citizens and the market. But this has been more than prediction-based and focused upon the active construction of a desired future that highlights the agency of planners to determine what is built, where and in what style; it has also represented an inherent conservatism in the culture of planning: 'the positivist planner is interested in control and order. Matters of predictability and forecasting are aligned with modernism, determinism, and functionalism' (Connell, 2009, p.95). In comparing equilibrist resilience approaches to planning, Davoudi argued that 'the quest for spatial equilibrium has a long and enduring legacy going back to the modernist visions of a "good city" through to positivist planning and its quest to order space and time [where] a resilient system is one which may undergo significant fluctuation but still return to either the old or a new stable state' (Davoudi, 2012, p.301). Essentially, the function of planning has traditionally been to 'normalize the future' by increasing stability, which is associated with control, predictability and overall confidence, and ontological security:

> Planning helps deal with the consequences of making decisions about an open future [by] maximising what is known and by minimising what is unknown [...] [and] presents the idea of the future in socially acceptable terms. (Connell, 2009, p.92)

The rise of urban resilience throws such ideas into turmoil and turns 'the assumptions of positivist social science – those hallmarks of certainty, blueprints, forecasting and equilibrium that doggedly persist in planning – on their head' (Porter and Davoudi, 2012, p.329). Resilience is thus increasingly forcing planners to work with uncertainty to devise a range of alternative visions of the future and to advance more interpretivist methods. In this sense urban resilience can be transformative – on the one hand a new normative philosophy for shaping change, producing active citizens and facilitating self-securing agency (Welsh, 2014, p.21) or simply governing complexity in an uncertain world, while on the other hand an inherently localist and contextual approach to planning multiple future visions with multiple publics. As Evans (2011, p.224) noted, 'adaptation requires localised, applied knowledge, [and] adaptive governance that abandon the Modernist dream of total control, acknowledging the inherently unpredictable and unplannable nature of cities'.

Throughout the book we have highlighted how attempts to manage change pragmatically, through the transformation of existing management and governance networks, is impeded by locally embedded institutional practices and political allegiances which affect how national and international planning policy is interpreted and actioned on the ground. Here pragmatic change is intertwined with broader issues of public sector reform and cultural change and involves compromise, experimentation, creativity, innovation and the ability to work across conventional boundaries with non-conventional partners in new strategic alliances and networks. In many countries the resilience turn in urban policy and practice is beginning to shift the traditional and obdurate culture of the planning profession in new and exciting ways. Donnelly (2015), writing in *Planning* magazine in the UK, argues in short that 'planning needs to move away from trying to predict the future (and then trying to create it) to building in ways to make cities more resilient against future challenges'. He cites urbanist Professor Greg Clarke who further notes that planning needs to modify its traditional structure and evolve a new modus operandi:

> [This is about creating] not a planned city, but a resilient city, one that is flexible, one that is adaptable, one that is able to innovate, one that is able perhaps to utilise new forms of data, new forms of technology, new forms of coordination.

The future of urban resilience

Urban resilience is in transition between survivalist and equilibrist narratives of 'business as usual', defined by top-down, techno-rational and often disaster response narratives of bounce-back with no Plan B, towards a more progressive alternative where local and socially driven transformation embrace flexibility, adaptability and multiple alternate pathways of action. What urban resilience *is* has become far less important than what it *does* and how it successfully becomes interpreted and translated into local planning practice. As we have demonstrated throughout, this is not a straightforward process and reveals a set of the tensions and contradictions between an (inter)national policy dynamic which seeks to encourage locally contingent solutions to be developed for localised problems and the centralising tendencies of the national state (and increasingly international coalitions) which result in prescribed 'blueprints' and 'models' being developed for local policy delivery.

Closing the implementation gap

The majority of work in the burgeoning field of urban resilience has not until recently been grounded within the everyday practices of planners. In the early years of the twenty-first century the rhetoric of resilience has abounded in policy and government narratives surrounding cities and planning – with *Time* magazine famously giving it the distinction of buzzword of the year in 2013. Here the focus was on the use of resilience as a new form of risk management to cope with the complexities of large integrated systems and reflecting an overall consensus about the necessity of adaptation to the uncertainty of future threats. Now that such a consensus has emerged it is vital that planners begin implementing resilience rather than just highlighting its merits (Coaffee and Clarke, 2015). Such an implementation gap has notably been illuminated by the impact of Hurricane Sandy in New York in 2012 with the independent Wilson Center noting that:

> [T]he word 'resilience' was everywhere – even on the sides of buses touting New Jersey as 'A State of Resilience'. *But evidence of actual planning for resilience was scant.* Resilience, the ability of human and natural systems to respond to change and sustain the key components of our lives that are necessary for human well-being, can be improved by reducing risk, responding quickly and efficiently to crises when they occur, and planning for these kinds of shocks. (De Souza and Parker, 2014, emphasis added)

Many urban resilience measures to date have focused upon fragmented incremental and short-term mitigation measures rather than adaptive and long-term transformative action that would fundamentally alter the nature of urban and regional planning (UN-Habitat, 2011). The behaviour of urban and regional planners towards the goals of enhancing resilience is, like all planning operations, highly related to organisational context that can have a huge effect on the ability of the planning system, or individual planners, to act effectively to mitigate the impact of disruptive challenge. Sometimes planners fail to act and adapt to changing circumstances where new risk and threats emerge and on other occasions planning responses might be deemed inappropriate or inflexible – in short maladaptive. They have what UN-Habitat (2011) referred to as 'adaptation deficit' where there is the lack of adaptive capacity to enhance resilience. Commonly, planning authorities with their often siloed ways of working, requirement to meet immediate goals, change averseness and fragmentation of roles, combined with the constant necessity for upskilling and retraining to enhance the knowledge of available options, have struggled to action much-needed resilience requirements. Here the status quo and falling back on past assumptions are mainstreamed and 'locked in' to the planning system and process. In this sense learning from prior approaches and adapting them to current reality and long-term future needs becomes of paramount importance for the planning community.

Moreover, accepting that risk cannot be eradicated – a move from ideas of 'fail-safe' to a 'safe-to-fail' mindset – is required (Ahern, 2011). There is a need to embrace the challenge of uncertainty with innovation; thinking outside of a traditionally conservative planning mindset and embracing flexibility and adaptability. This relates not only to the material designs of resilience interventions but also the range of scenarios that should be considered. Planners need to look to advance a range of innovative adaptive pathways to enhance diversity and redundancy, and seek ways that resiliency interventions can be blended with other policy priorities so there is a co-benefit which will not only be innovative but more often than not increase the effectiveness, social acceptance and cost of measures.

Learning the lessons when things go wrong or fail, as Fisher (2012) acknowledges, is often an inevitable part of the urban development process. Such reflexivity should be used as a learning experience to better enable planners to identify plans or decision making that is simply poor, unsuitable or can contribute to wider vulnerability, which will in turn enable adaptations to be undertaken that will enhance resilience. But it is not just the nature of the intervention that is of importance. The intended timescale of action is also crucial. Urban resilience measures that are claimed to be about adaptation are often short term, ad hoc or retrofitted.

Moving from rhetoric to implementation in urban resilience is thus not without its challenges. What is clear from debates about urban resilience is that planners cannot function in isolation and must be part of a more integrated urban management nexus. There is a need to advance adaptive governance strategies where there is coherent and transparent vertical as well as horizontal integration. Traditional command and control structures, although useful at certain points of the urban resilience cycle, should not predominate. Rather, local level integration of functions should be prioritised along with a sustained effort to actively engage citizens and communities in the urban resilience effort. Local communities need to know what risks they face and how to prepare for them. Our approach to constructing resilience should begin at the community level so that factors which existing datasets cannot measure may be captured and utilised; for example, local, traditional or tacit knowledge that is invaluable in advancing community-owned resilience plans. Here planners have a key role to play as an advocate for local communities and in particular the more marginalised sections of communities that need to be brought more fully into the resiliency effort.

Although it is relatively easy to highlight an institutional inertia within a range of built environment professions as a barrier until now to collaborative working in urban resilience (Bosher and Coaffee, 2008; Coaffee and Bosher, 2008), we should not forget the key role that planning education can play in better aligning effort in this crucial area. The key role of training and skills development to raise awareness of options that are available to *all* built environment professionals involved in the decision-making process or that hold a stake in developments is vital (Chmutina *et al.*, 2014). As the urban resilience agenda gains further traction then education and training are seen as key to reshaping the epistemic planning community in new and emergent ways and in helping to create what has been termed the 'resilience dividend' for urban society (Rodin, 2015). Here enhancing resilience:

> enable[s] individuals, communities and organisations to better withstand a disruption more effectively, and it enables them to improve their current systems or situation. But it also enables them to build new relationships, take on new endeavours and initiatives, and reach out for new opportunities, ones that may never have been imagined before. (ibid., p.316)

In practice, such a dividend can come through student-centred courses or through continual professional development, where adaptive capacity skills can be forged in a multidisciplinary and multi-professional environment, mirroring, to some extent, the complex reality of urban resilience problems on the ground. In the evolving epistemic planning community, educational needs in urban resilience have been partially addressed through the advancement of bespoke training programmes or the development of decision support platforms that can assist urban and regional planners to think differently about risk and resilience. Such available training is often specific to a particular risk type. For example, in the European Union, a guidance document has been produced for municipal planners and others responsible for civil protection in relation to flood resilience, highlighting the *Six Steps to Flood Resilience* which take the user through a decision-making cycle with regard to the installation of flood resilience technologies. This process highlights the key role of planners and the planning system and also interacts with other stakeholders and communities (for further details see www.smartfloodprotection.com). A similar decision support framework for built environment professionals has been advanced for security-driven urban resilience highlighting how the planning profession in particular can seek advice about how they might design in counter-terrorist measures to the built environment. The *Resilient Design Tool* aims to help key decision makers consider the proportionate use of counter-terrorism design features in new and existing developments planned for crowded public places (i.e. anywhere in, or adjacent to, locations to which large numbers of the general public have access). This UK-centred work was an attempt at improving the skills of planners and also led to the development of bespoke workshops run by the National Counter Terrorism Security Office for planners, where the planning profession and security professionals came together to see how the formal planning systems and their various delivery vehicles might be able to assist in the advancement of urban resilience (Coaffee, 2010).

From the perspective of advancing thinking about urban resilience with respect to both flooding and security and an array of other risks, the temporal phasing of action becomes of key importance. As we have highlighted previously, the engagement of urban and regional planners, and other key stakeholders, at the earliest possible stage of planning is vital in ensuring optimal results – both in terms of performance of adaptation measures and in terms of cost. Thus by considering resilience at the earliest stage of a development or in refurbishment, project decision makers can develop the design and construction strategy in an effective and cost-effective manner. For example, in their Integrated Security and Resilience framework Chmutina *et al.* (2014) highlight a cyclical approach to enhancing urban resilience, starting with hazard identification and moving through the assessment of vulnerability and the identification of the level of risk to assessing what risk mitigation measures are available and then prioritising them within a particular context. Similarly, under the World Bank's *Resilient Cities Program*, a rapid diagnostic tool – *City Strength* – has been advanced that aims to help cities enhance their resilience to a variety of shocks and encourages them to take a holistic and integrated approach, advising collaboration between sectors in order to more effectively and efficiently tackle issues and to unlock opportunities within their own cities (World Bank, 2015).

While many countries have been slow to adopt such an integrated approach across a range of planning and planning-related professions we can look to the recently emerging US model to see what might be achieved in training a range of built environment professionals to deliver pre-emptive urban resilience. In May 2014 a collective industry statement on implementing urban resilience was signed by representatives of the US's design and construction industry (including the bodies for planners, architects, chartered surveyors, interior designers, landscape architects and engineers) which noted that 'contemporary planning, building materials, and design, construction and operational techniques can make our communities more resilient to these threats [...] Together, our organizations are committed to build a more resilient future' (American Institute of Architects, 2014). Amongst its fundamental commitments to pro-actively plan for the future in sustainable ways, the key role for continual professional development was highlighted:

> We *educate* our profession through continuous learning. Through coordinated and continuous learning, design, construction and operations professionals can provide their clients with proven best practices and utilize the latest systems and materials to create more resilient communities. (ibid.)

A radical and transformative planning approach?

Urban resilience has the power to radically change how we imagine and analyse cities of tomorrow and implement planning practice. It is more than a fad, a buzzword, or a passing phase. Planning for risk, crisis and uncertainty, as Christopherson *et al.* (2010, p.4) highlighted, challenges our 'basic assumptions and measures of success and failure'. In reflecting upon urban resilience measures taken by urban and regional planners in a range of global contexts, we have identified a number of key principles that are fundamental to advancing an integrated and holistic approach towards resilience action at the urban level:

- There is a need to move beyond siloed governance approaches. Policies should include new and innovative approaches that support multi-scale and multi-sector action, rooted in the different expectations of a wide range of partners. Through embracing the principles of urban resilience, cities can develop a more integrated system of urban and regional planning with, for example, disaster-resistant infrastructure, smart zoning, good building codes and standards or integrated urban plans that accommodate responses to a range of risks simultaneously.
- Urban resilience policies should address both near-term and longer term issues and needs. Here scenario planning, informed by prior lessons, can help urban and regional planners and other decision makers understand and deal with future urban uncertainties. In particular, planners should better understand and appreciate the spatially uneven nature of risk and resilience and take this into account in policy measures.
- A diversity of options should be encouraged so that redundancy and flexibility are designed into the approach from the outset through a range of adaptation pathways and/or spare capacity, developed in order to accommodate and adapt to a range of disruptive challenges or changing circumstances. This may, for example, come through technological innovation or simply through the reorganisation of existing practices.
- Urban resilience should be proactive and encourage a front-loaded approach – planning issues should, if possible, be dealt with at the drawing board stage of any development. We must break out of the cycle of being reactive to crises and instead anticipate, plan and prepare for future risk and uncertainty.
- Policies should emphasise, encourage and reward innovative design and planning that produce 'synergies' and 'co-benefits' (i.e. what policies can do to achieve a number of policy goals simultaneously) in order to create value for developments where environmental sustainability and social equity are pursued in tandem with strong financial returns.
- Urban resilience should be a socially just and inclusive process emphasising good governance and shared responsibility. Moreover, urban resilience measures should be developed to be safe, robust and proportionate to the risks faced, finance available and as appropriate according to social, political and economic criteria.

- Training and skills development is key to enhancing the adaptive capacity and resourcefulness of planners to respond to a multitude of disruptive challenges and in raising awareness of options that are available to all those involved in the decision-making process, or that hold a stake in developments.
- There is no prescriptive one-size-fits-all model for advancing urban resilience. No single urban resilience policy is equally well suited to all cities and context should be paramount in planning and designing appropriate measures. The requirement for and capacity to influence urban resilience varies from city to city and from one country to another. Requiring that resilience plans are customised to suit the needs of each urban area depending on its risks profile and institutional capacities is paramount to successful urban resilience.
- Urban resilience is a continuous cyclical process and acts in accordance with feedback Thinking and planning in this way encourages continual reappraisal of plans and strategies, as well as placing greater emphasis on the enhancement of preparedness strategies and the advance of adaptive capacity-building measures.

Urban resilience can be a progressive agenda that can transform our urban areas in socially and spatially just ways, giving local communities a voice and resources to contribute (Welsh, 2014) and if necessary resisting and engaging in counter-resilience strategies which challenge existing loci of power (Shaw, 2012a). Adapting to this new paradigm may require some short-term acceptance of sub-optimal use of space but with an acknowledgement of future adaptive needs.

The transition to so-called evolutionary resilience in urban and regional planning will require significant cultural change and the interweaving of principles of resilience practice and resilience thinking into the everyday repertoires of planning practice. It should become a consideration in everything a planner does across the different parts of the planning process – from initial concept design of development schemes and the granting of planning permission through to construction and, importantly, monitoring and maintenance of the built environment. Ideally this should be a process of utilising best practice rather than a compliance-based approach using regulation and statutory codes of practice. Blending the planning lifecycle with the resilience cycle of mitigation, preparation response and recovery in a continuous and dynamic way, although challenging, would significantly assist the advancement of holistic urban

Figure 10.2

Integrating planning into the resilience cycle

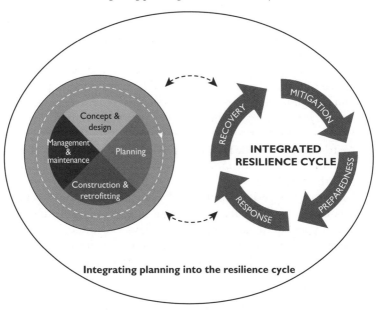

Integrating planning into the resilience cycle

resilience and its use in the practice of the planning community. This is represented schematically in Figure 10.2.

Urban resilience, if operationalised effectively, can provide a practical explanatory framework for urban and regional planners seeking to work with risk, crisis and uncertainty and the need for constant change, and to genuinely transform the way in which they work. Orchestrating such a coherently integrated framework for meeting the generational challenge of urban resilience will perhaps be the most significant challenge confronting planning practice – and its academic theoreticians – over the coming decades. The capacity and preparedness of planning systems to accommodate and promote such new approaches, technologies, assessment methods and resulting new urban forms will also be critical to the achievement of evolutionary urban resilience. At one extreme, urban and regional planning systems, and professional planners, have the ability to slow or stifle innovation, while at the other they may stimulate new lines of research and development, and new local and community endeavours in shaping urban resilience practices.

Postscript: Post-2015 dialogues and implications for planning practice

In response to the renegotiation of a number of interconnected global development agendas – notably for disaster risk reduction, sustainable development and climate change adaptation – the discourse and practices of resilience have been both explicitly and implicitly embedded within a set of (post-2015) dialogues aimed at advancing effective global policy that would come into effect from 2016.

The Sendai Framework was the first major agreement of the post-2015 development agenda, with seven targets and four priorities for action, and replaces the ten-year international disaster risk reduction plan, The Hyogo Framework for Action 2005–2015 (HFA): *Building the Resilience of Nations and Communities to Disasters.* On 18 March 2015 a revised international framework for risk reduction from disasters (Sendai Framework for Disaster Risk Reduction – SFDRR 2015–2030) was adopted by UN Member States at the World Conference on Disaster Risk Reduction (WCDRR) held in Sendai, Japan. This new framework emphasises a renewed commitment to and promotion of the local assessment of risk to disasters and the mainstreaming of these policies within a range of institutions and professions, notably urban and regional planning. The SFDRR highlights the urgency of building resilience to disasters and ensuring resilience is embedded within development plans, policies and procedures at all scales so as to complement, not hinder, sustainable development.

The SFDRR seeks to enhance implementation of disaster resilience by pledging to strengthen 'disaster risk governance for prevention, mitigation, preparedness, response, recovery and rehabilitation' and fostering *'collaboration and partnership across mechanisms and institutions'* for implementation (p.12, emphasis added). It also seeks to encourage the 'establishment of necessary mechanisms and incentives to ensure high levels of compliance including those addressing *land use and urban planning* [and] *building codes'*, and *'promote the mainstreaming of disaster risk assessments into land-use policy* [...] *including urban planning'* (p.15 emphasis added). The SFDRR also highlights the importance of anticipation and preparedness, noting that it is urgent and critical to anticipate, plan for and reduce disaster risk in order to 'more effectively protect persons, communities and countries, their livelihoods, health, cultural heritage, socioeconomic assets and ecosystems, and thus strengthen their resilience' (p.3). Moreover, it also recognises the importance of new technologies for warning and informing local communities about risk, urges an increased use of adaptive nature-based solutions for mitigating the impacts of climate change and encourages greater efforts in measuring and monitoring resilience at the local level.

Also presented at the Sendai Conference was a report commissioned by the UNISDR on economic losses from disasters, where Jerry Velasquez, UNISDR's Chief of Advocacy and Outreach, highlighted the key role of urban planning, noting that:

> [T]he way we do development is the reason why economic losses are so high. Development drivers are stronger drivers of the increase of risks than hazards themselves. In order to limit economic losses in the future, *we need to improve urban planning and make economic growth resilient.* (UNISDR, 2015a, emphasis added)

In September 2015 the UN released its much-anticipated Sustainable Development Goals (SDGs), replacing the former Millennium Goals, that set targets in relation to future international development up until 2030. Within the SDGs the discourse of resilience is utilised to highlight how we should respond proactively to a range of shocks and stresses and how we might collectively operationalise a joined-up response. Notably, Goal 11 is dedicated to *Make(ing) cities and human settlements inclusive, safe, resilient and sustainable.* This so-called 'urban SDG' marks the UN's strongest expression ever of the critical role of cities in the world's future, and in so doing raises the profile (and power) of urban areas in global dialogue.

Resilience discourse is also used in a number of other SDGs. Target 1.5 focuses upon community resilience: 'By 2030 build the resilience of the poor and those in vulnerable situations, and reduce their exposure and vulnerability to climate-related extreme events and other economic, social and environmental shocks and disasters'. The SDGs also promise to promote climate change adaptation: 'strengthen resilience and adaptive capacity to climate-related hazards and natural disasters in all countries' (Target 13.1); and critical infrastructure resilience: 'develop quality, reliable, sustainable and resilient infrastructure' (Target 9.1), 'build sustainable and resilient buildings utilizing local materials' (Target 11c). More holistically, and connecting to the Sendai Framework, Target 11b promises to:

> substantially increase the number of cities and human settlements adopting and implementing integrated policies and plans

towards inclusion, resource efficiency, mitigation and adaptation to climate change, resilience to disasters, develop and implement, in line with the Sendai Framework for Disaster Risk Reduction, holistic disaster risk management at all levels.

This includes, where possible a closer alignment with other UN commitments, notably the UN Framework Convention on Climate Change (December 2015) which will seek a legally binding treaty for dealing with climate change (Kelman, 2015).

The SDGs, in short, have begun a transformative conversation on the change required, in global discussions on urban development that combine poverty reduction, disaster risk reduction, safety and security, and climate change adaptation and mitigation and which provide more space and (hopefully) support for urban local governments who are being tasked with managing much of the sustainable development process. Notably the SDGs contain a reinvigorated notion of urban and regional planning that promotes more compact forms in cities with increase in population density, and encourages social diversity and mixed land use. This is an acknowledgement that the inability of many countries (particularly developing nations) to address sustainable development challenges stems largely from the absence of national urban policies and adequate urban planning systems. As Target 11.3 notes, the aim by 2030 is to 'enhance inclusive and sustainable urbanization and capacities for participatory, integrated and sustainable human settlement planning and management in all countries'.

This is a vision for sustainable development that chimes with the emerging discourse of urban resilience that is slowing but surely extending the ways in which urban and regional planners think about future sustainability issues, changing, in turn, the nature and practice of urban and regional planning.

The last, and arguably most significant, of the UN Post-2015 dialogues occurred at the United Nations Climate Change Conference (COP21), in Paris in December 2015 where the signatories to the UN Convention on Climate Change met to advance an agreement on future climate change adaptation. The agreement reached welcomed the adoption of both the Sendai Framework for Disaster Risk Reduction and the Sustainable Development Goals, while recognising the urgent threat climate change represents and thus requiring the widest possible international cooperation (United Nations Framework Convention on Climate Change, 2015). As with the other UN dialogues, the ideas of resilience and adaptation were explicit at the conference and in the eventual agreement reached.

On the third day of COP21, dubbed 'Resilience Day', the UN and a number of national governments announced major international partnerships to protect people who are most vulnerable to climate impacts. As the UN Assistant Secretary-General on Climate Change noted:

> Resilience is really important because the climate is already changing, and we need to be able to not just adapt to the changes but actually develop in a way that takes into account that in the future, climate will still change [...] So we need to adjust our development process, adjust our economic approach [...] and be more resilient to future changes that will happen. (cited in UN News Centre, 2015)

Citing recent urban resilience initiatives by the UNISDR and the Rockefeller Foundation (see Chapter 5) Peru's Minister of the Environment further noted that 'resilience – it is very important when we talk about climate change and its consequences' and:

> When we talk about resilience, we are talking about how can we resist [...] and avoid negative consequences to our human population [...] to the wildlife, to the habitat, to the ecosystems, to the water, to the ocean – that is why we have the 'Resilience Day'. If climate change is going to bring us natural disasters, we should have the objective of resilience as a way to face those kinds of consequences. (cited in ibid.)

The eventual agreement that emerged from COP21 made explicit the focus upon future urban resilience and how vulnerabilities could be reduced through climate proofing and climate resilience measures. Article 2, for example, noted that 'increasing the ability to adapt to the adverse impacts of climate change and foster climate resilience and low greenhouse gas emissions development, in a manner that does not threaten food production' should be encouraged, while Article 7, drawing on the lexicon of urban resilience and connecting adaptation alongside mitigation, noted: 'Parties hereby establish the global goal on adaptation of enhancing adaptive capacity, strengthening resilience and reducing vulnerability to climate change, with a view to contributing to sustainable development' (United Nations Framework Convention on Climate Change, 2015).

Overall, these three post-2015 dialogues highlight the importance and utility of ideas and practices of resilience in tackling the integrated and complex urban issues of reducing the risk of disasters, advancing sustainable development and mitigating and adapting to climate change. These core agendas, and their framing in resilience thinking, will ensure that urban resilience will be a vital area of study in urban and regional planning for years to come.

Bibliography

Abu Dhabi Government (2008) *Economic Vision 2030,* www.ecouncil.ae/ PublicationsEn/economic-vision-2030-full-versionEn.pdf, accessed 12 February 2013.

Abu Dhabi Government (2011) *2030 Urban Structure Framework Plan,* www.upc. gov.ae/abu-dhabi-2030.aspx?lang=en-US, accessed 12 February 2013.

Abu Dhabi Urban Planning Council (2013) *Abu Dhabi Safety and Security Planning Manual* (SSPM) (Abu Dhabi: Abu Dhabi Urban Planning Council).

Adey, P. and Anderson, B. (2012) 'Anticipating Emergencies: Technologies of Preparedness and the Matter of Security', *Security Dialogue, 43,* 99–117.

Adger, N. (2000) 'Social and Ecological Resilience: Are They Related?', *Progress in Human Geography, 24,* 3, 347–364.

Adger, W., Arnell, N. and Tompkins, E. (2005) 'Successful Adaptation to Climate Change Across Scales', *Global Environmental Change, 15,* 77–86.

Adger, N., Brown K. and Waters J. (2011) 'Resilience', in J. Dryzek, R. Norgaard and D. Schlosberg (eds) *The Oxford Handbook of Climate Change and Society,* pp. 696–710 (Oxford: Oxford University Press).

Aerts, J. C. J. H., Lin, N., Botzen, W. J. W., Emmanel, K. and Moel, H. D. (2013) 'Low-Probability Flood Risk Modeling for New York City', *Risk Analysis, 33,* 5, 772–788.

Agamben, G. (2005) *State of Exception* (Chicago, IL: University of Chicago Press).

Ahern, J. (2011) 'From Fail-safe to Safe-to-fail: Sustainability and Resilience in the New Urban World', *Landscape and Urban Planning, 100,* 341–343.

Akinci, A., Malagnini, L. and Sabetta, F. (2010) 'Characteristics of the Strong Ground Motions from the 6 April 2009 L'Aquila Earthquake, Italy', *Soil Dynamics and Earthquake Engineering, 30,* 5, 320–335.

Albers, M. and Deppisch, S. (2012) 'Resilience in the Light of Climate Change: Useful Approach or Empty Phrase for Spatial Planning?', *European Planning Studies,* http://dx.doi.org/10.1080/09654313.2012.722961, 1–13, published online 10 September 2012.

Alexander, D. E. (2013) 'Resilience and Disaster Risk Reduction: An Etymological Journey', *Natural Hazards and Earth System Science, 13,* 11, 2707–2716.

Allmendinger, P. (2002) *Planning Theory* (Basingstoke: Palgrave).

Alsnih, R. and Stopher, P. (2004) 'Review of Procedures Associated with Devising Emergency Evacuation Plans', *Transportation Research Record, 1865,* 89–97.

Ambrose, S. (2001) 'Man vs. Nature: The Great Mississippi Flood of 1927', *National Geographic,* May 1, http://news.nationalgeographic.com/news/2001/05/0501_ river4.html, accessed 1 February 2012.

American Institute of Architects (2014) *Industry Statement on Resilience,* www.aia. org/press/AIAB103807, accessed 29 May 2014.

Amin, A. (2013) 'Surviving the Turbulent Future', *Environment and Planning D, 31,* 140–156.

Anderson, B. (2007) 'Hope for Nanotechnology: Anticipatory Knowledge and the Governance of Affect', *Area*, 39, 2, 156–165.

Anderson, B. (2015) 'What Kind of Thing is Resilience?', *Politics*, 35, 1, 60–66.

Ando, M. (2011, 15 November) 'Interviews with Survivors of Tohoku Earthquake Provide Insights Into Fatality Rate', *Eos*, 92, 46, 411–412.

Argonne National Laboratory (2010) *Constructing a Resilience Index for the Enhanced Critical Infrastructure Programme* (Chicago, ANL).

Arias, G. V. (2011) 'The Normalisation of Exception in the Biopolitical Security Dispositif', *International Social Science Journal*, 62, 363–375.

Arup (2014) *City Resilience Framework*, www.arup.com/cri, accessed 15 September 2014.

Baer, M., Heron, K., Morton, O. and Ratliff, E. (2005) *Safe: The Race to Protect Ourselves in a Newly Dangerous World* (New York: HarperCollins).

Bailey, I., Hopkins, R. and Wilson, G. (2010) 'Some Things Old, Some Things New: The Spatial Representations of Politics of Change of the Peak Oil Relocalisation Movement', *Geoforum*, 41, 595–605.

Barker K. (2004) *Delivering Stability: Securing Our Future Housing Needs* (London: HM Treasury).

Barnett, J. and O'Neill, S. (2010) 'Maladaptation', *Global Environmental Change*, 20, 2, 211–213.

Bayley, S. (2007, 18 November) 'From Car Bombs to Carbuncles', *The Observer*.

BBC (2013) 'Bangladesh Government "Scared to Enforce Regulations"', www.bbc. co.uk/news/world-asia-22286117, accessed 24 April 2013.

BBC/Experian (2010a) 'Spending Cuts "To Hit North Harder"' www.bbc.co.uk/ news/business-11233799, accessed 15 March 2015.

BBC/Experian (2010b) 'Spending review – Resilience rankings explained', 9 September 2010, www.bbc.co.uk/news/business-11177161, accessed 6 January 2016.

Beatty, C. and Fothergill, S. (1996) 'Labour Market Adjustment in Areas of Chronic Industrial Decline: The Case of the UK Coalfields', *Regional Studies*, 30, 627–640.

Beatty, C. and Fothergill, S. (1998) 'Registered and Hidden Unemployment in the UK Coalfields', in P. Lawless, R. Martin and S. Hardy (eds) *Unemployment and Social Exclusion: Landscapes of Labour Inequality* (London: Jessica Kingsley Publishers and The Regional Studies Association).

Beatty, C., Fothergill, S. and Lawless, P. (1997) Geographical Variation in the Labour-market Adjustment Process: The UK Coalfields 1981–91. *Environment and Planning A*, 29, 2041–2060.

Beck, U. (1992a) *Risk Society – Towards a New Modernity* (London: Sage).

Beck, U. (1992b) 'From Industrial Society to the Risk Society: Questions of Survival, Social Structure and Ecological Enlightenment', *Theory, Culture and Society*, 9, 97–123.

Beck, U. (1994) The Reinvention of Politics: Towards a Theory of Reflexive Modernization', in U. Beck, A. Giddens and S. Lash (eds) *Reflexive Modernization. Politics, Tradition and Aesthetics in the Modern Social Order*, pp. 1–55 (Stanford: Stanford University Press).

Beck, U. (1996) *The Reinvention of Politics: Rethinking Modernity in the Global Social Order* (Cambridge: Polity Press).

Beilin, R. and Wilkinson, C. (2015) 'Introduction: Governing for Urban Resilience', *Urban Studies*, 52, 1205–1217.

Béné, C., Godfrey Wood, R., Newsham, A. and Davies, M (2012) 'Resilience: New Utopia or New Tyranny? Reflection about the Potentials and Limits of the Concept of Resilience in Relation to Vulnerability Reduction Programmes', *Institute of Development Studies Working Paper* No. 405, September 2012 (IDS: Brighton).

Benton-Short, L. (2007) 'Bollards, Bunkers, and Barriers: Securing the National Mall in Washington DC', *Environment and Planning D: Society and Space*, 25, 3, 424–446.

Berke, P., Kartez, J. and Wenger, D (1993) 'Recovery After Disaster: Achieving Sustainable Development, Mitigation, and Equity', *Disasters*, 17, 2, 93–109.

Biermann, F. (2014) 'The Anthropocene: A Governance Perspective, *The Anthropocene Review*, 1, 1, 57–61.

Birmingham City Council (2015) 'Social Impact Factors and Resilience of Wards in Birmingham', Presentation by Richard Browne, The University of Birmingham, 23 February 2015.

Boddy, T. (2007) 'Architecture Emblematic: Hardened Sites and Softened Symbols', in Michael Sorkin (ed.) *Indefensible Space*, pp. 277–304 (Abingdon: Routledge).

Booth, R. (2010, 24 February) 'Ambassador, You are Spoiling our View of the Thames with this Boring Glass Cube', *The Guardian*, 13.

Boschma, R (2015) 'Towards an Evolutionary Perspective on Regional Resilience', *Regional Studies*, 49, 5, 733–751(19).

Bosher L. S., (ed.) (2008) *Hazards and the Built Environment: Attaining Built-in Resilience* (London: Taylor & Francis).

Bosher, L. and Coaffee, J. (2008) 'Urban Resilience: an International Perspective', *Proceedings of the Institute of Civil Engineers: Urban Design and Planning*, 161, 145–146.

Bosher, L., Dainty, A., Carillo, P. and Glass, J. (2007) 'Built-in Resilience to Disasters: A Pre-emptive Approach', *Engineering, Construction and Architectural Management*, 14, 5, 434–446.

Bourdieu, P. (1977) *Outline of a Theory of Practice* (Cambridge: Cambridge University Press).

Boyd, E. and Folke, C. (eds) (2012) *Adapting Institutions: Governance, Complexity and Social-Ecological Resilience* (Cambridge: Cambridge University Press).

Boyd, E. and Juhola, S. (2015) 'Adaptive Climate Change Governance for Urban Resilience', *Urban Studies*, 52, 7, 1234–1264.

Brand, F. S. and Jax, K. (2007) 'Focusing the Meaning(s) of Resilience: Resilience as a Descriptive Concept and a Boundary Object', *Ecology and Society*, 12, 1, 23.

Brenner, N. (2004) *New State Spaces: Urban Governance and the Rescaling of Statehood* (Oxford: Oxford University Press).

Briggs, R. (2005) 'Invisible Security: The Impact of Counter-terrorism on the Built Environment', in R. Briggs (ed.) *Joining Forces: From National Security to Networked Security*, pp. 68–90 (London: Demos).

Brisbane City Council (2011a) *Brisbane Flood 2011: Independent Review of Brisbane City Council's Response*, www.brisbane.qld.gov.au/sites/default/files/emergency_management_Independent_Review_of_BCCs_Response_Final_Report_v4.pdf, accessed 20 July 2012.

Brisbane City Council (2011b) *Water Sensitive Urban Design: Streetscape Planning and Design Package*, www.brisbane.qld.gov.au/sites/default/files/WSUD%20Streetscape_Brio%20New.pdf, accessed 12 December 2014.

Brisbane City Council (2013a) Brisbane Vision 2031, www.brisbane.qld.gov.au/sites/default/files/Brisbane_Vision_2031_full_document.pdf, accessed 12 December 2014.

Brisbane City Council (2013b) *Brisbane's Total Water Cycle Management Plan*, www.brisbane.qld.gov.au/sites/default/files/brisbanes_total_water_cycle_management_plan_2013.pdf, accessed 4 January 2014.

Bristow, G. and Healy, A. (2014) Regional Resilience: An Agency Perspective, *Regional Studies*, 48, 5, 923–935, http://dx.doi.org/10.1080/00343404.2013.854879

Brown, G. (2007a) 'Statement on Security', 25 July 2007.

Brown, G. (2007b) House of Commons Debate, 14 November 2007. Col. 667.

Brown, K. (2012) 'Policy Discourses of Resilience', in M. Pelling, D. Manuel-Navarrete and M. Redclift (eds) *Climate Change and the Crisis of Capitalism*, pp. 37–50 (Abingdon: Routledge).

Brown, K. (2013) 'Global Environmental Change I: A Social Turn for Resilience?', *Progress in Human Geography*, 37, 1–11.

Brown, P. L. (1995, 28 May) 'Designs in a Land of Bombs and Guns', *New York Times*, 6.

Brown, S. (1985) 'Central Belfast's Security Segment: An Urban Phenomenon', *Area*, 17, 1, 1–8.

Bruneau, M., Chang, S. E., Eguchi, R. T., Lee, G. C., O'Rourke T. D. and Reinhorn, A. M. (2003) 'A Framework to Quantitatively Assess and Enhance the Seismic Resilience of Communities', *Earthquake Spectra*, 19, 4, 733–752.

Buckle, P., Mars, G. and Smale, S. (2000) 'New Approaches to Assessing Vulnerability and Resilience', *Australian Journal of Emergency Management*, 15, 2, 8–14.

Bulkeley, H. and Tuts, R. (2013) 'Understanding Urban Vulnerability, Adaptation and Resilience in the Context of Climate Change', *Local Environment*, 18, 6, 646–662.

Bull-Kamanga, L., Diagne, K., Lavell, A., Leon, E., Lerise, F. and MacGregor, H. (2003) 'From Everyday Hazards to Disasters: The Accumulation of Risk in Urban Areas', *Environment and Urbanisation*, 15, 1, 193–203.

Burby, R. J., Deyle, R. E., Godschalk, D. R. and Olshansky R. B. (2000) 'Creating Hazard Resilient Communities Through Land-use Planning', *Natural Hazards Review*, 1, 2, 99–106.

Burgess, J. (1999) 'Environmental Management and Sustainability', in P. Cloke, P. Crang and M. Goodwin (eds) *Introducing Human Geographies*, pp. 141–150 (London: Arnold).

Burton, C. (2014) 'A Validation of Metrics for Community Resilience to Natural Hazards and Disasters Using the Recovery from Hurricane Katrina as a Case Study', *Annals of the Association of American Geographers*, 105, 1, 67–86.

Cabinet Office (2003) *Dealing with Disaster (Revised Third Edition)* (London: Cabinet Office).

Cabinet Office (2008) *The National Security Strategy of the United Kingdom: Security in an Interdependent world* (London: The Stationery Office).

Cabinet Office (2011) *Strategic National Framework on Community Resilience* (Cabinet Office: London).

Campanella, T. (2006) 'Urban Resilience and the Recovery of New Orleans', *Journal of the American Planning Association*, 72, 2, 141–146.

Cannon, T. and Müller-Mahn, D. (2010) 'Vulnerability, Resilience and Development Discourses in Context of Climate Change', *Natural Hazards*, 55, 621–635.

Caputo, S., Caserio, M., Coles, R., Jankovic L. and Gaterell, M. (2015) 'Urban Resilience: Two Diverging Interpretations', *Journal of Urbanism: International Research on Placemaking and Urban Sustainability*, 8, 3, 1–19.

Caribbean Journal (2015, 4 March) 'Jamaica to launch $6 Million Climate Change Resilience Project', http://caribjournal.com/2015/03/04/jamaica-to-launch-6-million-climate-change-resilience-project/#, accessed 4 March 2015.

Carlson, J. and Doyle, J. (2000) 'Highly Optimized Tolerance: Robustness and Design in Complex Systems', *Phys Rev Lett*, 84, 11, 2529–2532.

Carp, J. (2012) 'The Study of Slow', in B. Goldstein (ed.) *Collaborative Resilience: Moving Through Crisis to Opportunity*, pp. 99–126 (Cambridge, MA: MIT Press).

Carpenter, S., Walker, B., Anderies, J. and Abel, N. (2001) 'From metaphor to measurement: resilience of what to what?', *Ecosystems*, 4, 8, 765–781.

Carpenter, S., Westley, F. and Turner, M. (2005) 'Surrogates for Resilience of Social–Ecological Systems', *Ecosystems*, 8, 941–944.

Carter, M., Little, P., Mogues, T. and Negatu, W. (2007) 'Poverty Traps and Natural Disasters in Ethiopia and Honduras', *World Development*, 35, 5, 835–856.

Centre for the Protection of National Infrastructure (2011) *Integrated Security: A Public Realm Design Guide for Hostile Vehicle Mitigation* (London: CPNI).

Chandler, D. (2012) 'Resilience and Human Security: The Post-Interventionist Paradigm', *Security Dialogue*, 4, 3, 213–229.

Chandler, D. (2014) *Resilience: The Governance of Complexity* (London: Routledge).

Chelleri, L. and Olazabal, M. (eds) (2012) *Multidisciplinary perspectives on Urban Resilience: A workshop report*, Basque Centre for Climate Change (BC3).

Chelleri, L., Water, J., Olazabal, M. and Minucci, G. (2015) 'Resilience trade-offs: addressing multiple scales and temporal aspects of urban resilience', *Environment and Urbanization*, doi: 10.1177/0956247814550780

Chmutina, K. and Bosher, L. (2014) 'Disaster Risk Reduction or Disaster Risk Production: The Role of Building Regulations in Mainstreaming DRR', *International Journal of Disaster Risk Reduction*, 13, 10–19.

Chmutina, K., Bosher, L., Coaffee, J. and Rowlands, R. (2014) 'Towards Integrated Security and Resilience Framework: A Tool for Decision-Makers', *Procedia Economics and Finance*, 18, 25–32.

Christopherson, S., Michie, J. and Tyler, P. (2010) 'Regional Resilience: Theoretical and Empirical Perspectives', *Cambridge Journal of Regions, Economy and Society*, 3, 1, 3–10.

City of New Orleans (2013) *Greater New Orleans Urban Water Plan*, http://livingwithwater.com/blog/urban_water_plan/reports/, accessed 1 February 2014.

City of New Orleans (2015) *Resilient New Orleans*, http://resilientnola.org, accessed 1 September 2015.

Clancy, H. (2014) 'Michael Berkowitz: Community is the Secret of Urban Resilience', *GreenBizblog*,www.greenbiz.com/blog/2014/08/12/michael-berkowitz-community-secret-ingredient-urban-resilience, accessed 12 August 2014.

CML (Council of Mortgage Lenders) (2008) 'CML Research, Table MM6', www.cml.org.uk/cml/statistics, accessed 23 February 2008.

CNN (2009) 'Court: Army Corps of Engineers Liable for Katrina Flooding', http://edition.cnn.com/2009/US/11/18/louisiana.katrina.lawsuit/, accessed 14 February 2010.

Coaffee, J. (2000) 'Fortification, Fragmentation and the Threat of Terrorism in the City of London', in Gold, J. R. and Revill, G. E. (eds) *Landscapes of Defence*, pp.114–129 (London: Addison Wesley Longman).

Coaffee, J. (2003) *Terrorism, Risk and the City: The Making of a Contemporary Urban Landscape* (Aldershot: Ashgate).

Coaffee, J. (2004) 'Rings of Steel, Rings of Concrete and Rings of Confidence: Designing out Terrorism in Central London Pre and Post 9/11', *International Journal of Urban and Regional Research*, 28, 1, 201–211.

Coaffee, J. (2006) 'From Counter-Terrorism to Resilience', *European Legacy – Journal of the International Society for the Study of European Ideas* (ISSEI), 1, 4, 389–403.

Coaffee, J. (2009) *Terrorism, Risk and the Global City – Towards Urban Resilience* (Farnham: Ashgate).

Coaffee, J. (2010) 'Protecting Vulnerable Cities: The UK Resilience Response to Defending Everyday Urban Infrastructure', *International Affairs*, 86, 4, 939–954.

Coaffee, J. (2013a) 'Rescaling and Responsibilising the Politics of Urban Resilience: From National Security to Local Place-Making', *Politics*, 33, 4, 240–252.

Coaffee, J. (2013b) 'From Securitisation to Integrated Place Making: Towards Next Generation Urban Resilience in Planning Practice', *Planning Practice and Research*, 28, 3, 323–339.

Coaffee, J (2014) 'The Uneven Geographies of the Olympic Carceral: From Exceptionalism to Normalisation', *The Geographical Journal*, doi: 10.1111/geoj.12081.

Coaffee, J. and Bosher, L. (2008) 'Integrating Counter-Terrorist Resilience into Sustainability', *Proceedings of the Institute of Civil Engineers: Urban Design and Planning*, 161, 75–84.

Coaffee, J. and Clarke, J. (2015) 'On Securing the Generational Challenge of Urban Resilience', *Town Planning Review*, 86, 3, 249–255.

Coaffee, J. and Fussey, P. (2015) 'Constructing Resilience through Security and Surveillance: The Practices and Tensions of Security-driven Resilience', *Security Dialogue*, 46, 1, 86–105.

Coaffee, J. and Healey P. (2003) 'My Voice My Place: Tracking Transformations in Urban Governance', *Urban Studies*, 40, 10, 1960–1978.

Coaffee, J. and O'Hare, P. (2008) 'Urban Resilience and National Security: The Role for Planners', *Proceeding of the Institute of Civil Engineers: Urban Design and Planning*, 161, DP4, 171–182.

Coaffee, J. and Rogers, P. (2008) 'Rebordering the City for New Security Challenges: From Counter Terrorism to Community Resilience', *Space and Polity*, 12, 2, 101–118.

Coaffee, J. and Wood, D. (2006) 'Security is Coming Home – Rethinking Scale and Constructing Resilience in the Global Urban Response to Terrorist Risk', *International Relations*, 20, 4, 503–517.

Coaffee, J., Moore, C., Fletcher, D. and Bosher, L. (2008a) 'Resilient Design for Community Safety and Terror-resistant Cities', *Proceedings of the Institute of Civil Engineers: Municipal Engineer*, 161, ME2, 103–110.

Coaffee, J., Murakami Wood, D. and Rogers, P. (2008b) *The Everyday Resilience of the City: How Cities Respond to Terrorism and Disaster* (London: Palgrave Macmillian).

Coaffee, J., O'Hare, P. and Hawkesworth, M. (2009) 'The Visibility of (In)security: The Aesthetics of Planning Urban Defences Against Terrorism', *Security Dialogue*, *40*, 489–511.

Coaffee, J., Rowlands, R. and Clarke, J. (2012) *DESURBS: Deliverable D1.1 – Security incidents analysis*, http://desurbs.eu/downloads/d1-1.pdf, accessed 12 July 2012.

COAG (Council of Australian Governments) (2011) *National Strategy for Disaster Resilience*, www.ag.gov.au/EmergencyManagement/Documents/NationalStrategyforDisasterResilience.PDF, accessed 11 December 2014.

Coleman, A. (1985) *Utopia on Trial: Vision and Reality in Planned Housing* (London: Hilary Shipman).

Collinge, C. and Gibney, J. (2010) 'Connecting Place, Policy and Leadership', *Policy Studies*, *31*, 4, 379–391.

Cornell, D. J. (2009) 'Planning and its Orientation to the Future', *International Planning Studies*, *14*, 1, 85–98.

Conzens, P., Saville, G. and Hillier, D. (2005) 'Crime Prevention Through Environmental Design (CPTED): A Review and Modern Bibliography', *Property Management*, *23*, 5, 328–356.

Conzens, P. M., Hillier, D. and Prescott, G. (2001) 'Crime and the Design of Residential Property. Exploring the Theoretical Background', *Property Management*, *19*, 2, 136–164.

Corburn, J. (2003) 'Bringing Local Knowledge into Environmental Decision Making: Improving Urban Planning for Communities at Risk, Journal of Planning Education and Research', *22*, 420–433. doi: 10.1177/0739456X03022004008.

Corner, J. (2004) 'Not Unlike Life Itself', *Harvard Design Magazine, 21*, 32–34.

Cote, M. and Nightingale, A. (2012) 'Resilience Thinking Meets Social Theory Situating Social Change in Socio-ecological Systems (SES) Research', *Progress in Human Geography, 36*, 4, 475–489.

Crawford, J. and French, W. (2008) 'A Low-carbon future: Spatial Planning's Role in Enhancing Technological Innovation in the Built Environment', *Energy Policy*, *36*, 4575–4579.

Cross, R. (2015, 30 April) 'Nepal earthquake: a disaster that shows quakes don't kill people, buildings do', *The Guardian*, www.theguardian.com/cities/2015/apr/30/nepal-earthquake-disaster-building-collapse-resilience-kathmandu, accessed 30 April 2015.

Cross, R., Mcnamara, H. and Pokrovskii, A. (2010) 'Memory of Recessions', Working Paper 10–09, Department of Economics, University of Strathclyde.

Cutter, S. L., Barnes, L., Berry, M., Burton, C., Evans, E., Tate, E. and Webb, J. (2008) 'A Place-based Model for Understanding Community Resilience to Natural Disasters', *Global Environmental Change, 18*, 598–606.

Cutter, S. L., Burton, C. G., and Emrich, C. T. (2010) 'Disaster Resilience Indicators for Benchmarking Baseline Conditions', *Journal of Homeland Security and Emergency Management*, 7, 1, Article 51.

Cyranoski, D. (2012) 'Rebuilding Japan: After the Deluge', *Nature*, *483*, 7388, 141–143.

Dainty, A. and Bosher, L. (2008) 'Afterword: Integrating Resilience into Construction Practice', in L. Bosher (ed.) *Hazards and the Built Environment: Attaining Built-in Resilience*, pp.357–372 (London: Taylor & Francis).

Davidoff, P. (1965) 'Advocacy and Pluralism in Planning', *Journal of the American Institute of Planners*, 31, 4, 331–338.

Davidson, D. (2010) 'The Applicability of the Concept of Resilience to Social Systems: Some Sources of Optimism and Nagging Doubts', *Society and Natural Resources*, 23, 12, 1135–1149.

Davis, M. (1990). *City of Quartz: Excavating the Future in Los Angeles* (London: Verso).

Davis, M. (1998) *Ecology of Fear: Los Angeles and the Imagination of Disaster* (New York: Metropolitan Books).

Davoudi, S. (2012) 'Resilience, a Bridging Concept or a Dead End?', *Planning Theory and Practice*, 13, 2, 299–307.

DCLG (Department for Communities and Local Government) (2006) Planning Policy Statement 3 (PPS3): Housing, London: Department for Communities and Local Government.

DCLG (Department for Communities and Local Government) (2007a) *National Indicators for Local Authorities and Local Authority Partnerships: Handbook of Definitions, Draft for Consultation* (London: DCLG).

DCLG (Department for Communities and Local Government) (2007b) 'Housing Market Assessments: Practice Guidance Version 2' (London: Office of the Deputy Prime Minister).

DCLG (2007c) 'Communities and Local Government Economics Paper 1: A Framework for Intervention' (London: Department for Communities and Local Government).

DCLG (Department for Communities and Local Government) (2010) *Total Place: A Whole Area Approach to Public Services* (London: TSO).

DCLG (Department for Communities and Local Government) (2011a) 'Live Table 244 Housebuilding: Permanent Dwellings Completed, by Tenure, England, Historical Calendar Year Series', www.communities.gov.uk/housing/housingresearch/housingstatistics/housingstatisticsby/housebuilding/livetables, accessed 24 June 2011.

DCLG (2011b) (Department for Communities and Local Government) 'Live Table 254 Housebuilding: Permanent Dwellings Completed, by House and Flat, Number of Bedroom and Tenure, England', www.communities.gov.uk/housing/housingresearch/housingstatistics/housingstatisticsby/housebuilding/livetables, accessed 29 June 2011.

DCLG (Department for Communities and Local Government) (2012) *National Planning Policy Framework* (London: TSO).

De Souza, R.M. and Parker, M. (2014) 'The Year That Resilience Gets Real', *New Security Beat*. www.newsecuritybeat.org/2014/01/year-resilience-real/, accessed 14 February 2014.

Dean (1999) *Governmentality: Power and Rule in Modern Society* (Thousand Oaks, CA: Sage).

de Goede, M. and Randalls, S. (2009) 'Precaution, Preemption: Arts and Technologies of the Actionable Future', *Environment and Planning D: Society and Space*, 27, 859–878.

Deleuze, G. (1992) 'Postscript on the Societies of Control' (trans. M. Joughin), *October*, 59, 3–7.

Delta Alliance (2014) *Towards a Comprehensive Framework for Adaptive Delta Management*, www.delta-alliance.org/media/default.aspx/emma/org/10848051/Towards+a+Comprehensive+Framework+for+Adaptive+Delta+Management. pdf, accessed 30 June 2014.

Delta Programme (2011). *Working on the Delta. Investing in a Safe and Attractive Netherlands, Now and in the Future*. Published by Ministry of Transport, Public Works and Water Management, Ministry of Agriculture, Nature, and Food Quality, Ministry of Housing, Spatial Planning and the Environment.

DETR (Department of the Environment, Transport and the Regions) (2000a) 'National Strategy for Neighbourhood Renewal. Report of Policy Action Team 7: Unpopular Housing' (London: HMSO).

DETR (Department of the Environment, Transport and the Regions) (2000b) 'Responding to Low Demand Housing and Unpopular Neighbourhoods: A Guide to Good Practice' (London: HMSO).

Department of Transport (1988) *Investigation into the Kings Cross Underground Fire*, www.railwaysarchive.co.uk/documents/DoT_KX1987.pdf, accessed 12 September 2012.

Dimmer, C. (2014) 'Evolving Place Governance Innovations and Pluralising Reconstruction Practices in Post-disaster Japan', *Planning Theory & Practice*, 15, 2, 260–265.

Dimmer, C. (2012) 'Letter from Tokyo – the challenges of creating more resilient architecture and infrastructure in earthquake- and tsunami-affected Japan', *Architectural Review Australia* (123), Special Issue 'The Resilient City', 25–35.

Doan, S., Ho Vo, B. and Collier, N. (2011) 'Tracking the Public Mood of Populations Affected by Natural Disasters as Well as an Early Warning System', *Lecture Notes of the Institute for Computer Sciences, Social Informatics and Telecommunications Engineering*, 91, 4, 58–66.

Doig, W (2014) 'The End of Our "Resilient Cities" Series Is Only the Beginning', https://nextcity.org/daily/entry/the-end-of-our-resilient-cities-series-is-only-the-beginning, accessed 19 September 2014.

Dolink, A. (2007) 'Assessing the Terrorist Threat to Singapore's Land Transportation Infrastructure', *Journal of Homeland Security and Emergency Management*, 4, 2, 1–22.

Donahue, A, and Tuohy, R. (2006) 'Lessons We Don't Learn: A Study of the Lessons of Disasters, Why We Repeat Them, and How We Can Learn Them', *Homeland Security Affairs*, 2, Article 4, www.hsaj.org/articles/167, accessed 14 September 2012.

Donnelly, M. (2015, 12 March) 'Planning "Should Focus on Resilience Rather than Trying to Predict the Future"', *Planning*, www.planningresource.co.uk/article/1337972/planning-should-focus-resilience-rather-trying-predict-future, accessed 12 March 2015.

Donofrio, J., Kuhn, Y., McWalter, K. and Winsor, M. (2009) 'Water Sensitive Urban Design: An Emerging Model in Sustainable Design and Comprehensive Water Cycle Management', *Environmental Practice*, 11, 3, 179–189.

Durodie, B. and Wessely, S. (2002) 'Resilience or Panic: the Public and Terrorism Attack', *The Lancet*, 130, 1901–1902.

Economics of Climate Adaptation Working Group (2009) *Shaping Climate-Resilient Development: A Framework for Decision-Making* (Zurich: Swiss Reinsurance).

Economist Intelligence Unit (2009) *European Green City Index: Assessing the environmental impact of Europe's major cities* www.thecrystal.org/assets/download/European-Green-City-Index.pdf, accessed 30 March 2015.

Edwards, C. (2009) *Resilient Nation* (London: Demos).

Ellin, N. (ed.) (1997) *Architecture of Fear* (New York: Princeton Architectural Press).

Elmer, G. and Opel, A. (2006) 'Surviving the Inevitable Future: Preemption in the Age of Faulty Intelligence', *Cultural Studies*, 20, 4/5, 447–492.

Environment Agency (2007) *Review of the 2007 Floods*, www.gov.uk/government/uploads/system/uploads/attachment_data/file/292924/geho1107bnmi-e-e.pdf, accessed 14 July 2012.

Environmental Systems Research Institute (2015) http://support.esri.com/en/knowledgebase/GISDictionary/term/spatial%20autocorrelation, accessed 30 March 2015.

Euronews (2015) Japan a world leader in disaster prevention, http://www.euronews.com/2015/03/30/japan-a-world-leader-in-disaster-prevention/, date accessed 30 March 2015.

Evans J. (2011) 'Resilience, Ecology and Adaptation in the Experimental City', *Transactions of the Institute of British Geographers*, 36, 223–237.

Evans, B. and Reid, J. (2014) *Resilient Life: The Art of Living Dangerously* (Cambridge: Polity Press).

Farazmand, A. (2007) 'Learning from the Katrina Crisis: A Global and International Perspective with Implications for Future Crisis Management', *Public Administration Review*, 67, s1, 149–159.

Ferrari, E. and Lee, P. (2010) *Building Sustainable Housing Markets: Lessons from a Decade of Changing Demand and Housing Market Renewal* (Coventry: Chartered Institute of Housing Practice Studies in collaboration with the Housing Studies Association).

Finch, P. (1996) 'The Fortress City is Not an Option', *The Architects' Journal*, February 15, 2.

Fischer, F. (2009) *Democracy and Expertise: Reorienting Policy Inquiry* (Oxford: Oxford University Press).

Fisher, T. (2012) *Designing to Avoid Disaster: The Nature of Fracture-critical Design*, (London: Routledge).

Fleischhauer, M., Birkmann, J., Greiving, S. and Stefansky, A. (2009) 'Climate-Proof Planning' *BBSR-Online-Publikation*, No. 26/2009.

Flinders, M. and Wood, M. (2014) 'Depoliticisation, Governance and the State', *Policy & Politics*, 42, 2, 135–149.

Flint, J. and Raco, M. (eds) (2012) *The Future of Sustainable Cities* (Bristol: Policy Press).

Flynn, S. (2007) *The Edge of Disaster: Rebuilding a Resilient Nation* (New York: Random House).

Flyvbjerg, B. (1998) *Rationality and Power: Democracy in Practice* (Chicago, IL: University of Chicago Press).

Folke, C. (2006) 'Resilience: The Emergence of a Perspective for Social–Ecological Systems Analysis', *Global Environmental Change*, 16, 253–267.

Folke, C., Carpenter, S., Walker, B., Chapin, T. and Rockström, J. (2010) 'Resilience Thinking: Integrating Resilience, Adaptability and Transformability', *Ecology and Society*, 15, 4, 20. Available at: www.ecologyandsociety.org/vol15/iss4/art20/, accessed 12 March 2015.

Forrest, R. and Murie, A. (1988) *Selling the Welfare State* (London: Routledge).

Franklin, J. (2014, 2 April) 'Chile Earthquake: Authorities Relieved at Apparent Low Levels of Casualties', *The Guardian*, www.theguardian.com/world/2014/apr/02/chile-earthquake-apparent-low-level-casualties, accessed 2 April 2014.

Fritz, H. M., Phillips, D. A., Okayasu, A., Shimozono, T., Liu, H., Mohammed, F., Skanavis, V., Synolakis, C. E. and Takahashi, T. (2012) 'The 2011 Japan Tsunami Current Velocity Measurements from Survivor Videos at Kesennuma Bay using LiDAR', *Geophysical Research Letters*, 39, 7, doi:10.1029/2011GL050686.

Frommer, D. (2011) 'Here's How The Japan Crisis Could Affect Apple iPad 2 Production and Other Tech Supply Chains', *Business Insider*, www.businessinsider.com/japan-supply-chain-2011-3, accessed 12 July 2011.

Fukushima Action Research (2013) 'Challenges of Decontamination, Community Regeneration and Livelihood Rehabilitation' 2nd Discussion Paper (Tokyo: Institute for Global Environmental Strategies).

Fünfgeld, H. and McEvoy, D. (2012) 'Resilience as a Useful Concept for Climate Change Adaptation?', *Planning Theory and Practice*, 13, 2, 324–328.

Furedi, F. (2006) *Culture of Fear Revisited*, 4th Edition, (Trowbridge: Continuum).

Galderisi, A. and Ferrara, F. F. (2012) 'Enhancing Urban Resilience in Face of Climate Change', *TeMA – Journal of Land Use, Mobility and Environment*, 69–87.

Gall, M. (2007) *Indices of Social Vulnerability to Natural Hazards: A Comparative Evaluation* (University of South Carolina: Columbia).

Garland, D. (1996) 'The Limits of the Sovereign State: Strategies of Crime Control in Contemporary Society', *British Journal of Criminology*, 36, 4, 445–471.

Gibney, J., Copeland, S. and Murie, A. (2009) 'Toward a "New" Strategic Leadership of Place for the Knowledge-based Economy', *Journal of Leadership*, 5, 1, 5–23.

Giddens, A. (1998) *The Third Way: The Renewal of Social Democracy* (Cambridge: Polity Press).

Giddens, A. (1991) *Modernity and Self-identity: Self and Society in the Late Modern Age* (Polity Press: Cambridge).

Gitay H., Wilson J. B. and Lee, W. G. (1996). 'Species Redundancy: A Redundant Concept?' *Journal of Ecology*, 84, 121–124.

Godschalk, D. R. (2003) 'Urban Hazard Mitigation: Creating Resilient Cities', *Natural Hazards Review*, 4, 3, 136–143.

Gold, J. R. and Revill, G. (eds) (2000) *Landscapes of Defence* (London: Prentice Hall).

Goldstein, B. (ed.) (2012) *Collaborative Resilience: Moving through Crisis to Opportunity* (Cambridge, MA: MIT Press).

Goldstein, B., Wessells, A., Lejano, R. and Butler, W. (2015) 'Narrating Resilience: Transforming Urban Systems Through Collaborative Storytelling', *Urban Studies*, 52, 7, 1285–1303.

Graham, S. (ed.) (2004) *Cities, War and Terrorism* (Oxford: Blackwell).

Greater New Orleans Urban Water Plan (2013) 'About', http://livingwithwater.com/blog/urban_water_plan/about/, accessed 1 December 2014.

Grosskopf, K. R. (2006) 'Evaluating the Societal Response to Antiterrorism Measures', *Journal of Homeland Security and Emergency Management*, 3, 2, 1–9.

Groves, R., Lee, P., Murie, A. and Nevin, B. (2001) 'Private Rented Housing in Liverpool: an Overview of Current Market Conditions', Research Report No. 3 (Liverpool: Liverpool City Council).

Gunderson, L. and Holling, C. S. (eds) (2002) *Panarchy: Understanding Transformations in Human and Natural Systems* (Washington: Island Press).

Gupta, K. (2007) 'Urban Flood Resilience Planning and Management Lessons for the Future: A Case Study of Mumbai, India', *Urban Water Journal*, 23, 1, 183–194.

Haas, P. (1992) 'Introduction: epistemic communities and international policy coordination', *International Organization* 46, 1, 1-35.

Haasnoot, M., Kwakkel, J., Walker, W. and ter Maat, J. (2013) 'Dynamic Adaptive Policy Pathways: A Method for Crafting Robust Decisions for a Deeply Uncertain World', *Global Environmental Change*, 23, 2, 485–498.

Hall, P. (1980) *Great Planning Disasters* (London: Weidenfeld).

Hall, P. (2002) *Cities of Tomorrow: An Intellectual History of Urban Planning and Design in the Twentieth Century* (Oxford: Blackwell).

Harding, A., Deas, I., Evans, R. and Wilks-Heeg, S. (2004) 'Reinventing cities in a Restructuring Region? The Rhetoric and Reality of Renaissance in Liverpool and Manchester', in M. Boddy and M. Parkinson (eds) *City Matters: Competitiveness, Cohesion and Urban Governance*, pp.33–50 (Bristol: Policy Press).

Hardt, M. and Negri, A. (2002) *Empire* (Cambridge, MA: Harvard University Press).

Harris, J., Tschudi, W. and Dyer, B. (2002) *U.S. Department of Energy Federal Energy Management Program: Securing Buildings and Saving Energy: Opportunities in the Federal Sector*, Presented at the US Green Building Conference, Austin Texas (Washington DC: US Green Building Council).

Harvey, D. (1989) 'From Managerialism to Entrepreneurialism: The Transformation in Urban Governance in Late Capitalism', Geografiska Annaler. Series B, *Human Geography*, 71, 1, The Roots of Geographical Change: 1973 to the Present (1989), 3–17.

Hasegawa, R. (2012) *Disaster Evacuation from Japan's 2011 Tsunami Disaster and the Fukushima Nuclear Accident, IDDRI Governance Study 5* (Paris: SciencesPo).

Haughton, G., Allmendinger, P., Counsell, D. and Vigar, G. (2010) *The New Spatial Planning: Territorial Management with Soft Spaces and Fuzzy Boundaries* (London: Routledge).

Hay, C. (2007) *Why We Hate Politics* (Cambridge: Polity Press).

Healey, P. (1996) 'The Communicative Turn in Planning Theory and its Implications for Spatial Strategy Formation', *Environment and Planning B: Planning and Design*, 23, 217–234.

Healey, P. (1997) *Collaborative Planning: Shaping Places in Fragmented Societies.* (Basingstoke: Macmillan).

Healey, P. (1998) 'Building Institutional Capacity Through Collaborative Approaches to Urban Planning', *Environment and Planning A, 30,* 9, 1531–1546.

Healey, P. (2006) *Collaborative Planning: Shaping Places in Fragmented Societies.* 2nd edition (London: Palgrave Macmillan).

Healey, P. (2007) *Urban Complexity and Spatial Strategies: Towards a Relational Planning for our Times* (London: Routledge).

Healey, P. (2010) *Making Better Places: The Planning Project in the Twenty-First Century* (London: Palgrave Macmillan).

Health and Safety Executive (2011) *Buncefield: Why did it Happen?*, www.hse.gov.uk/comah/buncefield/buncefield-report.pdf, accessed 2 July 2012.

Heng, Y. (2006) 'The Transformation of War Debate: Through the Looking Glass of Ulrich Beck's World Risk Society', *International Relations*, 20, 1, 69–91.

Hillier, J. (ed.) (2002) *Habitus: A Sense of Place* (Aldershot: Ashgate).

Hinkel, J. (2011) '"Indicators of Vulnerability and Adaptive Capacity": Towards a Clarification of the Science–Policy Interface', *Global Environmental Change, 21*, 1, 198–208.

Hinman, E. E. and Hammond, D. J. (1997) *Lessons from the Oklahoma City Bombing: Defensive Design Techniques* (Reston, Virginia: American Society of Civil Engineers).

Hollander, J. B. and Whitfield, C. (2005) 'The Appearance of Security Zones in US cities after 9/11', *Property Management, 23*, 4, 244–256.

Holling, C. S. (1973) 'Resilience and Stability of Ecological Systems', *Annual Review of Ecology Evolution and Systematics, 4*, 1–23.

Holling, C. S. (1996) 'Engineering Resilience Versus Ecological Resilience', in P. C. Schulze, (ed.) *Engineering within Ecological Constraints*, pp.31–43 (Washington, D.C., National Academy Press).

Holling, C. S. (2001) 'Understanding the Complexity of Economic, Ecological, and Social Systems', *Ecosystems, 4*, 390–405.

Holloway, J. (2012) 'Despite Fukushima Disaster, Global Nuclear Power Expansion Continues', http://arstechnica.com/science/2012/03/despite-fukushima-disaster-global-nuclear-power-expansion-continues/, accessed 26 May 2015.

Home Office (2006) *Countering International Terrorism: The United Kingdom's Strategy* (London: TSO).

Home Office (2009) *Working Together to Protect Crowded Places: A Consultation Document* (London: Home Office).

Home Office (2010a) *Crowded Places: The Planning System and Counter-Terrorism* (London: Home Office).

Home Office (2010b) *Protecting Crowded Places: Design and Technical Issues* (London: Home Office).

Home Office (2010c) *Working Together to Protect Crowded Places* (London: TSO).

Hopkins, R. (2008) *The Transition Handbook: From Oil Dependency to Local Resilience,* (Cambridge: Green Books).

Hopkins, R. (2011) *The Transition Companion: making your community more resilient in uncertain times,* (Cambridge, Green Books).

Hornbeck, R. and Naidu, S. (2014) 'When the Levee Breaks: Black Migration and Economic Development in the American South', *American Economic Review, 104*, 3, 963–990.

House of Commons (2006a) *Report of the Official Account of the Bombings in London on 7th July 2005,* www.gov.uk/government/uploads/system/uploads/attachment_data/file/228837/1087.pdf, accessed 2 July 2007.

House of Commons (2006b) 'Housing, Planning, Local Government and the Regions Committee: Affordability and the Supply of Housing' (Third Report of Session 2005–06), House of Commons, 1, 77 (London: HMSO).

Howe, J. and White, I. (2004) 'Like a Fish out of Water: The Relationship Between Planning and Flood Risk Management in the UK', *Planning Practice and Research, 19*, 4, 415–442.

Hower, M. (2015) 'Miami's Climate Vice: Budget Woes Stunt Urban Resilience', *GreenBiz*, www.greenbiz.com/article/miamis-vice-cash-flow-problems-curb-climate-resilience, accessed 17 September 2015.

HSSA (2011) Housing Strategy Statistical Appendix, www.communities.gov.uk/housing/housingresearch, accessed 14 June 2011.

Hurricane Sandy Rebuilding Task Force (2013) *Hurricane Sandy Rebuilding Strategy* (Washington: US Department of Housing and Urban Development).

Hussain, M. (2013, 5 March) 'Resilience: Meaningless Jargon or Development Solution?', *The Guardian*, www.theguardian.com/global-development-professionals-network/2013/mar/05/resilience-development-buzzwords, accessed 5 March 2013.

Hutter, G., Leibenath, M. and Mattissek, A. (2014) 'Governing Through Resilience? Exploring Flood Protection in Dresden, Germany', *Social Science*, 3, 272–287.

ICLEI (2011) *Financing the Resilient City: A Demand Driven Approach to Development, Disaster Risk Reduction and Climate Adaptation*, An ICLEI White Paper, ICLEI Global Report, http://resilient-cities.iclei.org/fileadmin/sites/resilient-cities/files/Frontend_user/Report-Financing_Resilient_City-Final.pdf, accessed 12 July 2012.

IPCC – Intergovernmental Panel on Climate Change (2007) *Climate Change 2007: The Scientific Basis. Contribution of Working Group I to the Fourth Assessment Report of the Intergovernmental Panel on Climate Change*, edited by S. Solomon *et al.* (New York: Cambridge University Press).

IPCC – Intergovernmental Panel on Climate Change (2012) *Managing the Risks of Extreme Events and Disasters to Advance Climate Change Adaptation: Special Report of the IPCC*, www.ipcc.ch/pdf/special-reports/srex/SREX_Full_Report. pdf, accessed 1 December 2012.

IPCC – Intergovernmental Panel on Climate Change (2014) *Climate Change 2014: Impacts, Adaptation, and Vulnerability. Part A: Global and Sectoral Aspects. Contribution of Working Group II to the Fifth Assessment Report of the Intergovernmental Panel on Climate Change*, https://ipcc-wg2.gov/AR5/images/uploads/WG2AR5_SPM_FINAL.pdf, accessed 13 January 2015.

Isin, E. (2004) 'The Neurotic Citizen', *Citizenship Studies*, 8, 3, 217–235.

Jabareen, Y. (2013) 'Planning the Resilient City: Concepts and Strategies for Coping with Climate Change and Environmental Risk', *Cities*, 31, 220–229.

Japan Cabinet Office (2011) *Disaster Management in Japan, Director General for Disaster Management* (Tokyo: Cabinet Office, Government of Japan).

Japan Statistics Bureau (1999) *Japan Statistical Yearbook 1999* (Tokyo: Ministry of Internal Affairs and Communications).

Japan Times (2015, 11 March) 'Survivors mark four years since 3/11 disasters', www.japantimes.co.jp/news/2015/03/11/national/survivors-mark-4-years-since-311-disasters/#.Vo_SXvmLTVZ, accessed 15th March 2015.

Japan Water Forum (2005) *Typhoon Isewan (Vera) and its Lessons* (Tokyo: Japan Water Forum).

Jeffery, C. R. (1971) *Crime Prevention through Environmental Design* (Beverley Hills: Sage).

Jerneck A. and Olsson L. (2008) 'Adaptation and the Poor: Development, Resilience and Transition', *Climate Policy*, 8, 170–182.

Jha, A. K. and Brecht, H. (2012) 'Building Urban Resilience in East Asia'. *An Eye on East Asia and Pacific*, 8 (Washington, DC: World Bank).

Jha, A. K., Miner, T. W. and Stanton-Geddes, Z. (eds) (2013) *Building Urban Resilience: Principles, Tools, and Practice* (Washington: International Bank for Reconstruction and Development).

Johnson, C. and Blackburn, S. (2012) 'Advocacy for Urban Resilience: UNISDR's Making Cities Resilient Campaign', *Environment and Urbanization*, 26, 1, 29–52.

Jones, L., Ludi, E. and Levine, S. (2010) 'Towards a Characterisation of Adaptive Capacity: A Framework for Analysing Adaptive Capacity at the Local Level', *Overseas Development Institute*, www.odi.org/publications/5177-adaptive-capacity-framework-local-level-climate, accessed 28 January 2015.

Joseph, J. (2013) 'Resilience as Embedded Neoliberalism: A Governmentality Approach', *Resilience: International Policies, Practices and Discourses*, 1, 38–52.

Kay, A. (2005) 'A Critique of the Use of Path Dependency in Policy Studies', *Public Administration*, 83, 3, 553.

Keck, M. and Sakdapolrak, P. (2013) 'What is Social Resilience? Lessons Learned and Ways Forward', *Erdkunde*, 67, 1, 5–18.

Kelman, I. (2015) 'Climate Change and the Sendai Framework for Disaster Risk Reduction', *International Journal of Disaster Risk Science*, 6, 117–127.

Klein, N. (2007) *The Shock Doctrine: The Rise of Disaster Capitalism* (London: Penguin).

Klijn F., Kreibich, H., de Moel, H. and Penning-Rowsell, E. (2015) 'Adaptive Flood Risk Management Planning Based on a Comprehensive Flood Risk Conceptualisation', *Mitigation and Adaptation Strategies for Global Change*, 20, 845–864.

Kuhlicke, C. and Steinfuhrer, A. (2013) 'Searching for Resilience or Building Social Capacities for Flood Risks?', *Planning Theory & Practice*, 14, 1, 114–120.

Landscape Institute (2011) 'Caldew and Carlisle City Flood Alleviation Scheme', www.landscapeinstitute.co.uk/casestudies/casestudy.php?id=70, accessed 14 July 2012.

Lee, P. (1999) 'Where are the Socially Excluded? Continuing Debates in the Identification of Poor Neighbourhoods', *Regional Studies*, 33, 5, 483–486.

Lee, P. (2010) 'Competitiveness and Social Exclusion: The Importance of Place and Rescaling in Housing and Regeneration Policies', in P. Malpass and R. Rowlands (eds) *Housing, Markets and Policy*, pp. 184–202 (London: Routledge).

Lee, P. and Murie, A. (1999) 'Spatial and Social Divisions within British Cities: Beyond Residualisation', *Housing Studies*, 14, 5, 625–640.

Lee, P. and Nevin, B. (2003) 'Changing Demand for Housing: Restructuring Markets and the Public Policy Framework', *Housing Studies*, 18, 1, 65–86.

Lee, P., Murie, A. and Gordon, D. (1995) 'Area Measures of Deprivation: A Study of Current Methods and Best Practices in the Identification of Poor Areas in Great Britain' (Birmingham: Centre for Urban and Regional Studies/Joseph Rowntree Foundation).

Lee, P., Nevin, B., Murie, A., Goodson, L. and Phillimore, J. (2001) 'The West Midlands Housing Markets: Changing Demand, Decentralisation and Urban Regeneration', West Midlands Housing Corporation.

Leichenko, R. (2011) 'Climate Change and Urban Resilience', *Current Opinion in Environmental Sustainability*, 3, 164–168.

Leverhulme Trust (2010) 'Application Material for a Research Programme Grant on Resilience' (London: Leverhulme Trust).

Lewis, M. and Conaty, P. (2012) *The Resilience Imperative: Cooperative Transitions to a Steady-state Economy* (Philadelphia: New Society Publishers).

Linkov, I., Bridges, T., Creutzig, F., Decker, J., Fox-Lent, C., Kröger, W. and Thiel-Clemen, T. (2014) 'Changing the Resilience Paradigm', *Nature Climate Change*, 4, 6, 407–409.

London Resilience Partnership (2013) 'Strategy Document', www.london.gov.uk/sites/default/files/gla_migrate_files_destination/London%20Resilience%20Partnership%20Strategy%20v1%20web%20version.pdf, accessed 1 February 2014.

Lowenthal, D. (1992) 'The Death of the Future', in S. Wallman (ed.) *Contemporary Futures: Perspectives from Social Anthropology*, pp. 23–35 (London, UK: Routledge).

Ludwig, D., Walker, B. and Holling, C. S. (1997) 'Sustainability, Stability, and Resilience', *Conservation Ecology*, 1, 1, 7. Available at: www.consecol.org/vol1/iss1/art7/, accessed 1 January 2012.

Luers, A., Lobell, D., Sklar, L. S., Addams, C. L. and Matson, P. M. (2003) 'A Method for Quantifying Vulnerability, applied to the Yaqui Valley, Mexico', *Global Environmental Change*, 13, 4, 255–267.

Lupton, D. (1999) *Risk* (London: Routledge).

Lyon, D. (2003) *Surveillance after September 11* (Cambridge: Polity).

MacKinnon, D. and Derickson, K. D. (2013) 'From Resilience to Resourcefulness: A Critique of Resilience Policy and Activism', *Progress in Human Geography*, 37, 2, 253–270.

Majoor, S. (2015) 'Resilient Practices: A Paradox-Oriented Approach for Large-Scale Development Projects', *Town Planning Review*, 86, 3, 257–277.

Malcolm, J. (2013) 'Project Argus and the Resilient Citizen', *Politics*, 33, 4, 311–321.

Manuel-Navarrete, D., Pelling, M. and Redclift, M. (2011) 'Critical Adaptation to Hurricanes in the Mexican Caribbean: Development Visions, Governance Structures, and Coping Strategies', *Global Environmental Change*, 21, 1, 249–258.

Marcuse, P. (2006) 'Security or Safety in Cities? The Threat of Terrorism after 9/11', *International Journal of Urban and Regional Research*, 30, 4, 919–929.

Martin, R. (2012) 'Regional Economic Resilience, Hysteresis and Recessionary Shocks', *Journal of Economic Geography*, 12, 1–32.

Martin, R. and Sunley, P. (2015) 'On the Notion of Regional Economic Resilience: Conceptualization and Explanation', *Journal of Economic Geography*, 15, 1, 1–42 doi:10.1093/jeg/lbu015.

Massumi, B. (ed) (1993) *The Everyday Politics of Fear* (Minneapolis: University of Minnesota Press).

Massumi, B. (2005) 'Fear (The Spectrum Said)', *Positions*, 13, 1, 31–48.

Matanle, P. and Rausch, A. (2011) *Japan's Shrinking Regions in the 21st Century: Contemporary Responses to Depopulation and Socioeconomic decline* (Amherst, NY: Cambria Press).

Mazur, L. (2015) 'Meet Obama's Chief Resilience Officer', *Grist*, http://grist.org/climate-energy/meet-obamas-chief-resilience-officer/, accessed 26 February 2015.

Mazur, L. and Fairchild, D. (2015) 'Is "resilience" the new sustainababble?', *Grist*, http://grist.org/article/is-resilience-the-new-sustainababble/, accessed 14 January 2015.

McEvoy, D., Fünfgeld, H. and Bosomworth, K. (2013) 'Resilience and Climate Change Adaptation: The Importance of Framing', *Planning Practice & Research*, 28, 3, 280–293.

McEvoy, D., Lindley, S. and Handley, J. (2006) 'Adaptation and Mitigation in Urban Areas: Synergies and Conflicts', *Proceedings of ICE, Municipal Engineer Special Issue: Climate Change*, 159, 4, 185–191.

McInroy, N. and Longlands, S. (2010) *Productive Local Economies: Creating Resilient Places* (Manchester: Centre for Local Economic Strategies).

Meyer H., Morris D. and Waggonner, D. (2009) *Dutch Dialogues – New Orleans– The Netherlands – Common Challenges in Urban Deltas* (Amsterdam: SUN).

Mguni, N. and Bacon, N. (2010) *Taking the Temperature of Local Communities: The Wellbeing and Resilience Measure* (London: The Young Foundation).

Minca, C. (2006) 'Giorgio Agamben and the New Biopolitical *Nomos*', *Geografiska Annaler: Series B, Human Geography*, 88, 4, 387–403.

Miyake, S. (2014) 'Post-disaster Reconstruction in Iwate and New Planning Challenges for Japan', *Planning Theory & Practice*, 15, 2, 246–250.

Mouffe, C. (2005) *On the Political* (Abingdon: Routledge).

Moynihan, D. (2009) *The Response to Hurricane Katrina, International Risk Governance Council*, http://irgc.org/wp-content/uploads/2012/04/Hurricane_Katrina_full_case_study_web.pdf, accessed 12 February 2010.

Murakami, K. and Murakami Wood, D. (2014) 'Planning Innovation and Post-disaster Reconstruction: The Case of Tohoku, Japan', *Planning Theory & Practice*, 15, 237–265.

Murie A., Nevin, B. and Leather P. (1998) 'Changing Demand and Unpopular Housing', Working Paper 4 (London: Housing Corporation).

Mustafa, D. (2005) 'The Terrible Geographicalness of Terrorism: Reflections of a Hazards Geographer', *Antipode*, 37, 1, 72–92.

Mythen, G. and Walklate, S. (2006) 'Communicating the Terrorist Risk: Harnessing a Culture of Fear', *Crime, Media and Culture*, 2, 2, 123–144.

NaCTSO (National Counter Terrorism Security Office) (2010) 'Argus Professional', http://designforsecurity.org/cpd-request-form/argus, accessed 14 July 2012.

Nadin, V. (2010) *European Spatial Planning and Territorial Cooperation* (London: Routledge).

National Academies (2012) *Disaster Resilience: A National Imperative* (Washington: National Academies Press).

National Academies of Science and Engineering (2014) *Resilien-Tech: 'Resilience by Design': A Strategy for the Technology Issues of the Future* (Berlin: acatech).

National Capital Planning Commission (2001) *The National Capital Urban Design and Security Plan: Designing and Testing of Perimeter Security Elements*, www.ncpc.gov/DocumentDepot/Publications/SecurityPlans/NCUDSP/NCUDSP_Section1.pdf, accessed 23 September 2002.

National Diet of Japan (2012) *The Fukushima Nuclear Accident Independent Investigation Commission* (Tokyo: The National Diet of Japan).

Neocleous, M. (2013) 'Resisting Resilience', *Radical Philosophy*, 178, 2–7.

Nevin, B., Lee, P., Goodson, L., Phillimore, J. and Murie, A. (2001) Changing Housing Markets and Urban Regeneration in the M62 Corridor, Housing Corporation, Manchester.

Newman, O. (1972) *Defensible Space: Crime Prevention through Urban Design* (New York: Macmillan).

Newman, O. (1973) *Defensible Space: People and Design in the Violent City* (London: Architectural Press).

New York Times (2012, 3 March) 'Mission Control, Built for Cities: I.B.M. Takes "Smarter Cities" Concept to Rio de Janeiro', www.nytimes.com/2012/03/04/business/ibm-takes-smarter-cities-concept-to-rio-de-janeiro.html?pagewanted=all&_r=0, accessed 3 March 2012.

Nirupama, N. and Simonovic, S. (2007) 'Increase of Flood Risk due to Urbanisation: A Canadian Example', *Natural Hazards, 40*, 1, 25–41.

Number 10 Press Briefing (2007, 14 November) 'Afternoon press briefing'.

NYS (2013) 'New York State 2100 Commission: Recommendations to Improve the Strength and Resilience of the Empire State's Infrastructure', www.rebuildbydesign.org/research/resources/36-resources/70/70, accessed 12 December 2013.

O'Malley, P. (2010) 'Resilient Subjects: Uncertainty, Warfare and Liberalism', *Economy and Society, 39*, 488–509.

O'Brien, G. and Read, P. (2005) 'The Future of UK Emergency Management: New Wine, Old Skin?', *Disaster Prevention and Management, 14*, 3, 353–361.

O'Hare, P. and White, I. (2013) 'Deconstructing Resilience: Lessons from Planning Practice', *Planning Practice & Research, 28*, 3, 275–279.

O'Hare, P., White, I. and Connelly, A. (2015) 'Insurance as Maladaptation: Resilience and the "Business as Usual" Paradox', *Environment and Planning C*, doi: 10.1177/0263774X15602022

ODPM (Office of the Deputy Prime Minister) (2004) Housing Market Assessment Manual, London: Office of the Deputy Prime Minister.

Olshansky, R. (2011) 'Review of Designing Resilience: Preparing for Extreme Events', *Journal of Comparative Policy Analysis: Research and Practice, 13*, 2, 233–235.

Olshansky, R. and Johnson, L. (2010) *Clear as Mud: Planning for the Rebuilding of New Orleans* (Chicago and Washington, DC: American Planning Association, Planners Press).

Olshansky, R. B. and Chang, S. (2009) 'Planning for Disaster Recovery: Emerging Research Needs and Challenges', in H. Blanco and M. Shaken Alberti (eds) 'Shrinking, Hot, Impoverished and Informal: Emerging Research Agendas in Planning', *Progress in Planning, 72*, 200–209.

Olshansky, R. B., Johnson, L. A. and Topping, K. C. (2006) 'Rebuilding Communities Following Disaster: Lessons from Kobe and Los Angeles', *Built Environment, 32*, 4, 354–374.

Onishi, N. (2011, 24 June) 'Safety Myth' Left Japan Ripe for Nuclear Crisis, *New York Times*, www.nytimes.com/2011/06/25/world/asia/25myth.html?_r=0, accessed 24 May 2015.

Osborne, D. and Gaebler, T. (1993) *Reinventing Government: How the Entrepreneurial Spirit is Transforming the Public Sector* (New York: Plume Publications).

Ougo, J. (2015, 26 January) 'Kenya: Why Urban Planning Is a National Security Priority', *The Star*, http://allafrica.com/stories/201501260326.html, accessed 27 September 2015.

Paganini, Z. (2015, April) 'Underwater: The Production of Informal Space though Discourses of Resilience in Canarsie, Brooklyn', address to the session on Planning for Resilience in a Neoliberal Age at the 2015 *Annual Meeting of the Association of American Geographers*, 25 April, 2015.

Parkinson, M., Ball, M., Blake, N. and Key, T. (2009) *The Credit Crunch and Regeneration: Impact and Implications*, London: Department for Communities and Local Government.

Pawley, M. (1998) *Terminal Architecture* (London: Reaktion).

Pawson, R. and Tilley, N. (1997) *Realistic Evaluation* (London: Sage).

Pelling, M. (2003) *The Vulnerability of Cities: Natural Disasters and Social Resilience*. (London: Earthscan).

Pelling, M. (2011) 'Urban Governance and Disaster Risk Reduction in the Caribbean: The Experiences of Oxfam GB', *Environment and Urbanization*, 23, 2, 383–400.

Pelling, M. and High, C. (2005) 'Understanding Adaptation: What Can Social Capital Offer Assessments of Adaptive Capacity?', *Global Environmental Change*, 15, 4, 308–319.

Pendall, R., Foster, K. and Cowell, M. (2010) 'Resilience and Regions: Building Understanding of the Metaphor', *Cambridge Journal of Regions Economy and Society*, 3, 1, 71–84.

Peterson, S. (2014) 'An Unflinching Look at Flood Risk', *Urban Land* http://urban-land.uli.org/sustainability/unflinching-look-flood-risk/, accessed 21 November 2015.

Pike, A., Dawley, S. and Tomaney, J. (2010) 'Resilience, Adaptation and Adaptability', *Cambridge Journal of Regions, Economy and Society*, 3, 1, 59–70.

Planning Commission General Economic Department (2014) Bangladesh Delta Plan 2100 Inception Report, Dhaka 2014, http://bangladesh.nlembassy.org/binaries/content/assets/postenweb/b/bangladesh/netherlands-embassy-in-dhaka/import/water-management/project-documents/bangladesh-delta-plan-2100/delta-plan-inception-report-version-3wf-30-09-2014.pdf, accessed 14 September 2014.

Planning Institute of Jamaica (2009) *Vision 2030: The National Development Plan – Planning for a Secure & Prosperous Future*, www.vision2030.gov.jm/Portals/0/NDP/Vision%202030%20Jamaica%20NDP%20Full%20No%20Cover%20(web).pdf, accessed 1 February 2014.

Porter, L. and Davoudi, S. (2012) 'The Politics of Resilience for Planning: A Cautionary Note', *Planning Theory & Practice*, 13, 2, 329–333.

Power, A. (1997) *Estates on the Edge: The Social Consequences of Mass Housing in Northern Europe* (London: Palgrave Macmillan).

Power, A. and Mumford, K. (1999) *The Slow Death of Great Cities? Urban Abandonment or Urban Renaissance* (York: Joseph Rowntree Foundation).

Prasad, N., Ranghieri, F., Shah, F., Trohanis, Z., Kessler, E. and Sinha, R. (2009) *Climate Resilient Cities: A Primer on Reducing Vulnerabilities to Disasters* (Washington, DC: International Bank for Reconstruction and Development/ World Bank).

Prior, T. and Hagmann, J. (2013) 'Measuring Resilience: Methodological and Political Challenges of a Trend Security Concept', *Journal of Risk Research*, 17, 3, 281–298, http://dx.doi.org/10.1080/13669877.2013.808686.

Pyati, A. (2015) 'Real Returns for Investing in Resilience', *Urban Land*, http://urban-land.uli.org/sustainability/real-returns-investing-resilience/, accessed 7 October 2015.

Raco, M. and Street, E. (2012) 'Resilience Planning, Economic Change and The Politics of Post-recession Development in London and Hong Kong', *Urban Studies*, 49, 5, 1065–1087.

Ravilious, K. (2015) 'Nepal Quake: Why Are Some Tremors so Deadly?', www.bbc.co.uk/news/32549706, accessed 1 May 2015.

Rebuild by Design (2014) www.rebuildbydesign.org/, accessed 18 December 2014.

Restemeyer, B., Woltjer, J. and van den Brink, M. (2014) *Exploring Adaptive Strategic Spatial Planning to Make Urban Regions More Flood Resilient: Adaptive Delta Management in the Netherlands and the Rotterdam Region*, paper presented at the AESOP conference, Utrecht, June.

Reuters (2015) 'Britain Needs Complete Rethink on Flood Defences after Swathes of England Hit', http://uk.reuters.com/article/us-britain-floods-idUKK-BN0UB16I20151229, accessed 29 December 2015.

Roberts, D. (2010) 'Prioritizing Climate Change Adaptation and Local Level Resilience in Durban, South Africa', *Environment and Urbanization*, 22, 397–413.

Robertson, D., McIntosh, I. and Smyth, J. (2010) 'Neighbourhood Identity: The Path Dependency of Class and Place', *Housing, Theory and Society*, 27, 3, 258–273.

Robertson, J. (2015, 23 March) 'Queensland to Create Permanent Disaster Recovery Agency', *The Guardian*, www.theguardian.com/australia-news/2015/mar/23/queensland-to-create-permanent-disaster-recovery-agency?CMP=share_btn_fb, accessed 23 March 2015.

Rockefeller Foundation (n.d) 'Rotterdam's Resilience Challenge', www.100resilientcities.org/cities/entry/rotterdams-resilience-challenge, accessed 14 September 2015.

Rockefeller Foundation (2013) *About 100 Resilient Cities*, www.100resilientcities.org/pages/about-us#/-_/, accessed 18 December 2013.

Rockefeller Foundation (2014a) *City Resilience Framework, April 2014* (New York and London: The Rockefeller Foundation: with Ove Arup & Partners International) http://publications.arup.com/~/media/Publications/Files/Publications/C/City_Resilience_Framework_pdf.ashx, accessed 10 March 2015.

Rockefeller Foundation (2014b) *City Resilience Index: Research Report Volume 1 Desk Study, April 2014* (New York and London: The Rockefeller Foundation: with Ove Arup & Partners International), http://publications.arup.com/~/media/Publications/Files/Publications/C/Volume_1_Desk_Study_Report.ashx, accessed 13 March 2015.

Rockefeller Foundation (2014c) *City Resilience Index: Research Report Volume 2 Fieldwork Data Analysis, April 2014* (New York and London: The Rockefeller Foundation: with Ove Arup & Partners International), http://publications.arup.com/~/media/Publications/Files/Publications/C/Volume_2_Fieldwork_Report.ashx , accessed 31 March 2015.

Rockefeller Foundation (2014d) *City Resilience Index: Research Report Volume 3 Urban Measurement Report, May 2014* (New York and London: The Rockefeller Foundation with Ove Arup & Partners International), http://publications.arup.com/Publications/C/City_Resilience_Framework.aspx, accessed 31 March 2015.

Rodin, J. (2015) *The Resilience Dividend: Being Strong in a World Where Things Go Wrong* (New York: Public Affairs).

Rogers, P. (2011) 'Development of Resilient Australia: Enhancing the PPRR Approach with Anticipation, Assessment and Registration of Risks', *The Australian Journal of Emergency Management*, 26, 1, 54–58.

Romão, X., Costa, A. A., Paupério, E., Rodrigues, H., Vicente, R., Varum, H. and Costa, A. (2013) 'Field Observations and Interpretation of the Structural Performance of Constructions After the 11 May 2011 Lorca Earthquake', *Engineering Failure Analysis*, 34, 670–692.

Romer, R. (2001) *Advanced Macroeconomics*. (New York: McGraw Hill).

Rose, N. (2000) 'Government and Control', *British Journal of Criminology*, 40, 2, 321–339.

Rose, N. (2007) 'Government and Control', in J. Muncie (ed.) *Criminal Justice and Crime Control* (London: Sage).

Roy, A., Wenger, S., Fletcher, T., Walsh, C., Ladson, A., Shuster, W., Thurston, H. and Brown, R. (2008) 'Impediments and Solutions to Sustainable, Watershed-scale Urban Stormwater Management: Lessons from Australia and the United States', *Environmental Management*, 42, 344–359.

Royal Society (2014) *Resilience to Extreme Weather* (London: Royal Society).

Rutter, M. (1985) 'Resilience in the Face of Adversity: Protective Factors and Resistance to Psychiatric Disorder', *British Journal of Psychiatry*, 147, 598–611.

Rydin, Y. (2010) *Governing for Sustainable Urban Development* (London: Earthscan).

Savitch, H. (2005) 'An Anatomy of Urban Terror: Lessons from Jerusalem and Elsewhere', *Urban Studies*, 42, 3, 361–395.

Schumpeter, J. (1976) *Capitalism, Socialism, and Democracy* (London: Allen and Unwin).

Scott, M. (2013) 'Living with Flood Risk,' *Planning Theory and Practice*, 14, 103–140.

Sendai City Council (2014) 'Sendai City Earthquake Disaster Reconstruction Plan, December 2011', www.city.sendai.jp/language/English.html, accessed 20 September 2014.

Serre, D. and Barroca, B (2013) 'Natural Hazard Resilient Cities', *Natural Hazards and Earth System Science*, 12, 2675–2678.

Shaw, K. (2012a) 'Reframing Resilience: Challenges for Planning Theory and Practice', *Planning Theory & Practice*, 13, 2, 308–312.

Shaw, K. (2012b) 'The Rise of the Resilient Local Authority?', *Local Government Studies*, 38, 3, 281–300.

Shirlow, P. and Murtagh, B. (2006) *Belfast: Segregation, Violence and the City* (London: Pluto Press).

Siemens (2013) *Toolkit for Resilient Cities*, http://w3.siemens.com/topics/global/en/sustainable-cities/resilience/Documents/pdf/Toolkit_for_Resilient_Cities_Summary.pdf, date accessed 14 January 2014.

Simmie, J. and Martin, R. (2010) 'The Economic Resilience of Regions: Towards an Evolutionary Approach', *Cambridge Journal of Regions, Economy and Society*, 3, 1, 27–43.

Smit, B. and Wandel, J. (2006) 'Adaptation, Adaptive Capacity and Vulnerability', *Global Environmental Change*, 16, 3, 282–292.

Smith, A., Stirling, A. and Berkhout, F. (2005) 'The Governance of Sustainable Socio-technical Transitions', *Research Policy*, 34, 1491–1510.

Smith, J. (2007) 'House of Commons Debate', 14 Nov 2007, Col 45WS.

Soffer, A. and Minghi, J. V. (1986) 'Israel's Security Landscapes: The Impact of Military Considerations on Land-use', *Political Geographer*, 38, 1, 28–41.

Stern, N. (2006) *Stern Review on The Economics of Climate Change* (London: HM Treasury).

Sternberg, E. and Lee, G. C. (2006) 'Meeting the Challenge of Facility Protection for Homeland Security', *Journal of Homeland Security and Emergency Management*, 3, 1, 1–19.

Strunz, S. (2012) 'Is Conceptual Vagueness an Asset? Arguments from Philosophy of Science Applied to the Concept of Resilience', *Ecological Economics*, 76, 112–118. doi:10.1016/j.ecolecon.2012.02.012.

Supkoff, L. M. (2012) 'Situating Resilience in Developmental Context', in M. Ungar (ed.) *The Social Ecology of Resilience: A Handbook of Theory and Practice*, pp. 127–142 (New York: Springer).

Suzuki, H. (2015) 'Interview with Professor Hiroshi Suzuki, Institute for Global Environmental Strategies', Kanagawa, Japan, Tuesday 3 March 2015.

Swyngedouw, E. (2005) 'Governance Innovation and the Citizen: The Janus Face of Governance-Beyond-the-State', *Urban Studies*, 42, 11, 1991–2006.

Swyngedouw, E. (2009) 'The Antinomies of the Postpolitical City: In Search of a Democratic Politics of Environmental Production', *International Journal of Urban and Regional Research*, 33, 3, 601–620.

Taleb, N. (2007) *The Black Swan: The Impact of the Highly Improbable* (London: Penguin).

Tewdwr-Jones, M. (1999) 'Discretion, Flexibility, and Certainty in British Planning: Emerging Ideological Conflicts and Inherent Political Tensions', *Journal of Planning Education and Research* 18, 3, 244–256.

Thoits, P. A. (1995) 'Stress, Coping, and Social Support Processes: Where Are We? What Next?', *Journal of Health and Social Behavior*, 35, 53–79.

Timmerman, P. (1981) *Vulnerability, Resilience and the Collapse of Society: A Review of Models and Possible Climatic Applications* (Toronto: Institute for Environmental Studies, University of Toronto).

Tomita, H. (2014) 'Reconstruction of Tsunami-devastated Fishing Villages in the Tohoku Region of Japan and the Challenges for Planning', *Planning Theory & Practice*, 15, 2, 242–246.

Trickett, L. and Lee, P. (2010) 'Leadership of "Sub-regional" Places in the Context of Growth', *Policy Studies*, 31, 4, 429–440.

Tricks, H. (2012, 9 August) 'Disaster and Demography in Japan - Generational Warfare', *The Economist*, www.economist.com/node/21559932, accessed 20 September 2014.

Ubauru, M. (2015, March) Reconstruction Initiatives Against the Great East Japan Earthquake and City Shrinkage, Presentation to Symposium on '*Challenges for Shrinking Cities – Land Use Planning, Resilience, Green Infrastructure*', The Japan Institute of Architects, Tokyo, Japan, 4–6 March 2015.

Uehara, M., Tadayoshi, I. and Gen, S. (2015) 'The Favorable Settlement Relocation Process After the 2011 Earthquake and Tsunami Disaster in Japan by Evaluating Site Environments and Accessibility'. *International Review for Spatial Planning and Sustainable Development*, 3, 1, 119–130.

UK Resilience Guidance (2005) *Central Government Arrangements for Responding to an Emergency* (UK Resilience: London).

UN-Habitat (2011) *Cities and Climate Change: Global Report on Human Settlements* (London: Earthscan).

UN-Habitat (2014) *Raising Standards of Urban Resilience – Dialogue 5 WUF7 Concept Note* (New York: UN Habitat).

UN-Habitat Press Release (2014) 'New Global Collaboration for Urban Resilience Announced at WUF7', http://unhabitat.org/new-global-collaboration-for-urban-resilience-announced-at-wuf7/, accessed 11 April 2014.

UNISDR (2012a) *How to Make Cities More Resilient: A Handbook for Local Government Leaders* (Geneva: International Strategy for Disaster Reduction), www.uclg.org/sites/default/files/toolkit_on_how_to_make_cities_resilient_0.pdf, accessed 20 January 2015.

UNISDR (2012b) Making Cities Resilient Report 2012 (New York: The United Nations Office for Disaster Risk Reduction), www.unisdr.org/files/28240_rcreport.pdf, date accessed 20 January 2015.

UNISDR (2014a) *UNISDR Disaster Resilience Scorecard for Cities: Frequently-Asked Questions* (New York: UNISDR with IBM and AECOM), www.unisdr.org/2014/campaign-cities/Scorecard%20FAQs%20March%2010th%202014.pdf, accessed 25 March 2015.

UNISDR (2014b) *Disaster Resilience Scorecard for Cities: Based on the "Ten Essentials" defined by the United Nations International Strategy for Disaster Risk Reduction (UNISDR) for Making Cities Resilient Developed for UNISDR by IBM and AECOM*, www.unisdr.org/2014/campaign-cities/Resilience%20Scorecard%20V1.5.pdf, accessed 25 March 2015.

UNISDR (2015a) *New Study Shows Little Prospect of Reducing Economic Losses from Disasters*, www.unisdr.org/archive/43261, accessed 18 March 2015.

UNISDR (2015b) *What is Disaster Risk Reduction?*, www.unisdr.org/who-we-are/what-is-drr, accessed 7 April 2015.

UNISDR Press Release (2015) 'ISO Standard for Disaster-Proof Cites', announced at UN Conference, www.unisdr.org/archive/43015, accessed 13 March 2015.

United Nations (1987) *Our Common Future – Brundtland Report* (Oxford: Oxford University Press).

United Nations (2012) *United Nations Secretary-General's High-Level Panel on Global Sustainability. Resilient people, resilient planet: a future worth choosing* (New York: United Nations).

United Nations (2014a) *Resilient Cities Acceleration Initiative,* www.un.org/climatechange/summit/wp-content/uploads/sites/2/2014/09/RESILIENCE-Resilient-Cities-Acceleration-Initiative.pdf, accessed 1 September 2014.

United Nations (2014b) *Compact of Mayors,* www.un.org/climatechange/summit/wp-content/uploads/sites/2/2014/09/CITIES-Mayors-compact.pdf, date accessed 1 September 2014.

United Nations (2015) 'Sendai Framework for Disaster Risk Reduction 2015–2030, www.preventionweb.net/files/43291_sendaiframeworkfordrren.pdf, accessed 2 December 2015.

United Nations Development Programme (UNDP) (2015) 'Sustainable Development Goals', www.undp.org/content/dam/undp/library/corporate/brochure/SDGs_Booklet_Web_En.pdf, accessed 2 December 2015.

United Nations Framework Convention on Climate Change (2015). *Adoption of the Paris Agreement,* http://unfccc.int/resource/docs/2015/cop21/eng/l09r01.pdf, accessed 12 December 2015.

UN News Centre (2015) 'COP21: on "Resilience Day", UN and partners launch initiatives to protect millions of people', www.un.org/apps/news/story.asp?NewsID=52710#.VnKiA2fnmUl, accessed 2 December 2015.

Unsworth, R. (2007) *City Living in Leeds* (Leeds: University of Leeds).

Urban Green Council (2013) *Building Resiliency Task Force: Report to Mayor Michael R. Bloomberg & Speaker Christine C. Quinn,* http://urbangreencouncil.org/sites/default/files/2013_brtf_summaryreport_0.pdf, accessed 27 September 2013.

Urban Land Institute (2015) *Returns on Resilience: The Business Case* (Washington: Urban Land Institute).

Urban Task Force (1999) *Towards an Urban Renaissance* (London: Department of Environment, Transport and the Regions).

USAID (2014) *Climate-Resilient Development: A Framework for Understanding and Addressing Climate Change* (Washington: USAID).

Valdes, H. M. and Purcell, H. P. (2013) 'Guidance on Resilience in Urban Planning', *International Journal of Disaster Resilience in the Built Environment*, 4, 1.

Vale, L. J. (2014) 'The Politics of Resilient Cities: Whose Resilience and Whose City? *Building Research & Information*, 42, 2, 191–201.

Vale, L. J. and Campanella, T. J. (eds) (2005) *The Resilient City: How Modern Cities Recover from Disaster* (Oxford: Oxford University Press).

Van Assche, K. (2007) 'Planning as/and/in Context: Towards a New Analysis of Context in Interactive Planning', *Journal of the Faculty of Architecture*, METU, 24, 2, 105–117.

van den Honert, R. and McAneney, J (2011) 'The 2011 Brisbane Floods: Causes, Impacts and Implications', *Water*, 3, 1149–1173.

Vanlandingham, M. (2015, 14 August) 'Post-Katrina, Vietnamese Success', *New York Times*, www.nytimes.com/2015/08/16/opinion/sunday/post-katrina-vietnamese-success.html?_r=0, accessed 14 August 2015.

Vernon, P. (2013) 'Is Resilience Too Accurate to Be Useful?', *New Security Beat blog*, www.newsecuritybeat.org/2013/06/resilience-accurate-useful/, accessed 15 June 2013.

Wagenaar, H. and Wilkinson, C. (2015) 'Enacting Resilience: A Performative Account of Governing for Urban Resilience', *Urban Studies*, 52, 7, 1265–1284.

Wagner, M., Chhetri, N. and Sturm, M. (2014). 'Adaptive Capacity in Light of Hurricane Sandy: The Need for Policy Engagement', *Applied Geography*, 50, 15–23.

Wainwright, O. (2015, 9 March) Bjarke Ingels on the New York Dryline: 'We Think of it as the Love-child of Robert Moses and Jane Jacobs', *The Guardian*, www.theguardian.com/cities/2015/mar/09/bjarke-ingels-new-york-dryline-park-flood-hurricane-sandy, accessed 9 March 2015.

Walker, B. and Salt, D. (2006) *Resilience Thinking: Sustaining Ecosystems and People in a Changing World* (Washington: Island Press).

Walker, B. and Salt, D. (2012) *Resilience Practice: Building Capacity to Absorb Disturbance and Maintain Function* (Washington: Island Press).

Walker, B., Holling, C. S., Carpenter, S. R. and Kinzig, A. (2004) 'Resilience, Adaptability and Transformability in Social–Ecological Systems', *Ecology and Society*, 9, 2, 5. Available at: www.ecologyandsociety.org/vol9/iss2/art5/, accessed 12 September 2014.

Walker, J. and Cooper, M. (2011) 'Genealogies of Resilience: From Systems Ecology to the Political Economy of Crisis Adaptation', *Security Dialogue*, 42, 2, 143–160.

Walsh, B. (2013) 'Adapt or Die: Why the environmental buzzword of 2013 will be resilience.' *Time: Science and Space*, http://science.time.com/2013/01/08/adapt-or-die-why-the-environmental-buzzword-of-2013-will-be-resilience/#ixzz2JeE6rFwE, accessed 8 January 2013.

Weichselgartner, J. and Kelman, I. (2014) 'Geographies of Resilience: Challenges and Opportunities of a Descriptive Concept', *Progress in Human Geography*, doi: 10.1177/0309132513518834.

Weizman, E. (2007) *Hollow Land: Israel's Architecture of Occupation* (London: Verso).

Welsh, M. (2014) 'Resilience and Responsibility: Governing Uncertainty in a Complex World', *The Geographical Journal*, 180, 1, 15–26.

White, I. (2008) 'The Absorbent City: Urban Form and Flood Risk Management', *Proceedings of the Institution of Civil Engineers: Urban Design and Planning*, 161, 151–161.

White, I. (2010) *Water and the City: Planning for Risk, Residence and a Sustainable Future* (London: Routledge).

White, I. (2013) 'The More We Know, the More We Know We Don't Know: Reflections on a Decade of Planning, Flood Risk Management and False Precision', *Planning Theory and Practice*, 14, 1, 106–112.

White, I. and Howe, J. (2002) 'Flooding and the Role of Planning in England and Wales: A Critical Review', *Journal of Environmental Planning and Management*, 45, 5, 735–745.

White, I. and O'Hare, P. (2014) 'From Rhetoric to Reality: Which Resilience, Why Resilience, and Whose Resilience in Spatial Planning?', *Environment and Planning C: Government and Policy*, 32, 934–950.

Wilbanks, T. and Kates, R. (2010) 'Beyond Adapting to Climate Change: Embedding Adaptation in Response to Multiple Threats and Stresses', *Annals of the Association of American Geographers*, 100, 4, 719–728.

Wilkinson, C. (2011) 'Social–Ecological Resilience: Insights and Issues for Planning Theory', *Planning Theory*, 11, 148–169.

Wilkinson, C. (2012) 'Urban Resilience: What Does it Mean in Planning Practice?', *Planning Theory and Practice*, 13, 2, 319–324.

Wilkinson, D. and Appelbee, E. (1999) *Implementing Holistic Government: Joined-up Action On the Ground* (London: Associated University Press).

Woods, D. and Branlat, M. (2011) 'Basic Patterns of How Adaptive Systems Fail', in E. Hollinagal, J. Paries, D. Woods and J. Wreathall (eds) *Resilience Engineering in Practice*, pp. 127–141 (Farnham: Ashgate).

World Bank (2015) *City Strength – Resilient Cities Program* www.worldbank.org/en/topic/urbandevelopment/brief/citystrength, date accessed 20 October 2015.

The Young Foundation (2010) *The State of Happiness: Can Public Policy Shape People's Wellbeing and Resilience?* (London: The Young Foundation).

Zanetti, L. A. and Carr, A. (2000) 'Contemporary Pragmatism and Public Administration: Exploring the Limitations of the 'Third Productive Reply', *Administration and Society*, 32, 4, 433–452.

Zebrowski, C. (2013) 'The Nature of Resilience', *Resilience: International Policies, Practices and Discourses*, 1, 159–173.

Žižek, S. (2008) *In Defence of Lost Causes* (London: Verso).

Zolli, A. (2012, 2 November) 'Learning to Bounce Back', *New York Times*, www.nytimes.com/2012/11/03/opinion/forget-sustainability-its-about-resilience.html?_r=1, accessed 4 November 2012.

Zolli, A. and Healy, A. (2013) *Resilience: Why Things Bounce Back* (London: Headline).

Index